Sled turned on side to hold team, in Stony Canyon, 1954.
From the Denali National Park and Preserve Archives.

Alaska Natural History Association is pleased to present *Denali—Symbol of the Alaskan Wild* by William E. Brown.

Alaska Natural History Association is a non-profit organization dedicated to enhancing the public's understanding and the conservation of Alaska's natural, cultural, and historical resources by working in cooperation with land management agencies and other educational organizations throughout Alaska.

We feel a special kinship with the history of the Denali-Mount McKinley area because our association was founded in the 1950s as a Mount McKinley National Park Association. Though our name has changed and our mission has broadened over the years, the Denali branch remains dedicated to furthering the educational and scientific efforts of the National Park Service at Denali.

We are proud to share our wonderful park with you through the engaging prose of our former Park Historian, Bill Brown.

Gina Soltis
Denali Branch Manager
Alaska Natural History Association

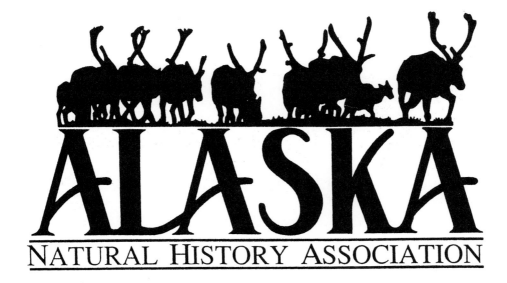

DENALI
Symbol of the Alaskan Wild

AN ILLUSTRATED HISTORY OF THE
DENALI-MOUNT McKINLEY REGION, ALASKA

BY WILLIAM E. BROWN

THE
DONNING COMPANY
PUBLISHERS

Photo previous page: S. H. Cathcart and S. R. Capps, silhouetted against a mountainous background, at work between headwaters of Savage and Sanctuary Rivers. Nenana district, Yukon region, Alaska. July 31, 1919. From the S. H. Cathcart Collection. Courtesy of the National Park Service.

The Donning Company/Publishers
184 Business Park Drive, Suite 106
Virginia Beach, VA 23462

Elizabeth B. Bobbitt, Editor
Mary Eliza Midgett, Designer
Barbara A. Bolton, Project Director
Tracey Emmons-Schneider, Project Research Coordinator

Library of Congress Cataloging in Publication Data:
Brown, William E. (William Edward), 1930–
Denali : symbol of the Alaskan wild : an illustrated history of the Denali-Mount McKinley region, Alaska / by William E. Brown.
p. cm.
Includes bibliographical references and index.
ISBN 0-89865-860-8 (acid-free paper).—ISBN 0-89865-861-6 (pbk. : acid-free paper)
1. Denali National Park and Preserve (Alaska)—History.
2. McKinley , Mount (Alaska)—History. 3. Denali National Park and Preserve (Alaska)—History—Pictorial works. 4. McKinley, Mount (Alaska)—History—Pictorial works. I. Title.
F912. M23B76 1993
979.8'3—dc20
93-569
CIP
Printed in the United States of America

Wolf tracks in the snow. From the Denali National Park and Preserve Archive.

Contents

Adventurous tourists sought out areas not reached by the road system. This pack train visited Polychrome Pass in the 1920s. From the Fritz Nyberg Collection, AMHA.

Preface

E ver since Congress enacted legislation to create Mt. McKinley National Park in 1917, park staff has saved newspaper clippings, correspondence, weathered old photos, and cabin journals in an effort to preserve a record of the park's history. Now, at last, the door to these archives has been opened wide illuminating Denali's rich past through these pages.

When noted historian William E. Brown first set pen to paper, university researchers, history buffs, local residents, and park staff eagerly awaited the outcome. The draft itself created a stir in 1991, fueling the excitement for this highly anticipated definitive history of the Mt. McKinley-Denali region.

William Brown is no newcomer to the authors' arena. His earlier work, *This Last Treasure*, established him as one of the respected chroniclers of Alaska's national park system.

Denali—Symbol of the Alaskan Wild: An Illustrated History of the Denali-Mount McKinley Region sets an important standard of professionalism for its accuracy, attention to detail, and honesty. It is, after all, a rare achievement to write an encyclopedic reference that is also eminently readable.

© 1991 DNP

Russ Berry
Superintendent, Denali National Park and Preserve

Fritz Nyberg and dog, Bos'n, in 1927. From the Denali National Park and Preserve Archive.

Acknowledgments

The end-notes for each chapter show my indebtedness to authors and archives that assisted this work. Original sources structure this history, and I thank the many archivists who extended themselves to help me—at the National Archives in Washington, D.C., San Bruno, California, and Seattle (Sand Point), Washington; the U.S. Geological Survey; the University of Alaska-Fairbanks Archives; and the Anchorage Museum of History and Art.

Regional Director John Cook made special arrangements so I could complete this narrative after my transfer to Southwest Region.

The privilege of working at Denali National Park and Preserve in 1988 and 1989 allowed me to benefit from the knowledge and kindness of the park's outstanding staff, including then Superintendent Robert C. Cunningham, who views history as a critical management tool. Many of the beautiful photographs are National Park Service photographs drawn from the Denali National Park and Preserve Archive.

My research colleagues in Anchorage, at Denali, and in the field know my obligation to them. Individuals who offered continuing encouragement and assistance include Leslie Hart and Kate Lidfors, Gail Evans (who shared her thesis research with me), George Wagner, and A. J. Lynch and the Mining Compliance field crews. Zorro Bradley, Ed Bearss, and Professor Steve Haycox of the University of Alaska-Anchorage reviewed and helped refine this history. Gina Soltis and Patty Ross did the accurate word processing, and Gina coordinated the publication effort for Alaska Natural History Association. Frank Norris helped me to catch errors and wrapped up the multitude of editorial, bibliographical, and indexing tasks that made publication possible.

W. E. B.
March 1993

U.S. *Geological Survey crew in the Kantishna district, 1931. J. C. Reed Collection, USGS.*

Introduction

BY CELIA HUNTER

My relationship with Mt. McKinley National Park began with my first visit to the park in the summer of 1947. Subsequently, my involvement became much more intimate, as I and my partners staked land just outside the then north boundary of the park near Wonder Lake, and created Camp Denali as a wilderness vacation camp, a unique experiment in providing guests with a natural history approach to this area. In the story of this fabulously beautiful, vibrant region of Alaska, my own saga becomes only one among many, all of them woven together into a colorful tapestry in this comprehensive and readable account by historian and yarn spinner Bill Brown.

Beginning with the pre-history of the lands and people surrounding Denali, "The Great One," Brown sketches the archaeological record of the Athabaskan natives who occupied this area for thousands of years prior to white men's explorations. He continues with accounts of these early ventures into the remote fastnesses of mountains, glaciers, forested lower slopes, and torrential streams. Like a magnet, Denali drew a hardy band of pioneering explorers, some to map and leave their names on outstanding landmarks, others intent on ascending both lesser peaks and "The Great One." Still others came in search of such varying goals as mineral wealth, and scientific knowledge of the flora and fauna.

Creation of the park was spurred by concerns over the preservation of its rich wildlife assets, with naturalist and big game hunter Charles Sheldon in the lead. From its earliest days, Mt. McKinley National Park was plagued with conflict between exploitive demands for development of its mineral and later of its tourism potential and the advocates of preserving its natural treasures for present and future generations to enjoy.

Brown does a masterful job of putting the park's evolution from 1917 to the present in perspective against a backdrop of the conditions existing in Alaska during those periods. His wealth of detail about exigencies faced by Harry Karstens, the first superintendent of the park, demonstrates that "the more things change, the more they stay the same." Later superintendents found themselves enmeshed in the same crosscurrents of political and economic forces which eventually forced Karstens' resignation.

Along the way, many divergent threads woven together created the present fortuitous mix of preservation and exploitation which manages to maintain a precarious and vital opportunity for visitors to witness free-roaming wildlife pursuing its natural activities.

Brown's final paragraph sums up the dilemma and the promise of Denali National Park and Preserve:

". . . will this park survive as symbol and standard of our civilization's higher aspirations, or will it be sacrificed to the lowest common denominator? The absolute relevance of this question today testifies to the enduring themes of the park's history, and its meaning to a society still trying to find its way."

Celia Hunter was one of the cofounders in 1952 of Camp Denali, a wilderness vacation camp in the Kantishna area. She was also involved in the 1960 creation of the Alaska Conservation Society, the first statewide conservation organization in Alaska. She has continued to be active in conservation activity since that time. From 1986 to 1992, she was also a board member of the Alaska Natural History Association.

Horseshoe Lake in summer of 1965, from the Overlook on the trail. Photograph by Verde Watson. From the Denali National Park and Preserve Archive.

Traditional Times

Near the geographic center of Alaska, Denali National Park and Preserve surrounds Mount McKinley, which hinges the great arc of the Alaska Range. The mountain, called Denali—The High One—by neighboring Athabaskan Indians, soars more than 20,300 feet above the sea, highest of North American peaks. It dominates its 17,400-foot consort, Mount Foraker, and the lesser elevations of the range as a monarch commands his court.

From the mountain's high buttresses and perpetual ice fields glaciers descend radially, sculpting great gorges in the granite and sediments of the clustered peaks that form the massif. Then the landscape falls away through barren rock canyons to lake-dotted tundra benches, flat and treeless, and, finally, to wide valleys formed by turbid glacial rivers, their braided beds flanked by stands of northern spruce forest.

On these lowlands more than 3 miles below the banner mountain, backdropped by the far-stretching range, roams a panoply of wildlife: caribou, bear, moose, wolf, fox, and, on the lower crags, the white mountain sheep of the north. In summer the animals blend into folds of landscape, moss-floored forest, and distant tundra moors. As migratory bands, as packs and family groups, or as solitaries, they forage the slopes and stream courses, building the reserves of fat to carry them through winter.

From earliest times, for at least 11 millennia, humans have been seasonally attracted to this remote and elevated country because of the concentrations of game animals. The migratory bands of caribou and sheep, the numerous moose and bear, and, in those earliest times, the relict bison and elk at the end of the last great ice age, have spurred human migration to the Denali region despite its isolation and forbidding terrain. In traditional times, a century and more ago, the people came from camps and villages on the many rivers fed by Denali's glaciers: Susitna, Chulitna, Kahiltna, Yentna flowing south; Kuskokwim flowing southwest; Kantishna, Toklat, Teklanika, Nenana flowing north. Some of the hunters cut the arc of the Alaska Range, travelling westward 200 miles from the Copper River basin. Others congregated from the Tanana or portaged from the Yukon. These people came to hunt the high, sparsely forested slopes and valleys and the funneling narrows of the passes. They came by boat as far as shoaling streams allowed, then overland to the killing sites. After the hunt, their meat and skins in tow, they left Denali's shelterless flanks and returned to the forested lands of the big rivers where logs for building and fuel, and migrating salmon for sustaining food, allowed survival through winter darkness and cold.

Migrations continue to this day. The animals still band together for their seasonal convocations. And people come from afar to behold this recurrent display of wildlife posed against the mountain. The great difference from the primeval scene is the migrant humans. Today, except on the fringes of the recently expanded parkland, they hunt with spotting scope and camera.

It was this gathering of wildlife, and fear that market hunting would destroy it, that inspired hunter-naturalist Charles Sheldon in the early years of this century. After extended visits to the Denali region in the years 1906-08, he turned his concerns into a vision: a park-refuge where Denali's vulnerable concentrations of game animals

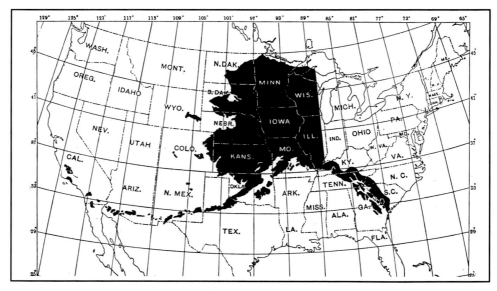

Alaska, superimposed on a map of the United States. From Alaska, A Guide Book Containing Descriptions of the Territory, *American Automobile Association, 1948, frontispiece.*

could roam and propagate unhunted—a reservoir that upon overflow would populate surrounding areas to the benefit of isolated mining camps and communities dependent on wild meat. He saw the fulfilling combination of protected wildlife and magnificent mountain scenery as a lure to visitors who would benefit the economy and development of Alaska.

After a decade of tireless efforts, Sheldon and the cohort of individuals and organizations that followed his lead joined with officials of the newly established National Park Service at the first National Parks Conference in January 1917, just weeks before Congress passed the Mount McKinley National Park establishment act. There he asked, in reference ". . . to descriptions of emotions evoked by the scenery of our national parks in this conference, why it . . . [is] that animals are not more mentioned as an adornment to the landscape." He cited the adornments of civilized landscapes—for example the spires and castles of Spain—then asserted:

Well, it's just exactly the same way in the wilderness. Does not, . . . like the spire in the civilized landscape, a wild animal, the product of . . . [the wilderness] environment, so adorn it that we feel that it is complete? That feeling, that completeness of all your feelings aroused by such wild scenery will in . . . [the Mount McKinley] region be gratified to the uttermost.[1]

Sheldon's vision of a park-refuge where visitors could view plentiful wildlife against the backdrop of stupendous mountains shaped the park's founding legislation; it inspired the policies and practices of the new park's first stewards and their successors through the years; it still determines the management philosophy and the visitor expectations of the expanded Denali National Park and Preserve created by Congress in 1980.

The relationship between Denali's mountains, wildlife, and people has changed drastically through the millennia that separate the ancient hunting parties and last summer's park visitors. In those first days remote geography and mountain ranges translated into time-and-energy barriers that hunters overcame in the quest for game. Today, modern transportation transforms distance into minutes and mountain barricades into scenery. The park ideal changed game into wildlife—the living adornment that, in Sheldon's synthesis, makes the scenery complete. These evolutions of human action and ideal, from traditional times to the present, form the backbone of the history that follows.

The first people to enter the Denali region were big game hunters, recently migrated from Asia over the Bering Land Bridge. They entered a world dominated by the brute physical facts of massive landforms, ice, roiling glacial rivers, and a climate usually frigid and only occasionally warm. The scenes that greeted them had evolved from ancient sea basins and colliding continents. These collisions and coalescings of migrant terrains had earlier raised great mountains, which had eroded and disappeared. Then another surge of plate tectonics some 10 million years ago gave birth to the young Alaska Range. Great forces fractured and faulted the mountains and the jigsaw fragments of land from which they had risen. Volcanoes spewed ash over this raw landscape. And torrent streams carried massive loads of gravel from the new mountains to fans, valleys, and lakes below.

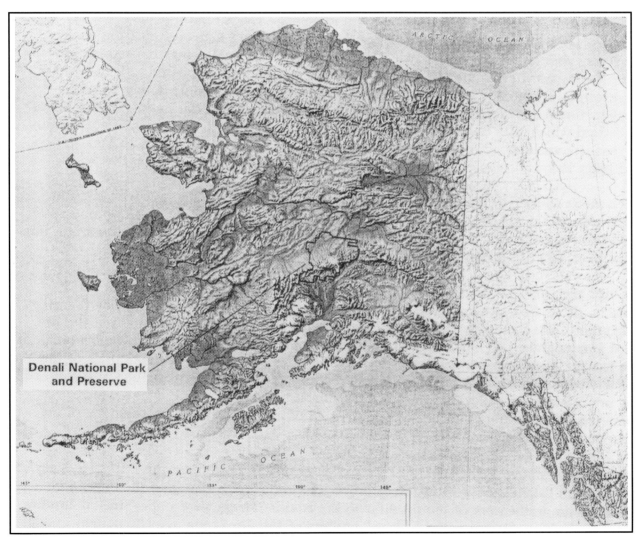

Alaska base map, showing location of Denali National Park and Preserve. From The National Atlas of the United States of America, U.S. *Geological Survey, 1970.*

Then came the ice of the Pleistocene epoch, in sheets and gouging glaciers. On the north side of the range, in the dry chill beyond the probing glacier snouts, grass-and-sage-covered steppes hosted an amazing array of Pleistocene mammals: mammoth, lion, giant bear and bison, wapiti or elk, horse, camel, antelope, and more.

Toward the very end of this time of dry cold and arctic steppes filled with herds of grazers, those first hunters appeared in the plateaus and foothills overseen by the great mountain. The changing climate—getting warmer and wetter—had diminished the dry, hard steppelands. Wetland bog and tundra occupied the stream-laced lowlands north of the range. Spruce and birch began to move in from the south. The mammals of the arctic steppe had by then largely disappeared, except for relict populations of bison and elk in the elevated valley-and-foothill refugium north of the range, where winds funneled through mountain passes maintained for awhile a micro-environment of the disappearing epoch.

On a terrace above Dry Creek, just west of present-day Healy and the Parks Highway, the hunters established a camp sited to overlook the creek valley and the crags and drainage amphitheaters of the foothills to the south. These were opportunistic hunters (as distinct from the specialized "drive" hunters of the Great Plains) who sought grazing sheep, bison, and elk. They came in small numbers, adult men, having left women, children, the aged and infirm at a central base camp in a more sheltered location. The hunting season was probably autumn, when the animals were fat, extending into winter. From their lookout the hunters spotted game, moved to kill it, then brought the butchered meat and skins back to camp for drying and fleshing. In the intervals between hunting and processing its products, they made and repaired the stone, bone, wood, and sinew tools of their trade.

The strategy of several seasonal hunting camps operating from a more stable base camp (as remains at Dry Creek suggest) fit well the opportunistic hunting techniques dictated by the kinds and numbers of game available. Dispersal of small hunting groups from a central camp to spike camps scattered through the country maintained

Native structure, either a shya *or a sweat house, John M. Brooks Collection, UA.*

16

the proper balance between human predators and their scattered prey. And the meat brought back to the central camp sustained the band between hunting forays. From evidence found at several other sites in Beringia (those parts of Alaska and Siberia bordering the former Bering Land Bridge), this Beringian pattern of big game hunting persisted from about 11,000 to 8,000 B.P. By the latter date the last remnants of the oversized Pleistocene mammals and all but patches of the arctic steppe had disappeared.

By then, also, the basic frame of flora and fauna that we see today had established itself in the Denali region. Tundra, brush, black-spruce bog, and forests of white spruce, birch and poplars occupied the old steppe grazing grounds. With extinction of the northern bison, some of the Beringian hunters may have migrated southward to the grasslands of the Great Plains where the buffalo still roamed. Moose and caribou, along with the persistent sheep, became the principal big game animals of the Denali region. In this evolving boreal forest environment, human hunters developed new seasonal and settlement patterns, which combined hunting for big game with fishing for migrating salmon, whose spawning runs up Alaskan rivers brought rich marine resources to the spare lands of the Interior. Seasonal rounds included hunting forays into the elevated valleys and foothills of the Alaska Range, with permanent or semi-permanent villages and camps located in the timbered, riverine lowlands for winter dwelling and fishing.[2]

Athabaskan Culture

Over succeeding thousands of years marked by unrecorded migrations and exchanges, a family of peoples evolved who later would be culturally and linguistically identified as Athabaskans. These Indians occupied and settled into the Interior geographies of present Alaska and neighboring Canada. Archeologists have noted the changing tool kits of the various and differentiated groups. They have traced a general change from a root Siberian-Beringian culture to one that showed progressive adaptation to North American boreal-forest conditions. Within that general pattern of adaptation would emerge the special refinements that allowed each group to fit effectively into its particular homeland environment. As centuries went by these special and constantly evolving variations of tools, clothing, food processing, travel, housing, and survival techniques would reflect ever more precisely each group's special knowledge of the demands and opportunities of its distinctive homeland.

As the millennia passed by, strong patterns emerged: some groups depended more on big game than on fish, and vice-versa. Others, closer to the sea, relied more on marine resources—either directly or by trade. Some groups controlled special assets, such as copper, which gave them trading advantages over their neighbors. Yet others, on the fringe of Eskimo territory, served as cultural and trading middlemen who transferred both ideas and goods across cultural boundaries. In these ways evolved differences in material culture, spiritual concepts, and language amongst the groups. On the eve of European penetration of the Denali region in the mid-nineteenth century, these differences marked each cultural group as a distinct tribe or nation: thus the Koyukon Athabaskans of the Yukon, lower Tanana, and Kantishna rivers; the Kolchan of the upper Kuskokwim River; the Tanana of the mid-Tanana and Nenana-Toklat rivers; the Tanaina of upper Cook Inlet and the Susitna drainage; and the Ahtna who were moving into the Denali region from the Copper River basin. Despite their cultural variations, all of these people belonged to the Athabaskan tradition, a generic lifeway developed over several thousand years of Interior Alaska living.

From the European perspective of linear cultural development—starting with the hunter-gatherer lifeway, progressing to pastoral, agricultural, and the urban, then the urban-industrial-technological forms of modern civilization—a hunter-gatherer culture of such long duration might represent a broken cultural clock. But such a judgment fits ill with a broader view of human history and the constraints of Interior Alaskan geography. We have all descended from hunter-gatherer societies. All of our ancestors spent endless millennia in lifeways that changed hardly at all and only gradually over time. When environments themselves changed, through climatic shifts or the like, then human inhabitants adapted to the new conditions, or migrated to other places, which in turn forced the new arrivals to modify their cultural patterns.

The archeological record for Interior Alaska exhibits constant change, territorial adjustments, and cultural dynamism from 11,000 B.P. to the end of the traditional period, ca. 1850. But these changes occurred within the frame of the generic hunter-gatherer pattern of life, for very good reasons. The subarctic Interior Alaska environment contained no animal species that could be domesticated and herded, thus eliminating the pastoral alternative. Nor, given rigorous climate, wet and frozen ground, and telescoped growing seasons, was this a place for agriculturalists. As top predators in landscapes usually hungry, only seasonally rich in biomass (as during caribou or salmon migrations), the Athabaskans and their precursors had to disperse in small bands during most of the year, barring "urban" concentrations (which would have required pastoral and agricultural hinterlands anyway).

As ecosystem (or living-off-the-land) people, deriving their entire stock of sustaining resources (food, clothing, tools, shelter) from the immediate environment in which they dwelt, the Athabaskans remained hunter-gatherers because there was no alternative in this place. This pattern holds true today in Interior Alaska for anyone who cuts the umbilical cords of imported goods and technology from warmer climes: wild meat and gathered wild vegetable products are the only foods available. And the same sort of thing can be said for other necessities of human livelihood.

It is in the endless refinement of knowledge—the traditional science of land and animals that allowed flexible response to environmental constraint and opportunity—and their rich spiritual life, all passed on with the embellishments of succeeding generations, that the Athabaskans demonstrate the depth and power of their culture. Over thousands of years in the isolation of their remote world, as integral parts of it, they grew to know this land as no other people ever will. In this light—illuminated by physical, intellectual, and spiritual union with the homeland—the traditional Athabaskans possessed a cultural inheritance very different from but every bit as rich and complex as that of the Europeans who would discover them.

The bands of Athabaskans who frequented the Denali region occupied the highland frontiers of their larger tribal territories. They roamed the upper rivers and foothills of the central Alaska Range, dominated by the great mountain. Compared to brethren bands on the main rivers—those arteries of salmon migration before dispersal into hundreds of spawning streams—the highland people depended more on big game. They tended to be more nomadic, spending less time congregated at winter villages or fish camps, more time in movement to intercept migrating caribou, more time dispersed in family hunting parties pursuing scattered winter game.

Illustrative of the lifeways of these upper river, highland bands were the people who ranged the northwest flank of the range. Their territories intersected in the Lake Minchumina vicinity at the divide between the Kuskokwim and Tanana drainages. Here lies a southwest-northeast trending lowland of forests, lakes, marshes, bogs, and streams. The Alaska Range and its outlying foothills parallel one side of this broad valley, the Kuskokwim Mountains the other. Mountain snows feed the waters that host fish and breeding waterfowl. Moose browse streamside willows and wade the lakes and marshes to feed on aquatic plants. Black bears haunt the forests; grizzlies wander over tundra and foothills. Bands of sheep and migrating caribou move through the flanking mountains, and in winter the caribou descend and disperse into sheltering forests and low hills. Fur bearers—so important for clothing—pursue their streamcourse-and-ridgeline rounds.

In Alaskan terms this is a rich environment for the subsistence of Indian hunters. The variety of accessible habitats, populated in the succession of seasons by many different animals, provided fresh meat at hunting and fish camps during times of plenty. Much of the meat from these intensive harvests was dried, smoked, or, in the fall, allowed to freeze, and, along with rendered fat, was stored to carry the people through the lean winter. And usually, in the hungry days of late winter, opportunistic hunters could find the solitary moose, the elusive caribou, the fat beaver, or the denning bear to bridge the final weeks before migrant birds returned to signal spring and freshen winter's monotonous diet—or save the day if the old meat were exhausted.

The Kuskokwim-Tanana Lowland runs from the forks of the Kuskokwim, near the present village of Nikolai, northeast 200 miles, passing through the environs of Telida village to the watershed and portage near Lake Minchumina. Thence it trends down the Kantishna River past traditional camps at the junctions of Birch Creek, Bearpaw River, and Toklat River, and on to the confluence of the Kantishna and Tanana rivers.

In late prehistoric and early historic times the Kolchan Indians of the upper Kuskokwim (represented by today's villages of Nikolai and Telida) maintained ties of trade and cultural interchange with their close linguistic relatives, the Lower Tanana people, who utilized the Kantishna and Nenana drainages. The two groups were probably in seasonal contact around Lake Minchumina and the upper Kantishna.

By the time of direct European contact Koyukon-speaking people had intruded into the Minchumina area, interdicting the traditional overlap between Kolchan and Lower Tanana groups. Family histories related by Minchumina elders trace the Koyukon settlers to the village of Coschaket at the mouth of the Cosna River, which is near the Tanana River's junction with the Yukon.[3]

In a recent ethnohistorical study, the authors comment: "This incursion of Koyukon speakers. . . [is consistent] with historic cultural patterns of movement, displacement and settlement."[4]

Lake Minchumina's favorable hunting and fishing location, astride a watershed-portage-trail complex that gave access to three great Interior rivers—Kuskokwim, Tanana, Yukon—made it a cultural frontier. Both the historical record and the prehistory revealed by archeology demonstrate a series of occupations by ancient and recent Indian groups, with strong evidence also of an Eskimo interlude of three centuries beginning some 1500 years ago.[5]

Trade and cultural interchange followed the trails radiating from Minchumina, making it a rather cosmopolitan place over a span of nearly three millennia. Yet, in the European experience, the Minchumina environs remained one of the last places explored in Alaska, and then with great difficulty, for it nested in the extreme upper reaches of tributary streams far from easily navigable major rivers. This contrast between ancient crossroads and historic-period remoteness tells us something about the skill with which Native peoples moved through daunting country that even now is seen mainly from the air.

Let us now glimpse the realities of day-to-day life in traditional times. In a 1983 report National Park Service anthropologist Susan Morton summarized the ethnography of the Birch Creek people, a Kolchan band of the Lake Minchumina-upper Kantishna River area. Her primary source was the work of Edward Hosley, ethnographer of the Kolchan. His reconstruction of their late-traditional lifeway typifies cultural patterns shared with localized variations by several Athabaskan bands in the Denali region. Morton's felicitous abstract, benefitting from her own interviews with Native elders, is quoted at length below as a convenient window on a lifeway now extinct:

The basic household unit for all Alaskan Athapaskans [alternate spelling of Athabaskan] including those of the Upper Kantishna was composed of two families. The two families shared a single dwelling and acted as a single economic unit throughout the seasonal round. Efficient exploitation of resources scattered throughout their territory required the cooperative efforts of anywhere from a few individuals to a large group. This flexibility involved several different levels of social and political organization.

The next level of social and political organization was the local band composed of from two to five households. A local band was usually made up of a large extended family, traditionally centered around two brothers, or a brother and his sister's husband along with their wives, children, and perhaps daughters, spouses and grandchildren. The group might number between fifteen and seventy-five, sometimes including more distant relatives.

The local band tended to stay together throughout the year, breaking up into individual households only when resources were scarce. The local band was usually exogamous, that is, members married outside of their own group into neighboring local bands.

Several local bands scattered along the same river drainage or foothill region were often linked by kinship, tradition, a shared dialect, and economic cooperation. This larger group has been called a regional band.

Individual local bands exploited territories that averaged 2500 square miles in size. Each band visited different locations in its territory on a regular basis in accordance with an established seasonal round. Winter encampments, which were the most sedentary phase of the annual cycle, were often located on the freshwater tributaries of the Kantishna or a lake. The entire winter season was customarily spent at one location, where permanent dwellings were built.

These dwellings were sometimes subterranean, oval or round in outline, and often had a dome-shaped roof. However, in winter sites predating Western influence (1850s and earlier), dwellings were rectangular, straight-sided, gable roofed, and usually excavated two or three feet into the ground. These structures were most often covered with layers of birchbark on willow or spruce pole framework, but caribou skins were sometimes used instead. Earth or snow was usually banked around the base of the dwelling for added insulation from the cold. Underground caches or pits held stored food.

During pre-contact times, the seasonal round focused almost entirely on hunting. During the winter months the most important species were beaver and bear; other sources of food were ptarmigan and hares. The people also hunted caribou whenever they were available during the winter months, although, in more recent times moose became more important. They turned to fishing only when other supplies of food failed.

About the end of March the people abandoned the winter settlement and began preparations for the spring caribou hunt. Prior to the break-up of the river ice, lightweight birchbark canoes and virtually all of a band's belongings would be loaded on hand-pulled toboggans and on dogs for the trip to the traditional caribou hunting grounds in the Alaska Range. Since the people were more mobile during the summer months, dwellings were usually less substantial than those built for winter. They were dome-shaped or more often conical tipi-like pole frames covered with caribou skins.

The spring and fall caribou hunts were usually cooperative hunts requiring two or more bands to come together and hunt as a single group. In pre-contact times, the entire summer season was frequently spent in the foothills of the Alaska Range hunting caribou, sheep, and occasionally a bear.

The band returned to the winter village just before or after winter freeze-up.

Each band was usually led by a family patriarch. Although a fair amount of social contact did take place between neighboring bands, each band was an independent unit. There was no concept of a large, political group beyond the regional band. The people did not recognize political leadership beyond the level of an informal headman, and such leadership often took the form of experienced elders offering advice to younger band members.

Kinship ties were the basis for social control within each band. Such ties meant there were strong obligations of mutual support and cooperation, especially for sharing food and other resources. Kinship ties, particularly among male siblings, were often the basis for relations within a band. However, a band might also form around a skinnah, a "partnership" bond between two men who often worked and hunted together. Sometimes they were also married to sisters or had exchanged sisters in marriage. The members of such a partnership were obligated to mutual support and hospitality. By extending the partner system to men of other bands, a man could be assured of a welcome wherever he went.

A man could also rely on such support and hospitality from fellow clan members whether in his own village or a distant community. The clan system which cross-cut the local and regional band structures consisted of three named groups. Clans were exogamous, members married outside their own group, and matrilineal, that is, descent and membership were traced through the mother's side of the family. Residence after marriage was usually with the wife's clan, at least temporarily.

Western influence came relatively late to the Upper Kantishna. The late 1830s saw traders from Kolmakovskiy Redoubt making regular trips to the Upper Kuskokwim for furs. They had established regular trade at Khunalinde (Vinasale) by early in the 1840s. Tanaina [Indians] from Cook Inlet were crossing the Alaska Range as early as 1844, acting as middlemen from Nikolaevskiy Redoubt and trading with Upper Kuskokwim (Kolchan). But in spite of additional explorations between 1834 and 1863, the Russians never reached farther into the interior.

So although many regions in Alaska had been visited and described by Westerners by the 1860s, the Upper Kantishna was one of the last areas to be explored by Europeans. The long period of indirect contact with Westerners had a profound effect anyway. The introduction of the fur trade and foreign trade goods by neighboring Native groups caused shifts in the annual cycle of subsistence activities and trading patterns. These economic shifts along with the spread of Western diseases brought about irreversible changes in the traditional way of life.

The relative isolation of Indian groups in the Minchumina area, sheltered by mountains and shoaling streams, meant that indirect contact with Europeans was the rule, with direct contacts the rare exceptions until after the turn of the century. Being once removed from the accessible coast and the navigable rivers, these Indians were able to perpetuate a modified traditional lifeway into the 1920s, a time of still living memory as this is written. Today's elders, who witnessed these times of change, have shared their experiences in a rich oral history. From the stories of their elders, and their own childhood experiences, today's tradition bearers remember the time of the homeland—the world that encompassed the history of their people, the hunting camps and villages, the ties of kinship, and the spiritual associations that gave meaning to each part of that world and each human act within it.

The area's isolation prolonged the history of an earlier Alaska in another way. When the first Westerners came into this country around 1900 there was a replay of the kinds of dependence on the local Indians that had long since faded in Alaska's more settled regions. The elders recall that time, too, when a lost army exploring expedition was saved and guided on its way, when the lore and the lay of the land was shared with other newcomers—traders, trappers, and prospectors. This theme punctuates the narratives of exploration that follow.[7]

✳

Horseshoe Lake in snow, from the Overlook on the trail. Photograph by Verde Watson. From the Denali National Park and Preserve Archive.

1. National Park Service, *Proceedings of the National Park Conference*, January 2-6, 1917 (Washington: Government Printing Office, 1917), 197.

2. This collage of ancient times was derived from R. Dale Guthrie, "Paleoecology of the Site and its Implications for Early Hunters," Chapter 6 in W. Roger Powers, et al., *Dry Creek, Archeology and Paleoecology of a late Pleistocene Alaskan Hunting Camp*, report prepared for the National Park Service (Fairbanks: University of Alaska, 1983); Howell Williams, ed. *Landscapes of Alaska* (Berkeley, University of California Press, 1958); Frederick Hadleigh West, "Excavations at Two Sites on the Teklanika River, Mount McKinley National Park, Alaska" (Fairbanks: University of Alaska, 1965); Robert M. Thorson, "The Ceaseless Contest," Chapter 1 in Jean S. Aigner, et al., *Interior Alaska, A Journey Through Time* (Anchorage: The Alaska Geographic Society, 1986).

3. Richard H. Bishop, *Subsistence Resource Use in the Proposed North Addition to Mt. McKinley National Park*, Occasional Paper Number 17, Anthropology and Historic Preservation, Cooperative Park Studies Unit (Fairbanks: Univ. of Alaska, 1978), 6-8.

4. William Schneider, Dianne Gudgel-Holmes, and John Dalle-Molle, *Land Use in the North Additions of Denali National Park and Preserve: An Historical Perspective*, Research/Resources Management Report AR-9 (Anchorage: National Park Service, 1984), 10

5. See Charles E. Holmes, *Lake Minchumina Prehistory: An Archeological Analysis*, in Aurora, Alaska Anthropological Association Monograph Series No. 2 (1986), for cultural sequence.

6. Susan Morton, "Geese House Report," prepared for the Doyon Cemetery and Historic Sites Committee (Fairbanks: Anthropology and Historic Preservation, Cooperative Park Studies Unit, University of Alaska, 1983).

7. Basic sources for Denali region traditional life include June Helm, ed., *Handbook of North American Indians*, Vol. 6, *Subarctic*, Alaska Plateau and South of the Alaska Range sections (Washington: Smithsonian Institution, 1981); Jean Aigner, "Footprints on the Land," in Aigner, et al., *Interior Alaska*; James VanStone, *Athapaskan Adaptations, Hunters and Fishermen of the Subarctic Forests* (Arlington Heights, Ill.: AHM Publishing Corp., 1974); Richard K. Nelson, *Make Prayers to the Raven, A Koyukon View of the Northern Forest* (Chicago: University of Chicago Press, 1983); Schneider, et al., *Land Use in the North Additions of Denali National Park*; Dianne Gudgel-Holmes, comp. and ed., "Kantishna Oral History Project," report prepared for National Park Service (Anchorage: Gudgel & Holmes Associates, 1983).

A U.S. Geological Survey party at work, near present-day Talkeetna. Courtesy of the Stephen R. Capps Collection, UAF.

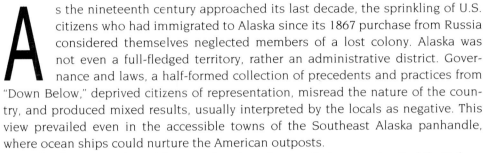

C H A P T E R 2
Early Exploration

As the nineteenth century approached its last decade, the sprinkling of U.S. citizens who had immigrated to Alaska since its 1867 purchase from Russia considered themselves neglected members of a lost colony. Alaska was not even a full-fledged territory, rather an administrative district. Governance and laws, a half-formed collection of precedents and practices from "Down Below," deprived citizens of representation, misread the nature of the country, and produced mixed results, usually interpreted by the locals as negative. This view prevailed even in the accessible towns of the Southeast Alaska panhandle, where ocean ships could nurture the American outposts.

In the distant reaches of the great Interior a few small steamboats plied the Yukon, whose forested banks opened occasionally for a log trading post or an Indian fish camp. Beyond the river, only scattered bands of hunters and the rare prospector roamed. Of government there was none. Over most of the Interior, for all one could see of "man sign," it was the world of Genesis before God's final creation. The Denali region and its approaches remained a blank space on the map, except for rough indications of mountains sighted from afar.

By the late 1880s the Arctic Mountains (later named the Brooks Range) had been partially explored—also the polar seas and coasts, the Yukon and its main tributaries, much of Southwest Alaska's delta lands, and, excepting mountain fastnesses, most of the Pacific rimlands. But at the center lay *terra incognita*.

In the main, the Russians had stayed near the coast. Beginning in the 1830s, having exhausted the populations of sea otter whose pelts had sustained the Tzar's enterprise in America for nearly a century, the Russian-American Company got serious about the Interior fur trade with establishment of posts on the lower or middle reaches of the Kuskokwim and Yukon rivers. Denali-region Indians participated indirectly in this trade via Indian middlemen who were based closer to Russian stations on the rivers and the coast.

British traders of the Hudson's Bay Company intruded Alaska in 1847 to establish Fort Yukon, far northeast of Denali on the upper Yukon River, and hundreds of miles from the nearest Russian post on the lower Yukon. Americans took over these posts after the purchase, linking the upper and lower river with additional stations along the middle Yukon, including several in the vicinity of the Yukon-Tanana confluence.

In time, direct contact began between American traders and the Indians of Denali, who floated downstream to trading posts and camps on the big rivers. The traders were content with this arrangement. There was no reason to labor up shallow rivers if the Indians would bring their furs down them. No other economic motivation existed to push settlement beyond the riverine highways—until the ever-roving prospectors began to find color around the outer margins of Denali.[1]

T H E   D E N A L I   M A S S I F

The first recorded reference to the Denali massif occurs in the 1794 journal of British explorer George Vancouver, who spent a month in Cook Inlet charting its waters—enough time for a break in the weather that gave him a view to the north. In his May 6 entry Vancouver named Cook Inlet in honor of his former captain on this same coast, James Cook, and noted "distant stupendous mountains covered with snow and apparently detached from each other,"[2] a certain description of McKinley and its consort, Mount Foraker, from the inlet. In 1834, during explorations for a trade route between the Kuskokwim drainage and Cook Inlet, the Russian Creole explorer Andrei Glazunov portaged from the Yukon and ascended the Kuskokwim and Stony rivers seeking a pass across the Alaska range. When his Ingalik Athabaskan guides turned back to their Kuskokwim homeland, Glazunov was forced to turn back toward his base at St. Michael near the mouth of the Yukon,[3] but not before noting on March 7 that he "saw a great mountain called 'Tenada, to the northeast."[4] At his location on the Stony River, Glazunov was nearly 200 miles from the mountain. His rendering of its name, Tenada, is traced to the Ingalik Dengadh. (The Koyukon name, Deenaalee, is the source of the modern Denali; all Athabaskan variants north of the Alaska Range mean "The High One.")[5]

Baron Ferdinand von Wrangell, governor of the Russian-American Company, had sponsored Glazunov's expedition to document previously unexplored areas of Yukon and Kuskokwim geography. The Wrangell map of 1839 shows the massif described by Glazunov, with the label "Tenada."[6] In later Russian maps the approximately located mountains and the name were dropped, ". . .as they were considered too far away to position accurately."[7] Thus the Native naming of the mountain faded from maps and memories.[8]

The naming of the Alaska Range followed explorations of the Western Union Telegraph Expedition in 1865-67—part of a scheme to link the Old World and the New by a telegraph line across Alaska and Siberia. William H. Dall, chief of the expedition's Scientific Corps had viewed the range from the Yukon and in 1868 proposed the name "Alaskan Range," which was modified to "Alaska Range" by local usage.[9]

The end of the Russian period in America reflected Russia's imperial competition with Great Britain and the massive debts inherited from the Crimean War. Alaska, on the farthest periphery, was no longer an asset but a drain. For these reasons Russian administration in the final years showed signs of atrophy.[10] The sale to the United States in 1867 kept Alaska out of British hands and it opened a new chapter in the expansion of the United States. American traders, prospectors, and military and geological survey explorers would take up where the Russians had left off and push the frontiers of Alaskan exploration to the edge of the mountain realm.

As in the Russian period, the coastline and major rivers would attract the first American pioneers. Alaska's size and difficult terrain, plus its great distance from the seat of federal government—fully engaged with settlement of its contiguous western territories—acted as brakes on penetration of the remote Interior. Systematic, government-sponsored exploration and mapping of the Denali region proper would be delayed for 30 years. Even prospectors drawn to the Yukon in the 1870s would take nearly 20 years to approach Denali's immediate vicinity. Thus it was by stages and dispersed probes of intervening geography that the mountain finally was approached.[11] A rich secondary literature[12] documents the details of Denali-region exploration, whose chronological highlights will be treated here, along with critical excerpts from original accounts.

As early as 1878 trader-prospectors Arthur Harper and Al Mayo ascended the Tanana River to the site of present Fairbanks, where they found fine gold in the river bars. Harper had earlier floated down the Tanana and seen the Alaska Range on the south horizon. Following his 1878 trip he reported ". . . a great ice mountain off to the south which was plainly visible. . . . one of the most remarkable things. . . . seen on this trip."[13]

According to Bradford Washburn, this is the first known record of Mount McKinley as a single peak reported from the Interior. Notably, Harper's son Walter, born of an Indian mother, would be the first man to set foot on McKinley's summit a generation later.[14]

As late as 1880 historian Ivan Petrov stated in the Tenth United States Census report that "civilized men" knew nothing of the Susitna country north of Cook Inlet despite a century of coastal occupation.

The Indians tell us that the rivers lead to lakes, and that the lakes are connected by rivers with other lakes again, until finally the waters flow into the basins of the Tennanah and the Yukon. But conflicting with this intermingling of the waters are stories of mountains visible for hundreds of miles. . . .[15]

Lt. Henry T. Allen's 1885 U.S. Army expedition defined the eastern march of the Denali region by linking the Copper and Tanana river basins via passage through the eastern part of the Alaska Range. Allen took note of "very high snow-clad peaks" south of the Tanana River's middle reaches.[16]

Prospector Frank Densmore and several companions crossed from the Tanana to the Kuskokwim Basin in 1889. They probably ascended the Kantishna River and portaged to the Kuskokwim via Lake Minchumina, an ancient route used by Indian travelers, and, within 20 years, to be well worn by miners and mail carriers. This traverse came closer to the mountain (within 65 miles) than any previously recorded. Densmore's enthusiastic descriptions of the great mountain to the southeast, as viewed from the Minchumina country, prompted fellow prospectors to call it "Densmore's Mountain."[17]

"MOUNT MCKINLEY"

Beginning in the mid-nineties placer gold discoveries on the Kenai Peninsula and along the shores of Cook Inlet attracted many prospectors into full view of the mountain—among them William A. Dickey, who would name the peak McKinley.[18]

Dickey's ascent of the Susitna River in 1896 followed by a decade his coming west to Seattle after graduation from Princeton, where he impressed people as a winning personality, a talented pitcher, and a mathematical genius. His career as a businessman never recovered from the destructive Seattle fire of 1889, so he eventually headed north to Alaska. His descriptions of the mountain, based on observations from prospecting camps on the Susitna, appeared in the *New York Sun* of January 24, 1897.[19]

His was one of a hundred parties spurred by Cook Inlet gold discoveries to enter the mud-flat delta of the Susitna in spring 1896. All but a handful gave up the struggle against the turbid current before reaching Susitna Station trading post some 25 miles upstream. Here Dickey and his three companions abandoned their heavy sea dory and whipsawed lumber for two Yukon-style river boats 25 feet long, 18 inches wide on the bottom, and 40 inches across at the gunnels. After two weeks of false channels, boat dragging, and wet skies they reached the great forks near present Talkeetna, where:

On the clearing up of the weather we obtained our first good view of the great mountain, occasional glimpses of which we had before, the first from near Tyonick [Tyonek], where we saw its cloudlike summit over (much lower) Sushitna [Susitna] Mountain. The great mountain is far in the interior from Cook's Inlet, and almost due north of Tyonick. All the Indians of Cooks Inlet call it the "Bulshoe" [from the Russian word for "big"] Mountain, which is their word for anything very large. As it now appeared to us, its huge peak towering far above the high rugged range encircling its base, it compelled our unbounded admiration. . . . On Puget Sound for years we had been admirers of Mount Rainier, over 14,000 feet high, but never before had we seen anything to compare with this mountain. My companion in the boat, Mr. Monks, was one of the few who made the ascent of Rainier the previous summer. In his opinion Rainier was about the same altitude as the range this side of the huge peak, which towered at least 6,000 feet above its neighbors. For days we had glorious views of this mountain range, many of whose glaciers emptied apparently into our river.

About seventy miles from the great forks we came to a small village of the Kuilchau, or Copper River Indians [Ahtna], tall and fine looking, and great hunters. Throughout the long and arduous winter they camp on the trail of the caribou. They build huge fires of logs, then erect a reflector of skins back from the fire, between which reflector and the fire they sleep, practically out of doors, although the temperature reaches 50° below zero. We were surprised to find them outfitted with cooking stoves, planes, saws, axes, knives, sleds sixteen feet in length, 1894 model rifles, etc. They were encamped near a fish trap which they had constructed across a small side stream, and were catching and drying red salmon. They had no permanent houses, living in Russian tents, with the entrance arranged like our own to keep out the gnats and mosquitoes. They informed us that we could go no further with our boats, as the Sushitna now entered an impassable cañon, whose upper end was blocked by a high waterfall. "Bulshoe!" they exclaimed, raising both hands high above their heads.

Unable to pass the falls on the main river we turned down the stream to the great forks. It was very exciting and dangerous running the rapids among the big boulders, the race-horse speed at which we travelled giving us no time to examine the river ahead. The boiling waves several times entered our boats, and we were constantly on the jump to keep them from swamping. We could make a greater distance down the stream in an hour than we could up in a day.

. . . We ascended Mount Sushitna near the mouth of the river and confirmed our previous observations on the upper river, namely, the extent of the broad, flat country, and the total absence of the great Alaska range as marked on the Government charts of Alaska.

We named our peak Mount McKinley, after William McKinley of Ohio, who had been nominated for the Presidency, and that fact was the first news we received on our way out of that wonderful wilderness. We have no doubt that this peak is the highest in North America, and estimate that it is over 20,000 feet high.[20]

When later asked why he named the mountain after McKinley, Dickey replied that the verbal bludgeoning he had received from free silver partisans had inspired him to retaliate with the name of the gold-standard champion.[21] For those dedicated to perpetuation of Native names on the land, beginning in the Denali-McKinley controversy with Charles Sheldon, this frivolous reason compounds the naming error.

Mountaineers responded with great interest to Dickey's claim, soon confirmed, that Mount McKinley was the highest mountain on the North American continent. Within a few years the pioneer climbers would begin the ongoing pilgrimage to this arctic giant's icy slopes. The turn of the century was the heyday of arctic exploration and the races for the poles. McKinley's lofty summit now joined the diminishing list of world-class objectives still left for those adventuring souls who mourned the earth's rapid domestication.

Gold!

In 1897, as Denali-Mount McKinley began its transformation into the dominant symbol of Alaska, the Klondike Gold Rush became an international phenomenon. The cadre of American prospectors who had probed and picked the Yukon country for the past quarter century had found some respectable placers, but never enough to ignite a full-scale rush. The Klondike discoveries in Yukon Territory in 1896 did the job. Those hardened rovers who had worked hard-rock mines and placer streams through the Rockies and Sierras, the Australian outback and the Canadian mountains, and the Yukon itself, led the stampede. From their stories and tales, and the bullion they shipped south, the vision of instant riches spread across oceans and continents. Clerks, farmers, merchants, students, and the displaced and dispirited of all descriptions—along with calculating predators and their henchmen—dropped whatever life they had been living and grabbed passage on any ship that could sail, and some that had been condemned. In short order the Klondike excitement spread across the goldfields of both Canada and Alaska.

Suddenly, the United States government, whose citizens comprised the great majority of stampeders, had a stake and responsibilities in Alaska. How could the mass of inexperienced gold-seekers get to the Klondike? How would they be supplied? What were the conditions of life in remote streams that were locked in ice and darkness for a good part of the year? Charlatans foisted false maps and manuals on the innocents, leading them astray, contributing to the potential disaster of marooned camps and death from scurvy and starvation. Boomers, shippers, and outfitters fed the excitement with rumors of new strikes. Hardly a stream in Yukon Territory or Alaska wasn't paved with nuggets that could change desperate lives into the stuff of dreams. Thus worked the alchemy of the Klondike Gold Rush—thought by its participants to be the last great adventure.

GOVERMENT SURVEYS

In 1898 responding to the demands of the Gold Rush, the Congress mandated that the U.S. Geological Survey should become the Nation's chief trailblazer in Alaska. Its task was to provide the public with accurate maps and information about the goldfields, including routes to them and the data of survival. At this time the Denali region was still marked "unexplored" on USGS maps. Separately, or in cooperation with the U.S. Army, the USGS launched several expeditions that year. Two of them would close in on the Denali region.[22]

One of these, headed by J. E. Spurr, geologist, with W. S. Post, topographer, dragged canoes up the Susitna River's tributary, the Yentna, then followed up that stream's tributary, the Skwentna, to portage over the Alaska Range. The party then proceeded down the Kuskokwim to that great river's mouth and conducted further explorations along the coast. This remarkable trip through unexplored areas included the first recorded crossing of the Alaska Range in the Denali region.[23]

Also in 1898 George H. Eldridge and Robert Muldrow of the Survey mapped the Susitna River, traveling by boat and backpack. They reached the Nenana River (then called the Cantwell), tributary to the Tanana, then returned to the coast down the Susitna. Aside from exploratory mapping, this expedition provided hard data on the mountain and reported an idea that would later take root and shape the future of the Denali region. Muldrow made the first professional instrument determinations of Mount McKinley's altitude and position, confirming that its height exceeded 20,000 feet above the sea.[24] Eldridge, the leader of the expedition, fulfilled his charge to find a pass through the Alaska Range suitable for "the location of a railroad or wagon route from Cook Inlet to the Tanana."[25] In his report Eldridge made the prescient point that a feature of the ". . . route that should not be overlooked is its picturesqueness. It would be at the very foot of Mount McKinley and would pass through one of the grandest ranges on the North American Continent."[26] (In 1902 and 1903 private

Junction of Muldrow and Traleika Glaciers, looking south, 1967. Photograph by P. G. Sanchez. From the Denali National Park and Preserve Archive.

engineers made preliminary surveys for a railroad from the Pacific Coast to the Tanana via Susitna Valley and Broad Pass. Construction of a privately financed railroad began in 1903 at the new town of Seward on the coast. The line eventually reached the Turnagain Arm of Cook Inlet. It would later be bought and incorporated into the government railroad system.)[27]

Army expeditions in 1898 and 1899 included reconnaissance surveys by Sgt. William Yanert and Pvt. George Vanschoonoven into the Susitna-Tanana divide area. These expeditions were elements of a larger Army effort under command of Capt. E. F. Glenn to define transportation routes to the Interior goldfields. The Susitna River was deemed navigable for small steamers as far as the great forks near present Talkeetna. And the Susitna Valley-Broad Pass-Nenana River route to the Tanana Valley passed Captain Glenn's tests of feasibility for construction of a railroad or wagon road. Among the advantages of this route, the wide valleys and passes would avert avalanche dangers. Sub-reports from Captain Glenn's command noted the well-worn trails used by Indian traders and hunters in their travels between the Susitna Valley and the Kuskokwim, Tanana, and Copper drainages. Yanert found the remains of a Tanana Indian hunting camp on the north side of Broad Pass. The condition of Natives at Tyonek and Susitna Station ranged from pitiable to fair, with many of the

Indians in advanced stages of pulmonary afflictions. By contrast, the Indians living at camps removed from the trading stations appeared healthy and provident, still engaged in traditional hunting and fishing for their livelihood.[28]

The 1899 expedition of 1st Lt. Joseph Herron, Eighth Cavalry, was the last of the Army efforts under Captain Glenn to find an overland all-American route to the Interior goldfields, one that could not be interdicted by Canadian constraints or regulations. Herron's party crossed the Alaska Range via the Yentna and Kichatna rivers at Simpson Pass. Then, abandoned by their Tanaina Indian guides (perhaps because of fear of the upper Kuskokwim Indians), Herron and his men wandered to the brink of starvation or death-by-exposure through the maze of tributaries and swamps in the upper Kuskokwim drainage. Fortunately rescued, sheltered, outfitted, and guided by Indians of Telida village, the expedition eventually reached newly established Fort Gibbon at the Tanana-Yukon junction, using the Lake Minchumina-Cosna River trail to the Tanana.

Herron's trip, notable for its hardships and the saving help from the Indians, proved the infeasibility of the wet and stream-laced Kuskokwim-Tanana lowlands for road construction. (The Valdez Trail from tidewater to the Fortymile country and Eagle on the Yukon—scouted by another Army unit—became the all-American route.)

Herron's extended stay at Telida gave him splendid views of the north side of the Alaska Range, including Mount McKinley's 17,400-foot consort peak, which he named Foraker after yet another Ohio politician, U.S. Senator J. B. Foraker. (Indian names, according to Orth, included variants on Denali—thus treating Foraker as part of the massif—and "Sultana" and "Menlali," meaning Denali's Wife.)[29]

Herron, an 1891 graduate of West Point, had crossed 500 miles of unexplored country in a total of 1,000 miles traveled. His was the first instance in modern exploration of a Cook Inlet-Yukon River traverse. His official account, published in 1901 by the War Department,[30] offered a case study of do's and don'ts for future travelers in Alaska's varied terrains, especially the difficulties of summer travel in Interior lowlands and the limitations of horses for such work.

Doubtless Herron and his companions would have perished in the onsetting winter had not Chief Sesui and his Telida people succored them. The expedition had been reduced to rags and tatters, and as the season advanced constant immersion in cold water, along with the wet snows that avalanched from trees as they plunged through thick forests and thickets of brush preyed on the men's energy and will. The upper streams, blocked by drift piles and sweepers, could not be rafted—

Nenana natives, 1917. Courtesy of the Stephen Foster Collection, UAF.

they had lost critical gear in a raft upset. The pack horses had weakened and been let go. So here were these weakened men trying to haul on their backs, with improvised canvas-and-rope packs, what gear remained, thrashing through brush, timber, and swamp.

Chief Sesui, hunting from Telida, killed the bear that had just robbed the Herron party's cache. Gutting the bear, Sesui discovered bacon, which meant that white men were near. Chief Sesui backtracked the bear and found the explorers lost and staggering through the swamps. It was September 19, with winter on the march, and, as Herron emphasized, he and his men both blessed the recently cursed bear and gave sincere welcome to the chief. Sesui took them to Telida, sheltering and feeding them for two months while the ground hardened, snow for travel fell, and the Indian women made winter clothes for them. Equipped with Indian snowshoes, transport provided by Indian dogs and sleds, and following Indian guides, Herron's party departed Telida November 25 and reached Fort Gibbon 3 weeks later.[31]

Chief Thomas of the Birch Creek Athabaskans, at Nenana, 1917. Courtesy of the Stephen Foster Collection, UAF.

Carl Sesui and his wife, 1919. Courtesy of the Stephen Foster Collection, UAF.

Roosevelt John and his wife, 1919. Courtesy of the Stephen Foster Collection, UAF.

KUSKOKWIM ATHABASKANS

The Herron-Chief Sesui episode has impelled anthropologist William Schneider to interesting commentary on the situation of the upper Kuskokwim people as direct contact with European culture began:[32]

The Upper Kuskokwim people were ready to assist Herron on his way through and they were ready to assist the hundreds of others that came in the early years of the twentieth century on their way to the gold strikes farther down river and at Nome. This readiness is rather unique for Indian groups which experienced gold rush activities and can be credited to a number of factors. A prolonged period of indirect contact [with both Russians and Americans] facilitated cultural integrity. The Upper Kuskokwim is geographically distant from the major western supply lines; therefore, Native services were vital to travelers. The Upper Kuskokwim Natives had flexibility to develop culturally appropriate and economically remunerative roles in activities of the gold rush—activities such as running roadhouses, supplying fish and game, and serving as dog team mail carriers.

In 1908 the Iditarod Trail was surveyed and became a winter route of travel for prospectors headed for Southwest and Northwest Alaska. In 1923, with the completion of the Alaska Railroad, the Kantishna/Upper Kuskokwim trail also became an important winter travel route. These two trails crossed the Upper Kuskokwim and were traveled by many people headed for the distant gold mining areas.

Strikes in Fairbanks in 1902 and Kantishna in 1905 also brought gold seekers who spilled over into the Upper Kuskokwim. To support the newcomers, roadhouses were built along the trails, and Upper Kuskokwim Natives were employed to work at these sites, and to provide food for the travelers and their dog teams. Some Natives were employed to carry the mail. In some cases the roadhouses were run and owned by Natives.

The introduction of fishwheels by 1918 on the upper river signalled a major technological advance that permitted Upper Kuskokwim people to catch large quantities of salmon on the main river. Fish were also caught in traps in the streams and sold to the roadhouses to feed travelers and their dog teams. The dramatic picture that emerges is of a small Native population which very quickly and effectively provided basic services on the trails and at the roadhouses. The services involved some skills that they had used all of their lives: hunting, fishing, and dog team driving. The introduction of the fishwheels was advantageous and, along with the traditional fish traps, provided a ready source of fish near the main travel routes. The ownership of roadhouses and the entrepreneurial skills that this demanded are of considerable interest.

The Upper Kuskokwim presented unique problems of supply. In summer, river steamers could operate dependably as far up river as McGrath, but the roadhouses farther up river had to depend on shallow-draft boats, and, of course, winter supply over the trails. One suspects that for these roadhouses, local—meaning Native—supply was very important, more important than elsewhere where white traders could depend upon steamboats for supply. The geographical remoteness from outside supply necessitated a dependance on local resources, and therefore permitted a relatively high degree of local control, paralleling in some respects the situation Herron found himself in during his stay at Telida.

Unfortunately, the period of employment and entrepreneurship was short-lived, lasting only until the 1930s when the airplane signalled an end to dog team mail delivery. Many of the roadhouses and even the trails ceased to be important. The employment opportunities decreased dramatically. By then the hordes of prospectors were gone. Those who had found paying quantities of gold were established in a few locales, most outside the Upper Kuskokwim. The traffic had decreased, the wage labor opportunities were few, and people returned to much of the trapping life that they had practiced before, only now the area was less isolated and white trappers shared in the rich fur resources.

Reflecting on the historical events surrounding Herron and the gold seekers, we are left with the strong feeling that the Upper Kuskokwim Natives not only culturally survived but thrived during the early phases of direct contact. . . .

Unlike many other parts of Alaska where direct contact in a home territory followed rather quickly after indirect contact and necessitated immediate change, the Upper Kuskokwim people maintained insulation for a long time, absorbing what they wanted and declining what they did not want. For many years they dealt with strangers on their own terms, and that may have influenced their willingness to exploit the opportunities that finally developed in their home territory. The people who entered their territory had destinations elsewhere. They sought gold outside that territory and did not provide direct competition for the employment opportunities. A contact situation was thus created which permitted the resident population ample opportunity to maintain its integrity and to benefit from their geographically remote location.

The 1902 exploration along the northwest base of the Alaska Range by USGS geologist Alfred Hulse Brooks transected the Denali region, touched the slopes of the Denali-McKinley massif, and produced works of mapping, description, and data (including mountaineering recommendations) that remained the standard references on the region for half a century.[33] An 1894 graduate in geology from Harvard, Brooks had been called from studies in Paris to join USGS Alaskan explorations in 1898. Each year thenceforth he participated in or led Alaska field expeditions in anticipation of his Mount McKinley exploration. In 1903 he became chief of USGS mineral surveys in Alaska, and later Chief Alaskan Geologist for the Survey. In 1912-13 he was vice-chairman of the Alaska Railroad Commission, whose report prompted President Woodrow Wilson to choose the route for the government built-and-operated Alaska Railroad that runs "along the very foot of Mount McKinley." Brooks' distinguished service as chief geologist for the American Expeditionary Force in World War I was followed by further Alaskan work, and authorship of essays and papers that became a posthumously published book classic, *Blazing Alaska's Trails*.[34]

Brooks' leadership of a volunteer cadre of USGS geologists and topographers spurred that agency to excel in its mission as the Nation's chief trailblazer in Alaska. In the Denali-McKinley region, his work effectively brought to a close the period of early exploration and charted the course for mining, mountaineering, and railroad transportation, which, in combination, would open an unexplored land to the world.[35]

Brooks' McKinley expedition of 1902 comprised 7 men and 20 pack horses, with D. L. Reaburn, topographer, and L. M. Prindle, geologic assistant. Their traverse began on June 2 at Tyonek near the head of Cook Inlet, and ended at Rampart on the Yukon. The route ran northwest across the Skwentna River to the Kichatna, then up that stream and across the Alaska Range through Rainy Pass—which Brooks named—to the Kuskokwim headwaters. Then for 200 miles the party followed the margin of the inland front of the range northeastward. On the northerly end of that course Brooks closely paralleled, and in places probably trod upon, the route of the present park

Mount McKinley, showing one of Brooks' campsites during his 1902 expedition. Courtesy of the A. H. Brooks Collection, USGS.

road, reaching the Nenana River via Hines and Riley creeks as do today's park road travelers. Thence the party aimed north via the Nenana River, crossing the Tanana Valley and arriving at Rampart on the Yukon, having traveled 800 miles in 105 days.[36]

The expedition accomplished with dispatch this long trek across some of Alaska's most trying terrain. Savage mosquitos, swamps, and swift glacial rivers combined with thick brush and timber and rugged topography to make many of the miles traveled seem like individual battlefields. Years of Alaska field experience gave Brooks and his professional colleagues both foresight in preparation and stamina in execution. Skilled horse wranglers and campmen simplified travel and camp routines so that men and animals could last the course. Sufficient minimums ruled in equipage, supply, and—to the extent possible—energy expended. And in the rich game country of the Denali region fresh meat was never lacking.[37]

Excerpts from Brooks' 1903 article[38] give a flavor of the Denali region's geography, landscapes, and wildlife—and the impact of the great mountain upon a skilled and literate observer:

[From the summit of Mount Susitna, near Tyonek] . . . the broad lowland of the Sushitna Valley lay spread before us, the dark greens of its spruce forest contrasting with the lighter greens of the open marshes and the bright gleam of small lakes or winding water courses. Beyond rose a range of highlands, and then, forming the sky-line, snow-covered Alaskan mountains. From our vantage point the rugged crest line seemed unbroken, and had we not known that it was in fact cleft by passes we might have despaired of finding a route through such a forbidding mountain mass.

As we gazed a mass of clouds hanging over what appeared to be the center of the range broke and revealed two majestic peaks, Mount McKinley and Mount Foraker, glistening in the slanting rays of the afternoon sun. Far above the crest line they towered, enormous mountains, even at a distance of 120 miles. Four years before, while making an exploration down the Tanana with canoes, I had seen the same peaks and at about the same distance, but from the opposite direction.

The task before us was to find a route across the swampy lowland, traverse the mountains, and, following their northern front, approach from the inland slope as near the base of this culminating peak of the continent as conditions and means would permit; we must map the country and incidentally explore a route which some time could be used by that mountaineer to whom should fall the honor of first setting foot on Mount McKinley.

From the forests we now entered a belt of foothills, which formed a northern spur of the main range, and once more obtained a clear view of Mount McKinley, still almost as far distant as when we first saw it from Mount Sushitna six weeks before. This was no cause for depression, however, for then we were separated from our goal by an apparently impenetrable swamp and a great, snow-covered range, whereas now there seemed no serious obstacles to our achieving our purpose.

Among these foothills, averaging a height of 3,000 or 4,000 feet, dwelt large numbers of mountain sheep, their pure white color, which in this region remains unchanged throughout the year, making them conspicuous objects on the bare rocks or moss-covered slopes. In the course of one morning's roaming over the hills, I counted more than 100 of these mountain dwellers. In fact, the abundance of sheep, bear, moose, and caribou found along the north slope of the Alaska Range rank it as one of the finest hunting grounds in North America.

Our descent from the foothills brought us to a gravel-floored plateau which butted directly upon the base of the range. Its smooth, moss-covered surface afforded such excellent footing and so few obstacles to progress that for days we hardly varied our direction a degree, heading straight for Mount McKinley. That mountain and its twin peak, Mount Foraker, now only 50 miles away, seemed to us to rise almost sheer from the gravel plain. We passed many large glaciers which debouched from the mountain valleys upon the plateau and discharged roaring, turbulent, bowlder-filled rivers, which were our most serious impediment.

An early climbing party on Mount McKinley. Courtesy of the Francis P. Farquhar Collection, UAF.

These were the happiest days of the summer. Cheered by the thought that every day's march was bringing us visibly nearer to our goal, we lent ourselves readily to the influence of the clear, invigorating air and the inspiration of that majestic peak ever looming before us, the highest mountain of North America, which we were to be the first to explore.

Our camp of August 1 was pitched in a grove of cottonwoods near the foot of a glacier which flowed down from the [ice] fields of Mount Foraker. This we called the "Herron Glacier," in honor of Capt. Joseph S. Herron, our predecessor in the exploration of the upper Kuskokwim Basin.

Two days later we made our nearest camp to Mount McKinley in a broad, shallow valley incised in the piedmont plateau and drained by a stream which found its source in the ice-clad slopes of the high mountain. We had reached the base of the peak, and part of our mission was accomplished, with a margin of six weeks left for its completion. This bade us make haste, for we still must traverse some 400 miles of unexplored region before we could hope to reach even the outposts of civilization. The ascent of Mount McKinley had never been part of our plan, for our mission was exploration and surveying, not mountaineering, but it now seemed very hard to us that we had neither time nor equipment to attempt the mastery of this highest peak of the continent.

[But the lure of the mountain was irrisistible, so on one clear day, Brooks scrambled up the mountain into the late afternoon when the falling ice made the climb very dangerous.]

Convinced at length that it would be utterly foolhardy, alone as I was, to attempt to reach the shoulder for which I was headed, at 7,500 feet I turned and cautiously retraced my steps, finding the descent to bare ground more perilous than the ascent.

On a prominent cliff near the base of the glacier which had turned me back I built a cairn, in which I buried a cartridge shell from my pistol, containing a brief account of the journey, together with a roster of the party. . . .

As I sat resting from my labors I surveyed a striking scene. Around me were bare rock, ice, and *snow; not a sign of life, the silence broken now and then by the roar of an avalanche loosened by the midday sun, tumbling like a waterfall over some cliff to find a resting place thousands of feet below. I gazed along the precipitous slopes of the mountain and tried to realize again its great altitude, with a thrill of satisfaction at being the first man to approach the summit, which was only 9 miles from where I smoked my pipe.*

The era of early exploration thus ended in contemplation of the great mountain. This lofty banner, visible for 200 miles, marked the center of a region long familiar to Indian hunters and now encircled and transected by newcomers upon the land. Their maps, photos, and written descriptions dissipated the mists of distance and filled the blank spaces recently marked "unexplored." The Denali region beckoned to prospectors, mountaineers, and engineers. Hunters, naturalists, and artists would soon follow. In time their experiences, reports, and renderings would cast a special meaning upon these mythic landscapes, the regal creatures that roamed them, and the towering massif that topped them all. Then would arise the notion that these scenes should be discovered anew by each generation. Despite their diverse callings, the second wave of pilgrims, like the first, would fall under the spell of this marvelous region. Purposefully or otherwise, they would all contribute to its dedication as a public treasure, a place of perpetual discovery.

❋

Fish camp at Cape of Good Hope, on Lake Minchumina. Courtesy of the Stephen Foster Collection, UAF.

1. J. M. Nielson, "Focus on Interior History," typescript report prepared for Alaska Historical Commission (Anchorage: 1980); Wendell H. Oswalt, "Historical Settlements Along the Kuskokwim River, Alaska," Alaska State Library Historical Monograph No. 7 (Juneau: Alaska Department of Education, 1980); Ronald T. Stanek, "Historical and Contemporary Trapping in the Western Susitna Basin," Technical Paper No. 134 (Anchorage: Alaska Department of Fish and Game, Subsistence Division, 1987); Melody Webb, *The Last Frontier, A History of the Yukon Basin of Canada and Alaska* (Albuquerque: University of New Mexico Press, 1985); Ted C. Hinckley, *The Americanization of Alaska*, 1867-1897 (Palo Alto, Calif.: Pacific Books, Publishers, 1972).

2. Quoted in Bradford Washburn, "Chronology of Events Related to the Exploration of the McKinley Massif, Alaska," draft typescript (Boston: Museum of Science, 1988), 1.

3. Oswalt, "Historic Settlements," 10.

4. Quoted in Gail E. H. Evans, "From Myth to Reality: Travel Experiences and Landscape Perceptions in the Shadow of Mount McKinley, Alaska, 1876-1938," master of arts thesis (Santa Barbara: University of California, 1987), 57.

5. James Kari, "The Tenada-Denali-Mount McKinley Controversy," Names, Vol. 34, No. 3 (September 1986), 347-350.

6. Ibid., 348; the Wrangell map, the best of Alaska in its time, is reprinted in Terris Moore, *Mt. McKinley: The Pioneer Climbs* (Fairbanks: University of Alaska Press, 1967), follows p. 2.

7. Washburn, "Chronology," 2.

8. Moore, *Mt. McKinley*, 5.

9. Webb, *Last Frontier*, 52-55; Washburn, "Chronology," 3; Donald J. Orth, *Dictionary of Alaska Place Names*, Geological Survey Professional Paper 567 (Washington: Government Printing Office, 1967), 61.

10. Webb, *Last Frontier*, 44-46.

11. See Morgan B. Sherwood, *Exploration of Alaska*, 1865-1900 (New Haven: Yale University Press, 1981), and Alfred Hulse Brooks, *Blazing Alaska's Trails* (Fairbanks: University of Alaska Press, 1973) for general sequence and progress of American exploration.

12. See, e.g., Terris Moore, *Mt. McKinley*; Brooks, *Blazing Alaska's Trails*; A. H. Brooks, *The Mount McKinley Region, Alaska*, USGS Professional Paper 70 (Washington: GPO, 1911); Stephen R. Capps, *Geology of Alaska Railroad Region*, USGS Bulletin 907 (Washington: GPO, 1940).

13. Quoted in Washburn, "Chronology," 4.

14. Ibid.; Moore, *Mt. McKinley*. 8.

15. Quoted in ibid.; 7.

16. Webb, *Last Frontier*, 7; Brooks, *Mount McKinley Region*, 26.

17. Capps, *Geology of Railroad Region*, 7.

18. Ibid.; Washburn, "Chronology," 5.

19. Moore, *Mt. McKinley*, 9, 10.

20. Quoted in ibid., 12-15.

21. Ibid., 17-20.

22. Capps, *Geology of Railroad Region*, 8; Evans, "From Myth to Reality," 62-65.

23. Capps, *Geology of Railroad Region*, 8; Gerald Fitzgerald, "Surveying and Mapping in Alaska," USGS Circular 101 (Washington: USGS, February 1951), 9; Washburn, "Chronology," 6.

24. Fitzgerald, "Surveying," 9.

25. Quoted in Washburn, "Chronology," 6.

26. Ibid.

27. Capps, *Geology of Railroad Region*, 9.

28. E. F. Glenn and subreports by William Yanert, George Vanschoonoven, George B. Thomas, and H. G. Learnard in *Compilation of Narratives of Exploration of Alaska*. Senate Reps., 56th Con., 1st sess., No. 1023 (1900), 642, 643, 654-667, 677-681, 733-737.

29. Orth, *Dictionary*, 345.

30. Joseph S. Herron, *Exploration in Alaska*, 1899 (Washington: War Department, 1901).

31. Ibid.; Moore, *Mount McKinley*, 20-25; William Schneider, "Chief Sesui and Lieutenant Herron: A Story of Who Controls the Bacon," *Alaska History*, Vol. 1, No. 2, Fall-Winter, 1985-86, 1-18.

32. Ibid., 11-16.

33. See especially Brooks, *The Mount McKInley Region*.

34. A. H. Brooks, *Blazing Alaska's Trails* (Fairbanks: University of Alaska and the Arctic Institute of North America, 1973).

35. For biographical data see Orth, *Dictionary*, 9; and biographical sketch in *Blazing Alaska's Trails*, xix-xxi.

36. See "Reconnaissance Map of Mount McKinley region," Plate III in Brooks, *The Mount McKinley Region*, end pocket; A. H. Brooks, "An Exploration to Mount McKinley, America's Highest Mountain," from the *Smithsoniam Report* for 1903 (Washington: GPO, 1904), 407-425.

37. Ibid., 409-410, 414, 415.

38. Ibid., (first published in the November 1903 *Journal of Geography*, Vol. 2, No. 9), 418-421.

Stuck, Karstens, and Harper climbed to the top of Mt. McKinley in 1913. This is
the south summit shown from the northeast as photographed by Bradford
Washburn in a later era. From the Denali National Park and Preserve Collection.

C H A P T E R 3

Challenge of the Mountain

The dozen years that followed the Brooks Expedition would set the pieces of the frame for the Denali region's future. Three men—Judge James Wickersham, Charles Sheldon, and Harry Karstens—would emerge as the moving forces whose interaction would create the park-refuge idea, carry it through to legislative enactment, then pioneer the new park on the ground.

Wickersham made the first attempt to ascend the mountain, one year after Brooks had gazed along its precipitous slopes. In so doing, the judge launched a heroic chapter in mountaineering, peopled by literate adventurers whose exploration and climbing accounts make a fascinating history of truth, falsehood, controversy, and final summit achievement. In aggregate, their published descriptions made Mount McKinley and its game-rich forelands household symbols of the Alaskan wild.

The placer mining claims that Wickersham's party staked in the Kantishna Hills, on the way to the mountain, created a minor gold rush that evolved into a long-term mining community whose hospitality and knowledge of the country would support and inform successive expeditions of mountaineers, hunters, and explorers.

The isolated miners of Kantishna and neighboring mining districts would seek government assistance to make their mining profitable and their lives more civilized. These demands contributed to government development of trail, mail, and rail services in the Denali region—the basic infrastructure that would in time provide access to Mount McKinley National Park.

The shared concerns of Charles Sheldon and Harry Karstens over the market hunting of Denali's game animals to supply mining camps and future railroad construction camps translated into the threat of wholesale slaughter of North America's premier wildlife assemblage. This threat, carried to Congress by Charles Sheldon and the cohort he led, motivated the legislators to create Mount McKinley National Park. Judge Wickersham—by then Alaska's Territorial Delegate to Congress—introduced the park bill. Karstens, with backing from Sheldon and Wickersham, became the pioneer superintendent of the new park-refuge.

Thus did the years 1903 through 1914 string the woof upon the loom: committed personalities, adventure and description, mining and hunting, definition of transportation needs and routes, the park-refuge idea. The warp would follow with Congressional action and early park development and access. Intervening history, from then until now, has been and continues to be woven on that same loom, with only variations of design.

In 1900 U.S. Judge James Wickersham set up District Court in Eagle, Alaska, under the terms of Alaska's new Civil Code, which followed hard upon the Gold Rush. His judicial district covered more than half of Alaska, centering upon the vast Interior. Wickersham won appointment to the judgeship after effective work as lawyer and political campaigner in Tacoma, Washington. His judicial and political career in Alaska would span more than 30 years. He helped guide Alaska's transition from orphan outpost to full territorial status in 1912, and subsequently served several terms as Alaska's Delegate to Congress.[1]

With the Fairbanks gold discoveries and stampede of 1902, the population of Wickersham's district gravitated to the new bonanza on the Tanana, and so, too, did the judge. After organizing his court and Fairbanks' civil offices in spring 1903, Wickersham considered what to do until his court convened in the fall. For him "...the most interesting object on the horizon was the massive dome that dominates the valleys of the Tanana, the Yukon, and the Kuskokwim—the monarch of North American mountains—Mount McKinley."[2]

After assembling four kindred spirits for the expedition, the judge set out for the mountain in May 1903. The party chose to approach as closely as possible by boat, thus pioneering steamboat access up the Kantishna River.[3] This route, down the Tanana and up the Kantishna to head of navigation, would be perfected with boat landings, trails, and supply points during the Kantishna gold rush of 1905, which was inspired by the Wickersham party's staking of placer claims.

Wickersham and his companions enjoyed their trip. His account sparkles with reflections on the virgin beauty of the land they had entered, well timbered, fertile—a valley scene that resembled the lower Mississippi more than the boreal Yukon drainage. Only the distant summits of the snowy range indicated their northern latitude.[4]

Along the river they found Tena (Tanana) Indians in traditional spring hunting camps in the neighborhood of the Toklat-Kantishna confluence. These people had left their winter villages on the lower Tanana in February, hauling their gear with dogs and toboggans. Foraging through the forests and foothills, they had taken moose and caribou, and now they hunted ducks migrating into the Kantishna's river-and-lake lowlands. The Indians shared their fresh meat and their knowledge of the landscape, pointing out the easiest route for the men and mules to the base of Mount McKinley—via Chitsia Creek, the lower birch-clad slopes of the Kantishna Hills (above the swamps and deep creeks), and the gap through those hills formed by Moose Creek and Wonder Lake.

Having off-loaded from their steamer, *Tanana Chief*, the men progressed with mules, backpacks, and a poling boat, *Mudlark*, which they had found and reconditioned near the mouth of the Kantishna. They encountered first one, then two more white trappers scouting the country for furbearers. The latter two had portaged from the Kuskokwim and after a year in the wilderness were en route to the Tanana trading posts with their furs.[5] Already the patterns of trade and transportation were being traced across a country unknown to white men just a few years earlier.

At the Telida Indian camp called *Anotoktilon*, near the mouth of Bearpaw River, Wickersham's party met Chief Sesui, rescuer of the Herron party. This band of hunters regularly pursued caribou and sheep on the plateau and in the headwater canyons below the Denali-McKinley massif. They gave detailed instructions for reaching the glaciers that descend from Denali's summit. They recommended that the poling boat be cached at this point for the trip across the foothills.[6]

The cross-country march took Wickersham and his companions past lakes alive with waterfowl and on to the flank of Chitsia Mountain, which they would climb for a magnificent view of the country. Chitsia or Heart Mountain (so-called because it is shaped like a moose heart) was a sacred place of the Tena Indians. During Wickersham's visit with them a few days earlier their blind shaman, Koonah, had told him of Yako, the Tena's origin hero. Yako had fathered the Tena people in the ancient past. He had magically created the Denali massif from giant sea waves sent to destroy him by

Totson the Raven Chief. During a later struggle, Tebay the White Sheep Chief had climbed to his Chitsia Mountain lookout to direct the enemies of Yako to his village on the banks of the Yukon. There the treacherous warriors from the southern sea were vanquished by Yako and his children so the Tena could live in peace.[7]

From Tebay's lookout, Wickersham describes the scene:

The little peak stands in the forefront of the mountain mass, the descent to the valley is abrupt; the Toclat spreads out at its base on the eastern slope, and is in view from the mountains in the south to its confluence with the Kantishna. Far to the east we can see the bluffs at Chena, and beyond, Fairbanks; the Tanana and the Tolovana hills are in view across the northern horizon, while the Nuchusala hills in the west rise hardly to our level. Minchumina Lake lies to the westward and glistens like silver in the sunlight. The view continues far south of Minchumina to the massive McKinley range. We can trace the course of the Kuskokwim into the Bull Moose hills and the portage from Minchumina lake to that river. The valley view from the Tebay's aerie is a widespread panorama of forest, lake, and river, stretching from the distant eastern horizon around by north and west to the western flanks of Mount McKinley due south of us. This three-quarters of a circle is a wide, flat valley, carpeted with an evergreen forest, marked by rivers and dotted with lakes. The sun shone in glorious radiance over Yako's land, and we now understood and better appreciated the vivid description of it given to us by Koonah, the blind shaman of lowland Kantishna.[8]

In succeeding days the party hunted and jerked caribou, found colors and staked claims on Chitsia Creek (the first mining claims in the Kantishna district), passed through the Moose Creek-Wonder Lake gap, and crossed the bars and channels of McKinley River, its silt and gravel plucked by Muldrow Glacier from the high walls of the mountain that now hung over them.[9]

The mountaineers set up base camp on the lower reaches of Peters Glacier. Ascending its main course they aimed for the northwest buttress of McKinley's North Peak as their route to the top. Turned by a chaotic icefall, crevasses, and sheer cliffs where Peters Glacier plunges through narrowed walls, Wickersham bore left up smaller Jeffery Glacier, which, in the towering topography and obscuring walls, seemed to offer access to the ascent ridge. After hours of careful toil avoiding crevasses and gingerly crossing snow bridges,

. . . we reached an arête or sharp ridge of bare rock at the extreme upper end of the bench glacier, and found, to our intense disappointment, that the glacier did not connect with the high ridge we were seeking to reach, which yet seemed as far above us as when we began the ascent. We are now about 10,000 feet above sea-level on a sharp ridge of rock. Here our bench glacier roadway ends, for over this arête which juts out from the mountain wall, the descent is almost perpendicular to the great bergs of the main glacier, far below as they crowd over each other to enter the narrow gorge. Here is a tremendous precipice beyond which we cannot go. Our only line of further ascent would be to climb the vertical wall of the mountain at our left, and that is impossible.[10]

That vertical wall, now known as Wickersham Wall, rises 14,000 feet from Peters Glacier to McKinley's North Peak.

The Wickersham climb, and another attempt the same year by Frederick Cook, served well as reconnaissance ventures. They showed that Peters Glacier was a dead end, at least for the pioneer climbers. The way to the top in the early days of Mount McKinley mountaineering awaited discovery of the ridge-hidden Muldrow Glacier route.

Wickersham's party returned to civilization by raft, boat, and steamboat after a glorious summer adventure. They had probed and mapped the approaches to the mountain. They had found traces of gold, and when they filed their claims at the Rampart recorder's office on the Yukon, they assured that others would come in force to the virgin lands of the Kantishna.

By 1903 Dr. Frederick A. Cook—a self-made man, medical doctor, and courageous member of four Arctic and Antarctic expeditions since 1901—had established impeccable credentials as an explorer. Among his admirers and former expedition colleagues were Robert E. Peary and Roald Amundsen of polar discovery fame.

Cook's 1903 attempt to climb Mount McKinley foundered in the maze of cliffs and drop-offs surrounding Peters Glacier and its upper basin, as had Wickersham's 2 months earlier. Cook and his companions managed to surmount the ice fall in the Peters Glacier canyon that had blocked the earlier party, and finally reached an elevation of about 11,000 feet on the North Peak's northwest buttress. From their highest camp, a hole chopped in a blue-ice precipice, the ridge

...led with an ever-increasing slope to a granite cliff which did not appear unclimbable from below. But at close range and in a good light we could see that farther progress ... was impossible. There were successive cliffs for four thousand feet.[11]

Acknowledging defeat, the party cached its extra food and fuel to lighten packs, then dashed 29 miles to the face of Peters Glacier.

Despite the mountain's dominance Cook's expedition that year brought richly deserved acclaim as a feat of exploration. His was the first circumnavigation of the McKinley massif. Paralleling Brooks' 1902 route from Tyonek, across the range, then along its northwest slope—with the climbing interlude at Peters Glacier—Cook scouted the unexplored heights northeasterly of Muldrow Glacier. There he found a pass negotiable by the party's pack horses via the extreme headwaters and intervening glaciers of the Toklat and Chulitna rivers. Thence, after abandoning the horses, the party rafted down the main courses of the Chulitna and the Susitna to Susitna Station and eventually came back to Tyonek.[12]

Had Doctor Cook ended his Mount McKinley career with this 3-month, 1,000-mile trek—its northern pass-finding arc through unexplored mountains—he would have capped a remarkable saga of exploration. But the lure of the mountain and the glory he sought would lead him to make false claims 3 years later to the destruction of his reputation.[13]

Cook's expedition demonstrated the terrible toll of even approaching the isolated mountain, much less

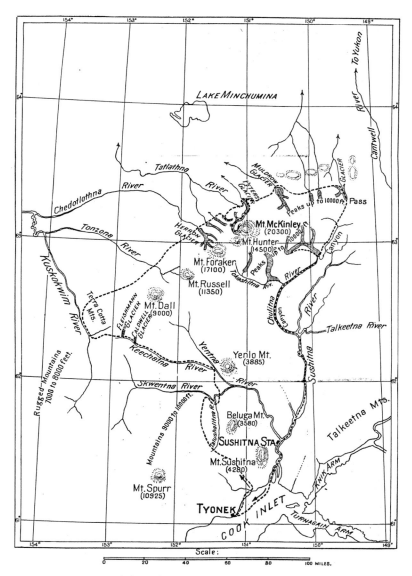

Route of the Cook Expedition. From The Shameless Diary of an Explorer, *by Robert Dunn, 1907.*

climbing it. Moreover, the narrow window imposed by subarctic seasons and weather nearly closed on Cook and his men as winter marched in step with them during their September dash across the range and down the Susitna.

Robert Dunn, a Harvard-educated journalist, accompanied Cook in 1903. Cook appointed him to a role best described as operational chief of the expedition, thus he labored and led the crew as a sweating participant, not as an observing reporter. Dunn's mentor, editor Lincoln Steffens, had charged him to write a completely truthful account of an exploring expedition—an expose of the rows, bickering, dissents, and demoralizations usually hidden behind the heroic prose of the exploring fraternity.[14]

The pages of Dunn's *The Shameless Diary of an Explorer* fulfilled that charge. They painted an ambivalent picture of Doctor Cook: sometimes hero, usually kind though often petulant, sometimes indecisive, on-again off-again as a leader and technically competent wilderness man. Dunn's descriptions of trail conditions, mishaps, and smoldering enmities amongst the party depict the attrition, physical and mental, of men and animals marooned except for their own unceasing labors in a wilderness beyond help of others.

First on the trail through the Skwentna River swamps:

By noon, it seemed that we'd been traveling a year, hewing down, down, stem by stem, among the iron-limbed alders. Winter snows flatten, toughen, bind, and bend them into tempered springs. You can't move an inch without an axe, or getting gouged in the face. And then to drive fourteen exhausted, half-wild bronchos, stampeding, snorting, as you hear the whooping-screeching rip of canvas—see the cinches dangling from the brush! Oh, our hot oaths as we hunt and gather the packs, chopping a clear place to pack, fighting mosquitoes! And for every foot the beasts travel we cover forty, dashing forward to head them, unsnarl, drag from the mud.

Mosquito netting was an integral part of the early surveyors' outfits. Courtesy of the Stephen R. Capps Collection, UAF.

We reached a big crick paralleling the river. The banks were slewed and clogged with drift and willows. We were an hour crossing and ploughing through the quicksands, finding the lead for trail beyond. . . .

Cutting trail with me on the other side and piling brush to keep the beasts from jumping into the crick where it turned and gouged the bank, Jack suddenly lost his temper for no reason I could see, and hurled off his axe murderously into the brush. Then he snagged his eye, and sat down, quivering for ten minutes on the sand-bar, his head in his hands, so no one dared to speak to him.[15]

Next, a moment of inspiration on a highpoint overlooking Peters Glacier:

The dizzy unworldliness of it all was intensified, compressed by perspective. You seemed suspended in air, infinitely near, yet infinitely far from ice or rock wall. The sky overhead was blue-black. The haze had dissolved, leaving rainbow islands of cloud at succeeding spheres of the shadowy cut, casting down abnormal shadows, swift darknesses, blazing revelations. Think of it—this mile-wide trail [Peters Glacier], unknown miles long, hemmed by one wall a mile high, another three sheer miles, and so straight you can hit its base with a snowball, as you look up at its summit, the apex of North America. Somewhere a snow-slide thunders, a tiny white cloud of fuzz like the puff from ten thousand cannon blurs the wall, its whisper dies away into the pre-creative silence.[16]

Finally, the doubt before choosing the doubtful exit from their plight, across the range and down the Susitna:

We've been discussing how to get out of the country, for ice is beginning to rim the river slews at night. Twelve days' rafting down the Peters stream should bring us to Tanana river and a Yukon trading post. But northeast stretches mile on mile, white with 10,000-foot alps, and the flat avenues of the world's biggest inland glaciers, ramifying like the tentacles of a cuttle-fish this supreme American range. And it is all unmapped, undiscovered, bleak and shriveled under the breath of autumn. And south across these mountains, to the Sushitna River and Cook Inlet, the Government Survey report we read between chapters of our one and only Tom Sawyer, says with familiar triteness that it is "extremely doubtful" if any pass exists.[18]

One of the true heroes of McKinley mountaineering was Belmore Browne. He was a man for all seasons: lumberjack, explorer, artist, hunter, artful writer, scholar, and right arm to Charles Sheldon in the political struggles of the McKinley park movement. Except for a sudden storm at the last moment and final steps of a great climb in 1912, he would have been the first man to achieve McKinley's summit. His love of Alaska took him to its farthest reaches over many decades, beginning as an 8-year-old boy in 1888. His career mingled with that of Doctor Cook, as colleague, then as critic. Regretfully, Browne and his partner Herschel Parker, would prove the falsehood of Cook's claim to conquest of the mountain in 1906.[18]

Browne's three expeditions to Mount McKinley during the period 1906-1912 gave him profound understanding of the mountain's challenge—particularly in the pre-aircraft era of the pioneer climbs. His book, *The Conquest of Mount McKinley* (1913), captures the perspective of that era—picturing the great mountain barricaded by distance, labyrinthine terrain, and arctic weather from those tiny mortals who stood at its base and longed to reach its top.

He describes the mountain as ". . . a gigantic mass of granite that was forced upward through the stratum of slate that overlaid it." The slate survives on the lower peaks, giving them "a strange, black-capped appearance."

A principal difficulty for the mountaineer is the low altitude from which the mountain rises. The plateaus of South America and Tibet allow climbers to hike halfway up to the peaks they seek to climb. But ascent of McKinley begins near sea level. After 30 miles of difficult ice-and-snow traverse on the glacial avenues that offer the only access through the gorges to the climbing heights—carrying all supplies in backpacks—the climber still looks up at 3 vertical miles of ice, snow, and forbidding cliffs, toward a peak still 10 or 12 miles distant, rimmed by sub-peaks and huge buttresses, which in themselves are major challenges, and beyond which (in those foot-slogging days without aerial reconnaissance) lie unseen gorges and ridges that may foil the climber's planned route. Even on the glacier approach polar equipment is

mandatory, and the time required for the climb and weather delays demands mountains of supplies. All this just to climb the mountain. Getting to the mountain,
geographically placed "in the most inaccessible position obtainable," was the other
half of the struggle.[19] Until the Alaska Railroad was completed in 1923 and glacier
piloting began in 1932, approach logistics consumed such prodigious energies and
supplies that many expeditions were whipped before they started the ascent.

With such depletions in mind, the mountain's other challenges, beyond technical
mountaineering, came to the fore: perennial arctic conditions above 10,000 feet—
constant cold at subzero temperatures; sudden storms, blinding snow, hurricane
winds, causing wind-chill factors well below minus 100 degrees; tents and equipment
ripped, lost, buried; trails laboriously broken, then erased by drifts, to be found and
broken again by people breathing and pumping like hummingbirds, counting to ten
between each step; climbers exhausted, disabled or dying from altitude sickness or
hypothermia; the loss of a mitt or a wet sock the difference between life and death. All
of this beyond avalanches, falls, crevasse disappearances, and the terrible toil of
simply moving upward in air nearly devoid of oxygen. These hazards still obtain, as
the mountain's constantly growing death toll demonstrates and despite modern
improvements of aircraft and high-tech mountaineering, medical, and rescue operations. That the pioneer climbers incrementally discovered the way up, made their
ascents, and came back to tell their stories is a testimonial to grit, frontier improvisation, and luck.[20]

Terris Moore's history of the pioneer climbs cites 11 distinct mountaineering
expeditions, beginning with Wickersham's, leading to the first completely successful
ascent of Mount McKinley in 1913. Only highlights of the balance of these efforts can
be presented in the context of this regional history.

S T R U G G L E   A N D   C O N T R O V E R S Y

Doctor Cook returned to Mount McKinley in 1906 in company with Herschel C.
Parker, professor of physics at Columbia University, and Belmore Browne, artist,
among others. This expedition resulted in a valuable reconnaissance and mapping of
the southern approaches to the mountain. The party used a pack train and a motor
launch to investigate the Susitna's tributaries and their heading glaciers on McKinley's
south flank. After 2 months of intense work without finding a route to the top, the
party returned to Cook Inlet, and its members went their separate ways. Doctor Cook
remained in the vicinity, and in early September with horse-packer Robert Barrill
made ". . . A LAST DESPERATE ATTEMPT ON MOUNT MCKINLEY,"[21] as Cook phrased
it in a dramatic telegram to Eastern backers. His subsequent claim that he had
dashed to the top and back in less than 2 weeks via Ruth Glacier inspired instant
skepticism amongst those familiar with the country, including Parker and Browne.
What came to be known as the Fake Ascent spawned a controversy between Cook
loyalists and mountaineering detectives that even now sputters on, despite overwhelming evidence that Cook lied.

Browne's *The Conquest of Mount McKinley* recounts his and Professor Parker's sleuth-
ing that identified a rock pinnacle in a side basin halfway up Ruth Glacier as the site of
Cook's famous "summit" photograph. This point is about 5,300 feet above the sea and
some 19 miles from McKinley's summit on a straight line. Cook trapped himself with
his own photography in a preliminary article and in his later book, *To the Top of the
Continent*. The book's unretouched summit photo, which shows a background peak
(not shown in the retouched article photo), plus contextual photos of the side basin

(claimed by Cook to be thousands of feet above its actual elevation) allowed Parker and Browne to pinpoint the rock pinnacle on the ground in 1910. Barrill, sworn to silence by Cook, later revealed the hoax in an affidavit, stating that Cook had dictated false entries for Barrill's diary. Brad Washburn assembled and critiqued all available evidence, including his own ground proofing, in his 1958 *American Alpine Journal* article, "Doctor Cook and Mount McKinley." Despite frost-action crumbling of the rotten rock pinnacle, which had altered its profile as shown in Cook's photos, the photos in Washburn's article show key remaining features of the pinnacle, and the tell-tale background mountain in a comparative photo essay. It was the "fingerprint" of this mountain (as Browne said, "No man can lie topographically") that had guided Parker and Browne to the pinnacle in 1910. Aside from all this physical evidence, the timetables, distances, logistics, and the route to the top described and mapped by Doctor Cook seemed immediately and were later proved incredible. After their own experiences with Cook earlier that summer of 1906, probing up the great tendril glaciers of McKinley's weather flank, Parker and Browne could not buy the 12-day up-and-back story from their first hearing of it.

As the Mount McKinley controversy grew riper, Doctor Cook threw another bombshell. In 1908 he claimed to have reached the North Pole, beating his former leader Robert Peary to the prize. This claim was immediately challenged by Peary and others, and another controversy erupted. This claim too was later disproved.

The combination of claims, suspicions, and rebuttals finally impelled the Explorers Club to call Doctor Cook before a committee of peers to clear himself. He refused to testify and disappeared. The Explorers Club, of which Doctor Cook had been president, expelled him in late 1909. He was also dropped from the rolls of the American Alpine Club and various geographical and learned societies.

The Parker-Brown Expedition — 1910

Then followed several mountaineering expeditions to Mount McKinley in 1910, both to attempt the ascent and to test Cook's claims. Two of these came back with authoritative evidence. Parker and Browne led the Explorers Club-American Geographical Society party that discovered the false peak. The distinguished experts who made up this expedition had been charged to find solid proof one way or the other respecting Cook's claim to have climbed the mountain. For the Cook controversies—both McKinley and North Pole—had turned ugly. The public suspected that Cook, their popular hero, was the victim of individual and institutional jealousies. Reputations were at stake—including those of such eminent third parties as Charles Sheldon and Alfred Hulse Brooks. who had contributed technical appendices to Cook's book, thereby implicitly endorsing his claims.

On the approach to Ruth Glacier in 1910, Parker and Browne encountered C. E. Rusk, leader of the Portland, Oregon Mazama Mountaineering Club expedition. The Mazamas wanted to track Cook's route as described in his writings and on his 1907 map. In this way they would assess his claims on the ground. Their sympathies lay with Cook but objectivity was their guide. The two expeditions joined in the quest for truth but proceeded separately. Weeks of hard hiking and glacier hazards, encumbered with polar equipment and supplies, brought the Mazamas up Ruth Glacier's vast trench to its great amphitheater and upper branches. At this point Rusk and his companions saw that Cook's map was the product of his imagination, for it matched in no way the actual scene before them. Cook had described a valley glacier route giving access northward to Muldrow Glacier, and thence to the top. A maze of mountains and glacial box canyons enclosed by cliffs greeted the Mazamas. Rusk would later close his meticulous report with this sad statement:[22]

Dr. Cook had many admirers who would have rejoiced to see his claims vindicated, and I too would have been glad to add my mite in clearing his name. But it could not be. Of his courage and resolution there can be no doubt. He is described as absolutely fearless. He is also considered as always willing to do his share and as an-all-around good fellow to be out with. His explorations around Mount McKinley were extensive. They were of interest and value to the world. Had he persevered, he doubtless would have reached the summit on some future expedition. He was the first to demonstrate the possibility of launch navigation up the Susitna and Chulitna Rivers. And that one trip alone—when with a single companion he braved the awful solitude of Ruth Glacier and penetrated the wild, crag-guarded region near the foot of McKinley—should have made him famous. But as we gazed upon the forbidding crags of the great mountain from far up the Ruth Glacier at the point of (Cook's and Barrill's) farthest advance and realized that it would require perhaps weeks or months more in which to explore a route to the summit, we realized how utterly impossible and absurd was the story of this man who, carrying a single pack, claims to have started from the Tokositna on the eighth of September, and to have stood on the highest point of McKinley on the sixteenth of the month. The man does not live who can perform such a feat. Let us draw the mantle of charity around him and believe, if we can, that there is a thread of insanity running through the woof of his brilliant mind . . . If he is mentally imbalanced, he is entitled to the pity of mankind. If he is not, there is no corner of the earth where he can hide from his past.

In mountaineering circles, the Cook controversy generated a mythos and a literature similar to the Custeriana that followed and still follows the Battle of the Little Bighorn.[23] But this study must move on, drawing once more the mantle of charity over a man whose genuine exploits and deserved reputation dissolved in falsehoods meant to enhance them.

The Kantishna gold rush of 1905 had come and gone by the time Doctor Cook's summit story hit the papers in 1906. Of the thousands who had followed Judge Wickersham to the Kantishna Hills only about 50 hard-core prospectors and miners remained, centered on the streams flowing into Moose Creek. These men were seasoned veterans who had taken over the best claims and were prepared for years of mine-development toil. Easy surface gold had been quickly exhausted; illusions of quick riches and those who held them had departed.

On the fringes of the isolated mining camps that year of 1906 roamed two other men important to this history, Harry Karstens and Charles Sheldon. Karstens was a bona fide Sourdough: Klondike stampeder, Seventymile River miner and cofounder of the nearby town of Eagle on the upper Yukon, and, lately, dog-team mail driver for the Kantishna camps. Sheldon himself was no stranger to Alaska and the Yukon country. A man of independent wealth, this distinguished member of the Eastern establishment combined the joy of the hunt with the pursuit of scientific knowledge and the collection of specimens for the scientific and museum communities. His special interest in the various species of the North American mountain sheep had drawn him northward from Mexico, through the Rockies, and on to British Columbia. Now he sought definitive knowledge of the life history of Alaska's white sheep, *Ovis dalli*. After extended tracking of these sheep along the Alaskan-Canadian borderlands, he came to the Denali region in the summer of 1906, accompanied by Harry Karstens. Of his guide and friend Sheldon stated:

. . . I recall no better fortune than that which befell me when Harry Karstens was engaged as assistant packer. . . . He is a tall, stalwart man, well poised, frank, and strictly honorable. One of the best dog drivers in the north, and peculiarly fitted by youth and experience for explorations in little-known regions, he proved a most efficient and congenial companion.[24]

49

For this cast now assembled on the north side of Denali's vast stage, the mountain and its approaches became a matter of daily experience. On clear days the miners, aware of the Wickersham and Cook climbing attempts, glassed the peak from highpoints in the Kantishna Hills. They speculated on the lay of the land and from their various observation points spotted glacial trenches and bordering ridges that might lead through the topographical maze toward the domed summit. From the Toklat area they saw that an upper basin sloped down from the top of the mountain.

During Sheldon's 1906-08 rambles on the piedmont plateau and foothills bordering the mountain massif, he had traced the lower course of Muldrow Glacier. He also spotted the icefall and ridges that led to the upper basin just below McKinley's two peaks. Sheldon became acquainted with miners Tom Lloyd and his partners, whose mining claims on a high ridge above Lloyd's cabin at the head of Glen Creek offered unexcelled views of Mount McKinley. From that ridge one day in January 1908, Sheldon and Lloyd viewed the mountain and Sheldon told of its double summit, North Peak and South Peak, and of the high glacier and icefalls descending from the basin between them. Sheldon believed that one of the ridges alongside that high glacier would give access to the top, as indeed one would 2 years later. As yet, no one knew the entire winding course of Muldrow Glacier—hidden by intervening ridges and mountains—which would soon serve as the broad avenue leading to the upper elevations and the peaks.[25]

THE SOURDOUGH EXPEDITION—1909-1910

The miners of Kantishna and their friends in Fairbanks shared in the skepticism bred by Doctor Cook's tale of whirlwind ascent. They knew the scale of the mountain. They believed that Alaskans, hardy men like themselves, should be the fittest and the first to scale McKinley's heights, not Outsiders who visited for a summer. The challenge galvanized Fairbanks. Backers and bettors urged the project along. Thus outfitted and assured prizes and glory, Tom Lloyd and his partners—Charley McGonagall, Billy Taylor, and Pete Anderson—left Fairbanks with dogs, horses, and a mule in late December 1909, en route to Denali's north flank. By early March 1910, after supply relays, establishment of a base camp at timberline near one of A. H. Brooks' old camps, and discovery of Glacier (now McGonagall) Pass, which accessed middle Muldrow Gla-

Members of the 1909-1910 Sourdough Expedition were (left to right): Charley McGonagall, Pete Anderson, Tom Lloyd (seated), and Billy Taylor. Courtesy of the Francis P. Farquhar Collection, UAF

cier, the reach for higher elevations began. Intermediate camps along the glacier led to the Sourdoughs' highest camp near the head of Muldrow at 11,000 feet. This was the highest point reached by the overweight Lloyd. But the three younger and stronger men—McGonagall, Anderson, and Taylor—set out for the top early on April 3 hauling a 14-foot-long spruce pole and a flag, which, emplanted on the peak, would prove their conquest. They pioneered the route via Karstens Ridge around the Harper Icefall to the upper basin, then struggled up Sourdough Gully to Pioneer Ridge. Somewhere around 18,000 or 19,000 feet the older McGonagall dropped out. His job was to get the pole within striking distance. He did that, and there was no reason to go any further, he later stated, because Pete and Billy were skookum (meaning strong and capable, from the coastal Chinook Indians) and didn't need any more help from him. So Anderson and Taylor went up the last hard ridge and planted their flag in a rock outcrop just below the North Peak summit.

According to later interview accounts from Taylor and McGonagall, their objective was to place the flag where it might be seen by telescope from Fairbanks. As they saw it, the peaks looked about the same height, but the South Peak could not be seen from Fairbanks.

Both contemporary and modern climbers have viewed with awe the amazing accomplishment of the Sourdoughs. Starting from their 11,000-foot camp, the 18-hour ascent and return, during which the pioneers negotiated some 8,500 feet of vertical rise over a route they discovered as they climbed, would tax the best climbers of any age. These miners were novice mountaineers with rudimentary, improvised equipment, wearing bib overalls, longjohns, and unlined parkas, and carrying a bag of doughnuts and a thermos of hot chocolate for provisions. But they were tough (as well as very lucky with the weather) and they proved the point that real Alaskans could climb that mountain if they set their minds to it. Aside from the sheer physical prowess of the Sourdoughs, the route they pioneered through McGonagall Pass, up the Muldrow, and around Harper Icefall via Karstens Ridge stood for more than 40 years as the only climbing route to McKinley's summit. Unfortunately Lloyd—first to return to Fairbanks—would claim that all four Sourdoughs reached the top. This tale clouded the party's real achievement, briefly relegating it to another Cook-like fantasy. But 3 years later the Karstens-Stuck party sighted the flagpole, and later interviews with Billy Taylor and Charley McGonagall distilled the truth from Lloyd's fictions.[26]

PARKER-BROWNE — 1912

The Parker-Browne expedition of 1912 was the first serious and technically competent effort by skilled alpinists to climb Mount McKinley. From their previous experiences—on the south flank with Cook in 1906 and in the east-side Ruth Glacier maze in 1910—plus their awareness of the 1903 failures on the western side, Parker and Browne were convinced that the northern approach via Muldrow Glacier offered the best chance for success. Moreover, knowing the scale of the country and the time required to complete logistical preparations for a serious assault, they determined on a winter approach march. They would in effect, two-stage their expedition: first, the long march from the coast, with establishment of a base camp on the piedmont plateau, then the climb itself. Wishing to explore the Alaska Range northwest of McKinley, Parker and Browne set their course in late January from the port of Seward to Susitna Station via Knik arm. Continuing their mushing with dog teams they ascended the Susitna Valley and followed up the Chulitna River to the then unnamed

Ohio Creek. At its head they crossed the range over glaciers and icefields, and finally, after 17 days on the ice, debouched at the lower curve of Muldrow Glacier. Thence they proceeded down Muldrow and cross-country to Clearwater Creek. In late April they established base camp on Cache Creek within easy reach of McGonagall Pass.

Though the Sourdoughs had come this same way, Browne did not know their precise route. His intensive study of McKinley's northeastern face set the climbing route and the approach to higher elevations. His probes through the blocking foothills led him up Cache Creek and to rediscovery of the pass onto Muldrow Glacier first found by McGonagall in 1910. There, at its midcourse, he tied the Muldrow together from its terminal moraine to the cliffs at its head, under the overhanging Harper Icefall. From various highpoints in the foothills he saw the advantages of yet unnamed Karstens Ridge as the route around that icefall and up into the big basin under the towering peaks. No better example of the logic of terrain could be found than Browne's independent rediscovery of the Sourdough route.

Almost immediately Browne and Parker, aided by Merl La Voy of Seattle, began supply relays with the dogs up Muldrow Glacier. At its head they cached their goods in a tarped and anchored sled at 11,000 feet, near the notch that gave access to Karstens Ridge. By May 8 they were back at base camp, which was run by the fourth, non-climbing member of the party, Arthur Aten of Valdez, Alaska. Then followed several weeks of rest, hunting, and equipment tending as the Denali spring changed the lower elevations into a paradise of flowered meadows, singing birds, and wandering game animals.

Except for a knee injury suffered earlier by La Voy, the three-man party started the big climb on June 5 in good shape. Their equipment was of the best alpine sort, and a balanced menu—based on energy-rich pemmican with a high-fat content—promised good strength to counter the effects of altitude and cold.

The attrition began early with a heavy snowstorm that trapped them on Muldrow for 3 days. Then they waited for avalanches to unload the snow-packed heights before threading the icefall narrows near Muldrow's head. After the excess snow had fallen they went on up to 11,000 feet, finding their sled-cache buried but intact, then climbed up on Karstens Ridge. In a series of exhausting advances and supply relays through deep snow they set up camps and snow shelters every 1,500 to 2,000 feet until reaching their final camp in the big basin at 16,500 feet. Throughout the advance La Voy's knee, reinjured in a crevasse fall, gave him trouble. Browne did double duty in the relay packing, hauling the heavy loads, and in breaking trail. The soft snow tripled their toil, and cold and altitude began sapping the men's energies. Sixty degree slopes overhanging drops of 2,000 to 5,000 feet demanded tight-wire concentration, not aided in the least by bouts of snow blindness and wind squalls that struck laden packers without warning. Slow progress through the snow forced more food relays from a cache nearly a mile below their upper camp. Then the source of their energy, the fatty pemmican, failed them. Beginning at 11,000 feet, the men began getting sick when they ate the pemmican. As they got higher their bodies absolutely refused to metabolize the fat, which became, in effect, a poison. Thus, just as they got set for the final climb, they were reduced to a starvation diet of tea, sugar, raisins, and hardtack. This snack fuel gave little heat and energy. So the daily rebound from toil and cold expected of solid food could not occur. As the climbers weakened under cumulative attrition, normal sleep became impossible, further eroding energies and resistance to cold.

On June 27 Browne and his companions set up their final camp in the big basin. Their frigid hollow grew colder as congealed air flowed down from the upper icefields.

To gather themselves they rested for one day in the tent, avoiding exposure and chill, and their spirits came back.

This was the third time that Parker and Browne had tried to climb this mountain. Now, poised at the base of the last big ridge leading toward the shoulder that marked final access to the summit, they could almost see their goal about 3,500 feet above.

Next morning, June 29, they felt good and the weather was clear. The sun began to moderate the stabbing cold. Browne noted in his diary, "There is nothing to stop us except a storm."[27] Leaving camp at 6 a.m. the climbers progressed almost as planned, though they could not meet their goal of 500 feet elevation gain each hour. Then in the lee of the ridge they hit soft snow, further slowing their pace. At nearly 19,000 feet they topped the big ridge and took a break at the base of the last slope to the summit. Browne describes the scene:

We had long dreamed of this moment, because, for the first time, we were able to look down into our [Ruth Glacier] battle-ground of 1910, and see all the glaciers and peaks that we had hobnobbed with in the "old days." But the views looking north-eastward along the Alaskan Range were even more magnificent. We could see the great wilderness of peaks and glaciers spread out below us like a map. On the northern side of the range there was not one cloud; the icy mountains blended into the rolling foothills which in turn melted into the dim blue of the timbered lowlands, that rolled away to the north, growing bluer and bluer until they were lost at the edge of the world. On the humid south side, a sea of clouds was rolling against the main range like surf on a rocky shore. The clouds rose as we watched. At one point a cloud would break through between two guarding peaks; beyond, a second serpentine mass would creep northward along a glacier gap in the range; soon every pass was filled with cloud battalions that joined forces on the northern side, and swept downward like a triumphant army over the northern foothills. It was a striking and impressive illustration of the war the elements are constantly waging along the Alaskan Range.[28]

Above them the way to the summit, whose edge they could plainly see, ". . . rose as innocently as a snow-covered tennis court and as we looked it over we grinned with relief—we *knew* the peak was ours."[29]

But just then the wind picked up and the sky darkened. The storm advancing from the south had found the final heights. In minutes a snow-laden gale enveloped the climbers. Visibility decreased as the blizzard gained force, but if they kept going uphill they must reach the summit. Forced to chop steps on the steeper slopes, their hands began to freeze and blowing ice particles blinded them. Cold now gripped their bodies entire, and they lost time desperately stomping and moving their extremities to keep feeling and life in them. Finally they emerged from a partially sheltering lee for the last few feet of ascent to the summit. In the full force of the wind they felt life ebbing. Browne, in the lead, was less than 200 feet below the summit elevation and only about 200 yards distant from it. At this farthest point of advance he realized that it would be suicidal to proceed. It had taken him several minutes to move only a few feet during his last upward exertions—blind, buffeted, and in places simply hunched in place as the hurricane battered him to a standstill. He turned back to La Voy and Parker and they huddled for a moment in a quickly chopped seat in the ice. But they could feel themselves freezing as they yelled against the wind. Browne screamed, "The game's up; we've got to get down."[30] Professor Parker wanted to go on, volunteering to chop the last steps. But the danger from freezing was now compounded by the packing snow filling their chopped steps and the wind erasing all signs of the trail back to their camp.

Slowly they retreated feeling their way and using the wind to guide them. Had it shifted they would have perished. By great good fortune they found the rocky spine of the ridge bounding the basin. Guided and sheltered by this line of rocks, they struggled to their tent.

Browne had got to the mountain top, halfway between the 20,125-foot summit shoulder and the true summit at 20,320 feet, but not to the very top of the mountain. Indeed, as he lamented, it had been a cruel and heartbreaking day.

Next day they rested and dosed themselves with boracic acid for snow blindness. They packed their rebellious stomachs with as much hardtack and raisins as they could stand. With great difficulty they dried out the frost particles that had penetrated every part of their clothing. Then they tried one more time. Leaving at 3 a.m. they got to the base of the final dome and began its ascent. Again they raced a rising storm. After an hour of vicious wind and blinding snow, they turned and stumbled wordlessly back to their tent. Browne remembered ". . . only a feeling of weakness and dumb despair; we had burned up and lived off our own tissue until we didn't care much what happened!"[31]

After a quick descent with its full share of obstacles and adventures the weary climbers reached their base camp where the faithful Aten awaited them. Rest, food, and recuperation followed. But even in this verdant resort, after a month on the mountain's ice and snow, Alaska's extremes tracked them down. The evening of July 6 grew ominous with heavy air and a sickly green sky. Then a great earthquake struck. The Alaska Range boomed and bellowed, then disappeared into snowy mists as avalanches and icefalls jolted from its cliffs and slopes. Fierce, debris-laden winds swept down from the mountains. The very ground they stood on heaved, split and slid. Streams crested with thick brown water from earth slides.

Later they learned of the great Katmai volcanic eruption on the Alaska Peninsula hundreds of miles to the south, of which this earthquake was an aftermath. Brad Washburn notes that had the pemmican not failed the Parker-Browne party they would have waited out the storms for another summit attempt. High on the unstable mountain ice they would have died without a trace in the earthquake's chaos.[32] (One year later, the Karstens-Stuck expedition would struggle though the vast debris of giant iceblocks that had tumbled from the mountain.)

For 36 hours the aftershocks persisted. Then the Parker-Browne party headed north, via the Kantishna mining camps, to the Yukon and home.[33]

To the Top — 1913

The mountaineering match-up of Sourdough Harry Karstens and Alaska's Episcopal Archdeacon Hudson Stuck produced both tensions and victory. It was an inevitable pairing in Alaska's small and interlocked community. Karstens' exploits of exploration and dog driving, and his 1906-08 expeditions with Charles Sheldon in the Denali country, made him a natural choice for pioneering co-leader when the eminent missionary set his sights on Denali's peak.

In 1904, shortly after coming into the country, Stuck first glimpsed Denali, whose Indian name he always preferred. Smitten with the mountain's beauty and its dominance over the Alaska Range, he determined that one day he would at least stand upon its foothills or ascend its flanks. In time, as Doctor Cook's fraudulent claims and the doubts spawned by Tom Lloyd's overblown story demeaned the mountain's majesty, Stuck vowed to climb it himself. The near success of Parker and Browne in 1912 spurred him on. He believed that starting from Fairbanks—instead of from the coast as they had—he could be successful.

As a traveling missionary through Alaska's Interior and Arctic regions, Hudson

Johnny Fredson, native Alaskan, drove a dog team at age 15 for Stuck and Karstens' climb of 1913, the same year he posed for this portrait. In 1942, he was a schoolteacher in Nome. From the Denali National Park and Preserve Archive.

Stuck was no stranger to the "strenuous life" that was the ideal of the times. He sledded and boated from village to village establishing missions and schools, and performing annual visits to the more isolated camps of his scattered Native adherents. He admired Native culture and their competence on the land, often clashing with superiors who would divorce Native peoples from their land-based way of life. He had emigrated from England in search of adventure. After divinity school he sought missionary challenge. He found both in Alaska.[34]

An enthusiastic but amateur mountaineer (with experience in the Rockies and Cascades, and a few days climbing in the Alps), he knew that he needed a partner who could lead ". . . in the face of difficulty and danger."[35] Karstens, a fellow Episcopalian in Fairbanks, fit the bill.[36] Karstens and Sourdough climber Charley McGonagall had once partnered in mail driving and they had worked claims together during the Kantishna gold rush. When Karstens later explored Denali with Charles Sheldon they had jointly studied the access ridge, later to bear Karstens' name, and agreed that it was the key to higher elevations. They even talked of climbing the mountain together. But, to Karstens' everlasting regret, Sheldon returned to the States and marriage, and never came back to Alaska. Stuck knew of the McGonagall-Karstens partnership and their shared knowledge of the route to the top. So it was that the Karstens-Stuck climbing expedition took shape.[37]

As finally assembled, the climbing party comprised the Archdeacon and Karstens as co-leaders (the former as organizer and cook, the latter as trail and climbing leader); robust Walter Harper, Stuck's 21-year-old aide and traveling companion, son of Yukon-Tanana explorer Arthur Harper and an Indian mother; and another able youth, Robert Tatum, a theology student whose recent services to the Episcopal missions included a heroic dog-team supply run to succor isolated mission women on the upper Tanana.

After many delays and frustrations, including non-arrival of previously ordered technical climbing gear—which forced Karstens to improvise critical equipment—the party left Fairbanks in mid-March 1913 by dog team. At the Nenana mission they picked up two teenage Indian lads, Esaias and Johnny Fredson, along with another dog team. These young students at the mission school proved invaluable assistants, both of them helping in the supply relays up Muldrow Glacier before Esaias had to return to Nenana, and Johnny remaining as the lonesome base-camp and dog-team keeper during the month-long absence of the climbing party.

Following established trails to the Kantishna mining camps (where final consultations with Sourdough climbers took place), the party broke trail past Wonder Lake, crossed McKinley River, and, on April 4, set up a wood-cutting camp at the last good spruce stand up Clearwater Creek. While wood was being gathered, Karstens went ahead and located the base camp at the forks of Cache Creek, just below McGonagall Pass. After transfer of the wood fuel up Cache Creek and preparation of rich mountain rations from caribou meat and marrow, the company began trailbreaking and supply relays up Muldrow Glacier on April 16.

The success of this pioneering expedition would be based on Karstens' pioneering experience and never-say-die toughness; on the shared knowledge of route and climbing conditions provided by his Sourdough-climb friends as well as Belmore Browne's recently published magazine account; and on the foresight, determination, and improvisational abilities of its members. Native foods in ample supply, locally hunted and processed for mountain transport, plus plenty of fuel and good bedding assured energy-rich nutrition and sleeping comfort throughout a long and storm-assaulted climb. Improved snow-goggles saved them from painful blindness. The climbers were mentally in the struggle for the duration, and they had the physical means to preserve their strength for the final push at high altitude.

Their way was not easy. Because this was no quick dash to the top (they knew they could not count on the Sourdoughs' luck with the weather), the immense physical labor required to assemble and transport equipment, supplies, and wood-fuel (the latter to the 11,000-foot camp) took its toll even in rare good weather. In the prevailing storms these labors were doubled. Storm-bound days confined to camp sapped will and gave rein to frustration. In these conditions even the best of friends get testy. Karstens and Stuck, because of temperament and style clashes, were hardly the best of friends.

Then there was the fire at their Muldrow camp: tents, socks, mitts, food destroyed or damaged. The devastation shook them. The expedition, so well prepared, faced defeat, victim of a stray spark and whipping winds. But Karstens said "Forget it," and the party improvised, making tents from sled covers, socks from Stuck's camel-hair sleeping bag liner, and so on. At one point, with the men sitting around sewing, the camp looked like a sweat shop. Deprived of such luxuries as sugar, powdered milk, and dried fruit—all burned—they still had the basics and they forged on.

Next they took on the access ridge, Karstens Ridge as named by Stuck. The steep and sheer, yet practicable pathway described by Belmore Browne was no more. Rising above them was a primordial shambles. Fringing the 3,000-foot high Harper Icefall, the ridge connected to the high basin formed by Harper Glacier. There was no other way to the final heights. They stared at the shattered ridge in disbelief, even as it dawned on them that the 1912 earthquake had created this chaos. They saw great blocks of ice, bigger than buildings, some the size of city blocks. They leaned, balanced, and honeycombed on each other on a thin ridge that fell more than 1,000 feet to Muldrow Glacier and 3,000 feet to its eastern branch, the Traleika.

For 3 weeks, as storms allowed, Karstens and Harper spent most of their time probing through this jumbled nightmare and chopping steps—3 miles of them—out of the concrete-like ice. They avoided the nearly sheer flanking slopes as much as possible, for avalanche danger was great, and the overhanging, unconsolidated blocks of ice balanced in defiance of gravity. In his diary Karstens noted that some of the blocks would fall if someone whispered at them. Stuck and Tatum began supply relays with backpacks as soon as the icy staircase reached flat spots where goods could be cached.

Finally, at 15,000 feet they passed beyond the ridge into the basin, above which rose Denali's great peaks. On June 3, at mid-point on Harper Glacier, Walter Harper spotted the Sourdoughs' flagpole on the North Peak. With the glasses everyone saw it, thus confirming the Taylor-Anderson ascent and McGonagall's hauling of the pole to nearly 19,000 feet.

In deliberate stages the men now advanced from camp to camp, always getting higher and closer to the South Peak. Their last camp at 17,500 feet—almost directly below Denali Pass between the peaks—put them about 1,000 feet higher for the final assault than Parker-Browne had been the year before. This was a critical advantage for 50-year-old Hudson Stuck, who was feeling the altitude much more than the youthful Harper and Tatum and the mid-30s Karstens. At that they still had nearly 3,000 feet to go vertically. But with all hands reasonably healthy, plenty of food, good bedding, and ample gas fuel for their stove, their objective was attainable.

Next morning, Saturday June 7, came on clear and cold, good weather for the climb. But except for Walter Harper, the men were suffering. For dinner the night before Harper had cooked noodles to thicken the caribou stew; at such altitude and lacking baking powder—also burned—the noodles were a half-done mess that wreaked havoc upon all digestive systems except the chef's. This, plus the last few day's extreme efforts at high altitude and excitement over the next day's climb, had made sleep impossible. Alone with his thoughts in the early hours, huddled over the gas stove, Stuck had stared at failure. All but Walter looked upon the new day with bad stomachs and wracking headaches. Karstens would have stayed in bed except that this was the day of the climb.

After a very light breakfast Karstens assigned the lead to the sturdy Walter, and at 4 a.m., with sun shining, a keen wind, and the thermometer marking minus 4 degrees F., the sorry company followed the indomitable young Indian toward the utmost heights. They carried lunch and scientific-instrument packs only. First they traversed the snow ridge that rose above their camp, then headed toward the final rises that still hid the summit. It was step by gasping step in bitter cold, which, aided by the wind, pierced their layered clothing and numbed their heavily clad hands and feet. Stuck relates that Karstens beat his freezing feet so violently against the packed snow that two of his nails later dropped off. On the margin between life and terrible damage or death by freezing, they pushed on. Behind a ridge, partially sheltered from the wind, the ascending sun gave a little warmth. Lunch and a thermos of hot tea helped.

As confidence grew, however, so did altitude. Hudson Stuck's oxygen deficiency nearly overcame him several times. He would black-out, then rest and recover. Walter Harper relieved him of the bulky mercurial barometer that Stuck had insisted on carrying.

At last, with Harper still in the lead and the first man there to stand, they got to the very top. Stuck, on the verge of unconsciousness had to be braced the last few steps by his companions.

After a few moments of recovery the climbers shook hands and gave thanks to an Almighty who seemed very near on this high place. Then the party set up the little instrument tent and began their measurements—temperature, altitude, and others.

From later expert calculations of their readings, the mountain's altitude averaged out at 20,700 feet. One of the experts, U.S. Geological Survey topographer C. E. Giffin, figured 20,374 feet above sea level, closest to the true 20,320.[38] (A 1909 Coast and Geodetic Survey observation had placed the altitude at 20,300, only 20 feet off the mark.)[39]

Finally, finished with the obligatory science, the men posed for photographs, which ended up double-exposed due to cold-numbed fingers. Then they looked about them.

Stuck gave thanks for a perfectly clear day in all directions—a rarity that the churchman could attribute only to God's design on the very day of their climb. In this providential moment Hudson Stuck touched the sublime in what he saw and how he described it:

Immediately before us, in the direction in which we had climbed, lay—nothing: a void, a sheer gulf many thousands of feet deep, and one shrank back instinctively from the little parapet of the [summit] snow basin when one had glanced at the awful profundity. Across the gulf . . . sprang most splendidly into view the great mass of Denali's Wife, or Mount Foraker . . . filling majestically all the middle distance. . . . And never was nobler sight displayed to man than that great, isolated mountain spread out completely, with all its spurs and ridges, its cliffs and its glaciers, lofty and mighty and yet far beneath us. . . . Beyond stretched, blue and vague to the southwest, the wide valley of the Kuskokwim, with an end of all mountains. To the north we looked right over the North Peak to the foot-hills below, patched with lakes and lingering snow, glittering with streams. . . .

It was, however, to the south and east that the most marvelous prospect opened before us. What infinite tangle of mountain ranges filled the whole scene, until gray sky, gray mountains, and gray sea merged in the ultimate distance! The near-by peaks and ridges stood out with dazzling distinction, the glaciation, the drainage, the relation of each part to the others all revealed.[40]

In the detachment that he felt from the world below, under the deep blue dome of the stratospheric sky, Hudson Stuck searched his feelings about their attainment:

There was no pride of conquest, no trace of that exultation of victory some enjoy upon the first ascent of a lofty peak, no gloating over good fortune that had hoisted us a few hundred feet higher than others who had struggled and been discomfited. Rather was the feeling that a privileged communion with the high places of the earth had been granted; that not only we had been permitted to lift up eager eyes to these summits, secret and solitary since the world began, but to enter boldly upon them, to take place, as it were, domestically in their hitherto sealed chambers, to inhabit them, and to cast our eyes down from them, seeing all things as they spread out from the windows of heaven itself.[41]

After an hour-and-a-half on the summit the remorseless cold cut contemplation and drove them downward. Next day, from their camp high in the basin, they descended rapidly in good spirits to the 11,000-foot camp on upper Muldrow. On June 9 they reached base camp on Cache Creek.

Young Johnny Fredson had been hearing voices for days as the climbers' absence stretched past the planned 2 weeks to the month that had passed since last farewells at the Muldrow camp. Finally the boy heard real voices and the ghosts became real men, weather beaten and hungry. Roast caribou and sheep greeted them, along with Johnny's share of sugar and milk for coffee, which he had religiously saved for them after theirs was lost in the fire. The well-kept dogs joined in the joyful reunion.

From there on out, excepting Tatum's near drowning in McKinley River—dragged down by his pack, pulled out by Karstens—and a series of foundering feeds with miner friends at the Kantishna camps, the return trip was routine. Their cached poling boat, named *Getaway* by Karstens, took them down the rivers to the town of Tanana, where they arrived June 20, more than 3 months after leaving Fairbanks.

As news of the first complete ascent of Mount McKinley flashed across the country, Cook supporters rallied to dispute this latest first-climb claim, but most everyone else accepted the missionary's word.

Despite Stuck's giving immediate and subsequent credit to Karstens as the true climbing leader, news stories about the exploit revolved around the Archdeacon, with only anonymous reference to his "companions." The resentments that Karstens had built up during the expedition—based partly on Stuck's sparse participation in camp duties, particularly his leaving the cooking to others, and partly on his literary airs and refined manner—now exploded. In an undated letter to Charles Sheldon, probably written in early August 1913, Karstens expanded upon both the technical aspects of the climb and his many complaints about Stuck. He lamented the fact that Sheldon had not climbed the mountain with him rather than the "preacher."

Despite Stuck's repeated attempts at reconciliation, the strong-willed Karstens never forgave him. Mutual avoidance was the only resolution. As can be inferred from the careful treatment of this feud by Stuck's biographer,[42] the chemistries and backgrounds of the two men—the rough-hewn pioneer versus the doctor of divinity—were so distinct that the rights and wrongs of the dispute probably were less important than differences of style. Unfortunately but predictably, Karstens' volatile temperament would raise its head again in this stalwart man's career. Yet the very singlemindedness that maintained Karstens' grudge would be one of his greatest strengths as a pioneering superintendent.

Beyond its unfortunate aftermath the climb had been, after all, a resounding success: well planned, well executed by men totally committed and able to surmount extreme physical challenges. Karstens' splendid pioneering ability and field leadership—as Hudson Stuck constantly reiterated—had been the key to that success.

It would be 19 years before the top-dwelling spirit of Denali would receive another visitor.[43]

1913 South Peak Expedition—Tatum, Esais, Karstens, Walter, and Stuck at the Clearwater Camp. From the Denali National Park and Preserve Archive.

1. Webb, *The Last Frontier*, 197-198; Ernest Gruening, *The State of Alaska*, (New York: Random House, 1954), 286-289.

2. James Wickersham, *Old Yukon: Tales—Trails—and Trials* (Washington: Washington Law Book Co., 1938), 203.

3. Ibid., 218-220

4. Ibid., 220.

5. Ibid., 222-237.

6. Ibid., 255-257.

7. Ibid., 243-253.

8. Ibid., 268.

9. Ibid., 268-277.

10. Ibid., 289; Washburn places them on a spur of Wickersham Wall at an elevation of 8,100 feet, "Chronology," 8.

11. Frederick A. Cook, *To the Top of the Continent* (New York: Doubleday, Page & Co., 1908), 69-70.

12. Washburn identifies the extreme eastern branch of the Toklat River as the entrance to Cook's yet unnamed pass, "Chronology," 9.

13. For accounts of Cook's 1903 journey see his book, 1-96; Moore, *Mt. McKinley*, 40-48; Robert Dunn, *The Shameless Diary of an Explorer* (New York: The Outing Pub. Co., 1907).

14. Moore, *Mt. McKinley*, 43.

15. Dunn, *Shameless Diary*, 59, 60.

16. Ibid., 196.

17. Ibid., 238.

18. See Bradford Washburn's Introduction to Belmore Browne's *The Conquest of Mount McKinley* (Boston: Houghton Mifflin Co., 1956, first published in 1913), for Browne's biography.

19. Ibid., 1-3.

20. This impression is derived from a mountainous literature on Mount McKinley. Brad Washburn's *Mount McKinley and the Alaska Range in Literature, a Descriptive Bibliography* (Boston: The Museum of Science, 1951) is a good start. His 265-item listing has probably been doubled, at least in the years since 1951. A modern account of a climbing tragedy, Joe Wilcox's *White Winds* (Los Alamitos, Calif.: Hwong Pub. Co., 1981), depicts the other-worldliness of Mount McKinley's upper regions.

21. Moore, *Mt. McKinley*, 53.

22. Quoted in ibid., 85. See Claude E. Rusk, "On the Trail of Dr. Cook," *Pacific Monthly*, October 1910, November 1910, January 1911 (reprinted in *Mazama*, 1945), for Rusk's full report.

23. See Bradford Washburn, "Doctor Cook and Mount McKinley," *American Alpine Journal* (1958), 1-30, for a full discussion of Cook's claims and countering eveidence, and the basic bibliography on the controversy.

24. Charles Sheldon, *The Wilderness of Denali* (New York: Charles Scribner's Sons, 1930), 4.

25. Sheldon, *Denali*, 274.

26. Terrence Cole, Ed., *The Sourdough Expeditions, Stories of the Pioneer Alaskans Who Climbed Mount McKinley in 1910* (Anchorage: Alaska Northwest Publishing Co., 1985), contains original accounts and critical evaluations thereof; Bradford Washburn, ed., *A Map of Mount McKinley* (Boston: The Museum of Science, 1977); Moore, *Mt. McKinley*, 69-75, 143-153; Francis P. Farquhar, "The Exploration and First Ascents of Mount McKinley," reprinted from *Sierra Club Bulletin*, June 1949, 95-109.

27. Browne, *Conquest*, 337.

28. Ibid., 339.

29. Ibid., 340.

30. Ibid., 344.

31. Ibid., 349.

32. Washburn, "Chronology," 11.

33. See Moore, *Mt. McKinley*, 87-104, for summary of the 1912 Parker-Browne attempt.

34. Paul E. Thompson, "Who Was Hudson Stuck?" *Alaska Journal*, Vol. 10, No. 1, Winter 1980, 62-65.

35. Hudson Stuck, *The Ascent of Denali* (New York: Scribner's, 1914), xii.

36. David M. Dean, *Breaking Trail, Hudson Stuck of Texas and Alaska* (Athens: Ohio University Press, 1988) ix-xi, 150-158; Karstens obituary, *Fairbanks News-Miner*, Nov. 29, 1955.

37. Dean, *Breaking Trail*, 159-160. These details derive in part from the Harry P. Karstens Papers, Dartmouth College Library, cited in Note 19, p. 318, of Dean's book.

38. Stuck, *Ascent*, 150-151.

39. Washburn, "Chronology," 11.

40. Stuck, *Ascent*, 101-102.

41. Ibid., 108-109.

42. Dean, *Breaking Trail*, 169-171, 178-181.

43. Basic sources used in the summary of the first ascent include Hudson Stuck, *The Ascent of Denali*, passim, with Bradford Washburn route photos and an appendix containing Walter Harper's climbing diary (in The Mountaineers 1977 paperback edition); Bradford Washburn, "The First Ascent of Mount McKinley, 1913, A Verbatim Copy of the Diary of Harry P. Karstens," *The American Alpine Journal* (1969), 339-348; Dean, *Breaking Trail*, 150-183; Clara Childs Mackenzie, *Wolf Smeller (Zhoh Gwatsan), A Biography of John Fredson, Native Alaskan* (Anchorage: Alaska Pacific University Press, 1985), 40-58; Harry P. Karstens undated letter to Charles Sheldon (ca. August 1913), in Charles Sheldon Collection, University of Alaska Archives, Fairbanks, Box 1, File 11; Moore, *Mt. McKinley*, 105-120; Bradford Washburn, "Guide to the Muldrow Glacier Route," undated typescript in Denali National Park library.

Mist on the East Toklat River, October 25, 1966. From the Denali National Park and Preserve Archive.

Miners whipsawing logs, a tough and thankless task. Courtesy of the Stephen R. Capps Collection, UAF.

C H A P T E R 4
The Kantishna and Nearby Mining Districts

GOLD — THE GLORY DAYS

When Karstens and the others came down from the mountain, they headed for Eureka, the mining camp at the junction of Eureka and Moose creeks, now known as Kantishna. There a miner named Hamilton fed them "like a Prince." Next day, they reached Joe and Fanny Quigley's place, where they enjoyed a "big feed." And the next day they had another big feed at Glacier City.[1]

Who were these miners, these dwellers of the far places for whom hospitality was code and communion? All the early travelers remarked of the miners that they were a special breed, men and women of everlasting hope. Failure they knew well. For gold was elusive: scattered in the gravels of rushing streams, clinched in rocky crevices, hidden under deep, sometimes hundreds-of-feet deep, sediments that overlay ancient watercourses. These were all variations of placer gold—gold already eroded from the country rock and concentrated here and there (but where?) by Nature's running waters. This kind of gold, when discovered, ran out fast in those early days, for much of the gold escaped the ingenious but crude traps set by the pioneer miners. All of them then used flows and charges of water—as Nature had already done, to a point—to move lighter rock and gravel, allowing the heavy gold to settle in the riffles of sluice boxes.

Stampedes brought mixed company, in waves. And the mining proceeded in stages. Some prospectors following, in Robert Dunn's phrase, "the old, relentless dream-trail,"[2] found paying colors. The word got out. First to the new Eldorado were prospectors and miners already in the country. Expert and efficient, they found and staked the better claims. The second wave of stampeders, often delayed until the next season, staked what was left or found work as laborers at the operating mines. Many of these latecomers lacked experience. Theirs, typically, was a life of leavings, pittance-pay hard labor (given mining-camp prices), and eventual return to more civilized precincts.

As surface-stream gold gave out, and if the geology were right, placer operations shifted to bench claims and deep-hole mining—probing old creek terraces or the ancestral streambeds far below. In the first primitive efforts, the miners melted through the frozen dirt with hot rocks or wood fires; later they used steam, generated by small, wood-fired boilers. They dug their shafts to bedrock where the old streams had concentrated the gold. By this time only hard-core miners remained, for intensive development work, often taking years, preceded any hope of pay, once the "sunburnt" gold was gone.

If the arduous bench and deep-hole efforts failed to fill their pokes, the miners began looking up the steep creeks toward the domes and ridges where the lode gold—the uneroded gold of creation—lay hidden in the solid rock. Then hard-rock mining began with dynamite and pick and pry-bar—into the very heart of the mountain, where veins of gold-bearing quartzite meandered through the fissures and fractures of geologic history.

Kantishna went fairly quickly from placer mining to lode prospecting. As improved

Top photo: *Bench mining on Glacier Creek, 1906. Courtesy of the L. M. Prindle Collection, USGS.*

Bottom photo: *Sluice boxes on Spruce Creek, Kantishna area, 1906, Courtesy of the L. M. Prindle Collection, USGS.*

placer techniques allowed, miners made their pay from placer benches and deep holes (and from reworking previously sifted surface-stream gravels) while they prospected and developed the lode claims.

Because all the Denali-region districts were remote and their pay locations spotty—without the vast extent of the Klondike, Fairbanks, and Nome fields—there was little corporate takeover and agglomeration of the mines as compared to the climax stage in those larger fields. Thus, continuity of people and ownership persisted clear into the '30s in some places. This was particularly true in the Kantishna. The mining camps scattered on the streams and ridges comprised a loose-knit community. Rugged topography—deep valleys and tortuous ridges—hindered casual visiting. But when someone did drop by on the way out to town, or back in, it was a special occasion. And being far from town, helpfulness—really going out of one's way—was not marked up as a debt owed, for tomorrow or next year, it might be yourself who needed the gathering-round of neighbors.

The principal gold fields of the Denali region include:

❋ *The Kantishna district with most of the mining concentrated in the southwest part of the Kantishna Hills, just north of Wonder Lake.*

❋ *The Bonnifield district to the northeast, tapping tributaries of the Tanana flowing north from the Alaska range.*

❋ *And the fields to the south of the range in the Susitna drainage—the hand-work and dredge placers on Cache and Peters creeks, draining the Dutch and Peters Hills; the upper Chulitna River lode mines; and the surface and deep-hole placers of the Valdez Creek area on the upper Susitna, east of Cantwell.*

All of these were remote fields, far removed from the big rivers that permitted easy steamboat transport of supplies and equipment to landings near mine sites. The Valdez Creek miners relied at first on overland transport from the military wagon road between Valdez and Eagle. (Later, when the Alaska Railroad reached Cantwell, they shifted their base of supply to that town.) The other districts used a combination of river and overland transport. Small steamers chugged up the tributaries as far as they could go. At the heads of navigation of these shoaling streams a "last chance" trading station might be established. From such stations goods went farther upstream in launches, poling boats, and horse-drawn scows. Finally, overland travel with dogsleds or horse-drawn sledges brought the goods to the mines. Each link in the transportation system cost money. Barring very rich diggings, the big financiers showed only passing interest in such fields. There was no profit after a big investment, as the era of company mining (1917-21) at Valdez Creek showed.[3] Thus the small-scale, labor-intensive mining of the pioneer field tended to persist in such places. Where stripped-down hydraulic and dredging and hard-rock operations did occur on the upper creeks, they were plagued by water shortages and equipment-maintenance problems. Improvisation and creative salvage and adaptation of any machined metal helped the miners to limp along.[4]

With construction of the Alaska Railroad (1915-23)—up the Susitna Valley through Broad Pass, and south from Fairbanks along the Nenana—leading to spur roads and trails from the rail line, transportation improved. But by then exhaustion of surface placers, and less-than-Bonanza prospects for more expensive mining, had reduced many of the camps to subsistence levels. With few exceptions up through the '30s, large-scale mining enterprises in these districts could not be made to pay. Typically, after two or three seasons of expense and labor to develop and put into operation such enterprises, they folded and the engineers left. Then the durable old-timers with modest expectations salvaged machinery, pipes, and other useful items from the abandoned company camps.

All of these districts started up about the same time, in the years 1903 to 1907.[5]

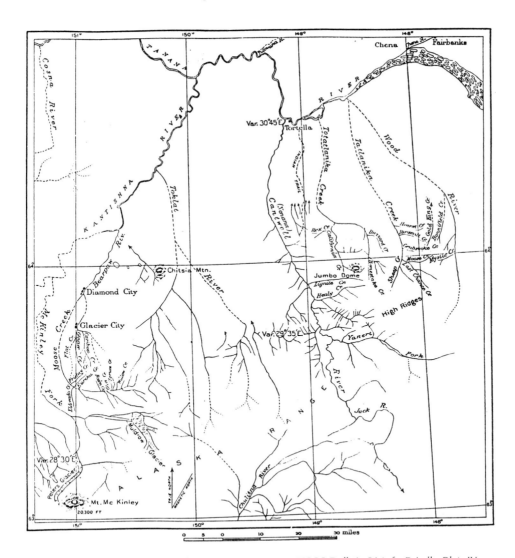

Map of the Bonnifield and Kantishna regions, 1906. From USGS Bulletin 314, by Prindle, Plate IV.

65

Claim No. 2a on Eureka, Kantishna area, 1906. *Courtesy of the* L. M. Prindle Collection, USGS.

Through the '30s they had similar sequences of boom and bust, then revival with modest investments of outside money, usually followed by disappointment. They all responded with flurries when the railroad came near and when, in 1933, President Franklin D. Roosevelt raised the price of gold to $35 an ounce.

Mines in these districts produced by-products (or in a few instances were primary producers) of other metals: silver, zinc, lead, antimony, or copper. But gold would always be the main lure and bring in all but a small fraction of the pay.

In the early days, coal—which would soon become Alaska's second most valuable mineral—was only of local consequence in the Denali region. Small outcrops and shallow beds occurred in many places, and if one of them was near a mining camp it could be exploited as fuel for domestic, forge, and machinery operations. For example, the Dunkle Mine on the south side supplied the nearby Golden Zone mine overlooking the Chulitna's West Fork, until the miners shifted to hydropower. Vast coal deposits—untappable without bulk transport—occupied the Matanuska and Nenana fields. This latent wealth and energy helped determine the route of the Alaska Railroad. The railroad would use the higher grade coals of the Matanuska field to fuel its locomotives while hauling the lower grade coal to Anchorage and Seward for domestic use. After the last spike was driven in 1923 the Nenana field—next door to the new National Park—supplied Fairbanks, and also local consumers, including the park. Many small coal mines flourished briefly along the railroad, e.g., the mine at Railroad Mile 341, now within the enlarged park. Another small mine, in the original Mount McKinley National Park, near the East Fork of the Toklat River, was operated by the Alaska Road Commission to supply its camps during construction of the park road for the National Park Service.[6]

The mining story in the Denali region began coincidentally with the mountaineering saga. A kind of symbiosis evolved between the two very differently engaged groups of people: The miners provided hospitality and knowledge of the country; the visitors (not just mountaineers, but also USGS parties and ramblers of assorted kinds) brought news of the outside world and, because most of them were genteel sorts, provided polite new sounding boards for old arguments and opinions long since dismissed by the host miner's steady company. It was, after all, a fair deal.

A by-product of these exchanges were the writings of the visitors, which give us a contemporary view of the progress of the country and the people in it.

In the flurry of stampedes to the Denali region that began in 1903, prospectors came from north and south. Overflow from the earlier Fairbanks strike populated the Bonnifield and Kantishna districts. Prospectors from the entry port of Valdez crossed glaciers and mountains to open the Valdez Creek district east of Denali. And latecomers to the Cook Inlet strikes headed up the Susitna and Chulitna to the fields on Denali's south side. Trading stations and roadhouses sprang up overnight. Primitive packhorse and winter trails to the mining camps were blazed and brushed from the boat landings at heads of navigation. At these off-loading sites stores, saloons, and boarding houses appeared as if by magic. For Alaska's goldrush population included a large contingent of gypsy caterers to miners' needs and appetites. The toll gates at these places worked both ways: stampeders going to the fields spent their grubstakes for supplies and necessities; on the way back out, if their pokes held gold, they satisfied their appetites for booze, gambling, and women. Many hopefuls never made it to the gold fields. They lingered too long in the saloons, blew their grubstakes, and returned crestfallen to the towns. Serious prospectors and miners worked first, and, among those so inclined, binged second.

The Kantishna district exhibited all of these sequences and stages and shall be the main focus of the narrative that follows.

Though Judge Wickersham's claims on Chitsia Creek never paid a dime, his recording of them in 1903 attracted experienced prospectors to the Kantishna Hills. Joe Dalton found colors on the Toklat in 1904. Joe Quigley and Jack Horn staked Glacier Creek early the next summer. Their filing of claims on a quick trip to Fairbanks caused excitement and the rush began. Meanwhile, Joe Dalton and his partner had shifted southwest from Crooked Creek of the Toklat drainage to Friday and Eureka creeks which flowed into Moose Creek. Their staking of these rich diggings coincided with the arrival of the first stampeders in mid-July. Within weeks the 2,000 to 3,000 argonauts had staked every drainage in the Kantishna from mouth to head, and some prospectors were already probing the benches and ridges. A small fleet of steamers and launches carried people, gear, and supplies up the Kantishna and Bearpaw rivers

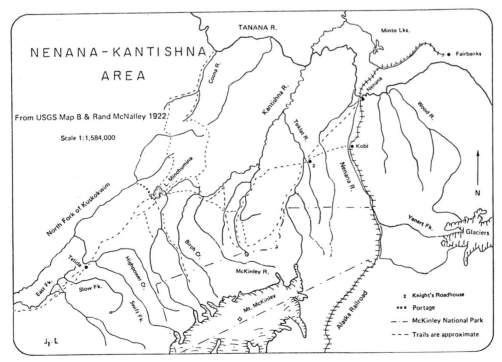

Trails in the Nenana Kantishna area, 1922. From Ethnohistory of Four Interior Waterbodies, *by Dianne Gudgel-Holmes, page 68.*

Placer miners in the Kantishna area, 1919.
Courtesy of the Stephen Foster Collection, UAF.

as far as they could go. Instant boom towns sprang up: Diamond and Glacier City on Bearpaw River; Roosevelt and Square Deal on the Kantishna. The tent metropolis of Eureka, at the Eureka-Moose Creek junction, was the last stop before the miners clambered and hauled themselves and gear up the creeks and over tundra ridges to the scattered claims.[7]

Within 6 months the rush was over. The real miners quickly scooped up the shallow, rich diggings, which were localized in a few streams. By February 1906, disappointment began driving the frustrated thousands out. Winter trails—around the north side of the Kantishna Hills via Glacier City and Diamond, or the pack trail up Myrtle Creek and across a low pass to Clearwater Fork of Toklat River—carried contrasting traffic: backtrail losers going out, and more supplies and equipment for the winners, going in.[8]

For all but a few the summer season of 1906 proved disappointing, and the gradual exodus became a rout. U.S. Geological Survey geologist L. M. Prindle visited the district late that summer. He saw many abandoned diggings. On September 1, after trekking down Glacier Creek where a few men were working, he noted in his trip diary, "town of Glacier, a long line of abandoned cabins & 2 stores."[9] Diamond inspired a similar entry. The town of Roosevelt, isolated by 18 miles of swampy tundra from the creeks, was practically deserted. The few hangers-on and the many empty cabins in these places ". . . testified with depressing emphasis to the decadence from the activities of the previous year."[10]

Thus ended the brief glory days and began the hard mining. About 50 people remained. Over the next 15 years or so the Kantishna district remained stable. Each year some 30 to 50 miners worked their claims. They all continued their placer work, at decreasing levels of pay, and some of them actively prospected and staked hard-rock claims on the ridges. When USGS geologist Stephen Capps visited the region in 1916 he found 35 people, most of them holdovers from the first stampede. At that time all pay still came from placer mines, but preliminary development of the hard-rock claims was underway. Capps forecast that eventually the lodes—containing gold, silver, and the sulphides of lead, zinc, and antimony—would probably outstrip the placers in value.[11] He noted that several miners wintered in the cabins at Glacier City, down in the timbered flats. It was better than hauling wood to their high summer camps in the barren hills,[12] and wintering game and furbearers could be taken in the woods.

This was the distilled Kantishna community, this small group of durable people, whose hospitality became legend, whose daily anecdotes, as transmuted by literate visitors became the stuff of myths. They all hoped for better times. If they could get good transportation, thus reducing mining costs, many of the marginal creeks could be made to pay. If an all-weather wagon road came their way, maybe from the rumored railroad that some said would go through Broad Pass, then they could get in heavy equipment and go for the lode deposits. Always there were these hopes—and petitions and letters to the authorities that stated them and asked for transportation relief. Meanwhile, they exploited the shallow bench claims. From local materials they built automatic dams—boomer dams—which filled with water, then dumped themselves and filled again. The "splashes" from these dams washed away the heavy overburden so the miners could get to pay gravel under the deeper creek deposits. They hauled in some pipe and big nozzles and diverted water behind header dams so they could carve away the benches hydraulically. They subsisted on a combination of placer mining, hunting, trapping, and gardening. And they kept hoping.

The toils, character, and relentless energy of the miners inspired many descriptions. Robert Dunn, in 1903, captured the spirit of those embarked on a gold rush:

Prospectors are coming into this valley for the first time. No strike has been made, no, but it's the last valley in Alaska still untouched. They have spent the late summer boating up their year's supplies from the head of the Inlet. Some have dogs, some hope to get them from somewhere before winter. They are the bedrock Alaskan article, the men to be first on the claims if an Eldorado is struck. They start their stampede the winter before, not in the spring, which is the tenderfoot way. Each has just waked from failure—in a rush camp, or looking for daily wages in Valdez. Again they take up the . . . trail to riches through the desolate and uncertain North. . . . Now the Eldorado is at hand, in this Sushitna valley, here is the place.[13]

Three years later Doctor Cook caught the ephemeral nature of the mining camps as prospectors swarmed the creeks and moved on if they didn't pay:

Youngstown, a kind of mythical miners' camp, the supposed head of navigation, was our ultimate destination. But we were a long time locating the town. Indeed the town was unable to locate itself, for it drifted with a shifting population of miners. At about ten o'clock we saw a big dory drifting down the stream. A corpulent miner with all kinds of things was in the boat. To our question, "How far to Youngstown?" he answered: "It used to be twenty miles above, but it just moved. I have the town in the dory and am taking it down the stream."[14]

A camp that stuck, the Kantishna, hosted Belmore Browne and Doctor Parker on the backtrail from their 1912 climb. Browne's relation of encounters with the durables of that community provides a cameo of them and their way of life.

Seeing the first strangers for months, the climbers at first were shy. But the welcome they received broke their sense of strangeness instantly. On Moose Creek they met two miners named Clark and Fink. They were working a lay, a claim owned by another miner who received a percentage of the pay. While the visitors learned how to eat at a table again, their hosts—"the best type of the Alaska pioneer"—told of the yearly round:

During the short mountain summer they worked constantly, sluicing the golden sand. In the winter they whip-sawed lumber, trapped, and hunted meat. Clark was an expert hunter of big game, and for a season he had killed the mountain sheep for the market. . . .

[The next day] we looked at Clark and Fink's ground. By digging a ditch they had brought water to the head of their claims. The water then ran through sluice boxes into which the gravel was thrown. At the lower end of the boxes the riffles caught the gold that had been separated from the gravel by the water, while the gravel, being lighter, continued onward with the water into Moose Creek. It is in this simple way that most of the gold in this part of Alaska is secured.

Later Browne and Parker passed through Joe Dalton's discovery claim on the way to his current diggings farther up Eureka Creek. There, they had been told, Dalton had cached some dog feed for them. From Dalton and others they learned of the Katmai eruption, which explained the distant boomings they had heard on the mountain, and the earthquake whose worst effects they had narrowly escaped. They reflected on these denizens of the far creeks:

Here were men from many different lands, but the hard life in the open, the search for gold, and the

Top photo: Moose hunt, November 1919. Fanny Quigley is at the far left. Joe Quigley is to her right. Courtesy of the Stephen Foster Collection, UAF.

Bottom photo: Miners and government men at the Quigley cabin, August 30, 1931. Shown from left to right, are: Mr. Edmonds (ARC), Fanny Quigley, Mrs. Edmonds, Philip Smith (USGS), and Joe Quigley. Courtesy of the Fanny Quigley Collection, UAF.

separation from civilization had stamped each with a certain undefinable air that gave them a personality of their own.

In nature's stamp mill they had been polished down until they represented a type.

Another Eureka Creek miner, Fred Hauselman, a Swiss, now guided them to Glacier Creek, where they were welcomed "to the palatial home" of Fanny and Joe Quigley. Fanny, originally from a Bohemian settlement in Nebraska, was known in Kantishna's early days as "Mother McKenzie." She was still the only woman in camp, providing that touch of home that the miners missed so much. Joining the Ninety-Eight rush to the Klondike, she had since migrated from camp to camp—cooking, and prospecting and mining in her own right. At Kantishna she met and in 1906 married Joe Quigley—first staker of Glacier Creek—a pre-gold rush prospector who had crossed the Chilkoot Pass in 1891. Their home was spacious and clean, well lighted and cheerful. Books and magazines bespoke lively intellectual interests. A flourishing garden, with flowers and vegetables, fed soul and stomach. Their permafrost cellar kept meat frozen, and their cooler kept vegetables fresh.

Though small of stature, Fanny was strong and rugged:

She lived the wild life as the men did, and was as much at home in the open with a rifle as a city woman is on a city avenue, and she could not only follow and hunt successfully the wild game of the region, but could do a man's share in packing the meat to camp. From a physical standpoint she was a living example of what nature had intended a woman to be, and, furthermore, while having the ability to do a man's work, she also enjoyed the life as a man does. No man could catch more grayling in a day than she, the miners said, and at the day's end she would shoulder her heavy catch and tramp homeward as happy as a boy.

Browne compared the meals she cooked to Roman feasts: meats, breads, vegetables, jellies, pies, and a wild rhubarb sauce that beat any tame rhubarb Browne had eaten. All was washed down with ice-cold potato beer, of which Fanny was master brewer. After dinner, their hosts—and Sourdough climber Charley McGonagall, who

Glacier City, 1906. Courtesy of the L. M. Prindle Collection, USGS.

had also joined them—told of mountains, hunting, the habits of animals, and the many adventures of wilderness life.

All too soon this visit ended and the surfeited mountaineers proceeded to Glacier City, some 12 miles away. Just before they began the trek, Pete Anderson, another of the Sourdoughs, passed by Quigley's and invited them to drop in at his cabin when they reached the old supply town.

The hike was long and it rained. They came upon the remains of a decrepit bridge over a slough, "a wonderful structure" in that wild, out-of-the-way place, a harbinger of civilization. Rain-soaked and tired, they finally discovered a line of moss-covered cabins, now overgrown with alders. Fronting them was the dim trail, also being recaptured by Nature, that led to Glacier City. A clearing and more lines of empty cabins marked the center of the town. Smoke from one of them, and a hail from Anderson, brought them to another stupendous meal, after a change to dry clothes that were relics of the stampede.

From Glacier City, they loaded their duffle on packhorses belonging to Sourdough Billy Taylor and quick-stepped the last leg of their march to the head of navigation on Moose Creek. Here, as urged by a miner named Greiss (whom they had met on Eureka Creek), they partook of his cabin and grub, including fresh garden greens, then they reconditioned an abandoned stampeder's boat, salvaged by Greiss, for the drift down the rivers to the Yukon.[15]

PROSPECTING AND TRAPPING

Another traveler of the same period, Lee R. Dice, a government fur warden, left us a picture of the prospector-fur trapper way of life in the Lake Minchumina area. Ben Anderson and James Johnson had located their cabin and prospects on a small creek draining a high dome between the lake and the upper North Fork of Kuskokwim River. They were working on one of several prospect holes that reached to bedrock when Dice called upon them in the winter of 1911. He had met them earlier at the Tanana trading station and was following up on their invitation to visit.

Anderson and Johnson were thawing the frozen ground with hot rocks heated in a wood fire. The rocks were lowered to the bottom of the shaft, covered with moss, and then after several hours, retrieved. The resulting foot or so of thawed muck was shoveled into a bucket by the man in the shaft; the man on top used a hand windlass to hoist the bucket loads to the surface. Then the whole process was repeated. The

Roosevelt, on the Kantishna River, ca. 1917. Courtesy of the Stephen Foster Collection, UAF.

Top photo: Sluicing in the Kantishna area in the early 1920s. Courtesy of the John M. Brooks Collection, UAF.

Bottom photo: The Hanson brothers, John, Einar, and Emil, were natives of Denmark who trapped in the Kantishna River area from 1916 to 1950. Courtesy of the Fabian Carey Collection, UAF.

holes at this prospect, which had yet to show colors, averaged 70 feet deep.

Dice learned from these men that the fur bearers around Lake Minchumina had been pretty well trapped out by the Indians who lived in a small village on the lake. His hosts, nearly done with their prospecting, invited Dice to move with them down the Kuskokwim to their trapping cabin. Dice accepted this proposition with alacrity and great appreciation, for they knew that part of his work involved trapping fur animals for scientific purposes, which would make him not only a guest but also a competitor of sorts.

They arrived in good country for fur: low hills covered with spruce and patches of birch, and plenty of creeks, lakes, and swamps. Marten and weasel were common. Abundant hares attracted lynx. Otter, beaver, and muskrat frequented lakes and streams.

Dice noted that in 1911-12, many prospectors and miners had shifted to trapping in the winter, even though this pursuit interfered with their search for gold and their accumulation of winter "dumps," the piles of pay dirt hauled out of the frozen ground in anticipation of spring sluicing. The furs would buy the grubstakes for the next season of mining.

In contrast was the seasonal round of the full-time trapper:

The man who planned to devote the major part of his time to trapping would probably select a locality far remote from civilization, because the more accessible regions had already been trapped out. It would probably take him most of the summer for him to get in his winter's supplies from the nearest trading post, travelling by poling boat up some river. The autumn would be spent in building a main cabin and perhaps several relay cabins and in cutting trap-line trails. If deadfalls were to be used, these must be built. By about November 15 the meager harvest would begin. From that time on the trapper must go over his trap-line twice a week if possible; dig out the traps that had drifted full of snow; reset those traps sprung by jays or other animals; change the location of traps where necessary; and skin such animals as he had taken. To walk ten to fifteen miles a day on snowshoes and do all the necessary work of trapping, cooking, and keeping up his camp is hard work for a strong and vigorous man.

The average season's catch of fur by an Alaskan trapper in 1912 was probably worth less than five hundred dollars. This amount would, at the high prices charged for supplies at the trading posts, just about buy the actual necessities for another winter of trapping. The trapper, therefore, unless he was unusually vigorous or very fortunate, made only a bare living. There were reported to be a few exceptions, but with the sparse distribution of fur-bearing animals in Alaska at that time, no great fortune was in prospect for most trappers.[16]

Dice admired the ingenuity of his generous companions, who, with nothing but a few hand tools, some line, and very few nails could fashion cabins, boats, buckets, furniture, winches, sluice boxes, and just about anything else from the trees that grew around them. Their improvisational genius is illustrated by this passage from Dice's manuscript:

These men had an old single-barrelled shotgun, very rusty and with several dents in the barrel. They called it the "gas-pipe" and it did look much like a piece of rusty iron pipe fastened to a broken wooden stock. The breech-lock would not fasten, so they had rigged a rope bandage, which for each shot was driven tight with a wooden wedge. The trigger would not work, so the hammer was held back with the thumb and let go when ready to fire. Their old brass shells had expanded and stuck tightly in the barrel. After being fired, each empty shell consequently had to be driven out of the barrel with a ramrod and a back of an ax. For powder they were using the poorest grade of black powder, which makes a terrific report and gives off a dense cloud of black smoke. The wads for their shells were cut with a pocket knife from birch bark and from the leaves of an old copy of Stevenson's "Treasure Island." All their lead shot had been used up, but they made a substitute by chopping wire and iron nails into short lengths with the ax. Thus equipped, the two men roamed the woods, one carrying the gun and the other the ramrod, ax, and extra shells. Amazingly, they secured a considerable quantity of game.[17]

THE DECLINE OF MINING

The coming of World War I accelerated a general decline of mining in Alaska, and led to the exodus of many miners who joined the armed forces or sought wartime wages in the States. Those who served the miners in towns and camps also gravitated to wartime economic opportunities Outside.

Quigley Hill from across Friday Creek, near Kantishna, shows the Quigley's mine on Red Top Claim, in the early 1930s. Courtesy of the Fanny Quigley Collection, UAF.

A hardcore of miners did remain. In the Kantishna, Joe Quigley and the Sourdoughs—Lloyd, Taylor, McGonagall, and Anderson—along with Charles A. Trundy and a few others continued lode prospecting, mainly for gold. These and earlier prospecting efforts had discovered antimony deposits on Slate, Caribou, and Stampede creeks, and some ore was extracted. But depressed market prices foiled the miners and the ore piles remained at the sites, too expensive to ship.

This lode prospecting for gold and other minerals opened up the possibility of a bright future—again, if good, all-weather transportation could be developed. Not until after the war would the Alaska Railroad and the spur roads and trails that it spawned bring this hope to any pitch of immediacy. But even then the isolation of the Kantishna and its neighboring districts would continue to inhibit large-scale development. Fluctuating market prices for metals other than gold added to the marginality of these distant prospects and mines, despite promising quantities and assay values.[18]

NATIVE MINERS

Until 1924, with the passage of the Indian Citizenship Act, Denali region Indians seldom engaged in mining as claim owners and operators. There were instances, as in the Valdez Creek district, where Indians leased or worked shares on white-owned claims.[19] But the legal status of Alaska Natives, set by the 1867 Treaty of Cession, forbad all but those totally assimilated to the dominant culture (i.e., "citizens") from owning claims. Given the biases of those times, few people of Native heritage qualified as citizens.[20]

Denali-region Natives worked as wage laborers, sometimes at the mines, more often in the transportation, and supply systems that supported mining. The exceptional Native entrepreneurial period of roadhouse, transportation, and hunting-fishing supply services in the Kantishna-Minchumina Lake area (cited in Chapter 2) was largely a function of isolation and a low level of economic activity, which was unattractive to non-Native enterprisers.

The philosophy of the Natives' subsistence way of life was to get enough meat and other necessities for comfortable living. When wage-labor opportunities came with mining into their areas, the Indians tended to adhere to that philosophy of moderation. Money was useful to a point. But subjecting oneself to wage labor for cash beyond necessity—that is, the year's store-bought supplies—made little sense. In fact it was nonsensical, because one had to hunt and fish for the family's true necessities, and wage-work shortened time on the land for those activities. Trapping, a more congenial way of earning cash than working for someone else, also took time. The complaints of mine operators about the Indians' poor work attendance took little account of this logic. Such complaints and such logic still contend today when Native Alaskans respond to traditional calls back to the land.

That Natives often successfully incorporated the new economic opportunities into the larger subsistence life-way was a positive adaptation. But some other effects of the breakdown of isolation and the weakening of traditional patterns led to disaster: addiction to liquor (used by unscrupulous traders to bilk the Natives of their furs); the spread of diseases (some with catastrophic effect); and—because of time taken for trapping furs, thus neglecting hunting and fishing—over-dependence on inferior store-bought foods. These, and much else in the baggage of "civilization," led to decline of physical health, which, combined with imported epidemics, caused die-offs of entire bands. Traditional social patterns of hunting, fishing, and sharing the harvest of the land were wrenched if not destroyed by these tribulations and the insidious workings of the cash economy. As elders died or their counsel was neglected, traditional knowledge for competent life on the land lapsed. This process accelerated as children went to schools (both mission and government), which, with few exceptions, worked to eliminate Native beliefs and modes of life.

In the more isolated areas, and in those places where the boom and bust of mining and all that came in its train was short-lived, the elders and the rudiments of tradition survived. Then, if there was a pause in the march of progress, and if non-Native hunters and trappers were not too numerous, Native families and bands could regroup to fashion a more balanced accommodation between modern and traditional influences. These struggles still go on.[21]

At the end of the early mining period the Denali region was still an isolated backwash—a few small mining camps and trading stations, connected with each other and the outer world by tenuous trails of transport and communication. These trails were marked by the occasional roadhouse and scattered Native settlements. As the railroad approached, it

Lillian Crosson, Fanny Quigley, and Joe Crosson at Kantishna in the early 1930s. Joe Crosson was the first pilot to land at the camp. Courtesy of the Fanny Quigley Collection, UAF.

spawned construction camps that would become modern towns. It would open the way for big-time coal mining on Healy Creek, just north of a new national park established by Congress in 1917 in the most remote part of the American land.

✳

1. Washburn, ed., "Karstens Diary," 348.

2. Dunn, *Shameless Diary*, 295.

3. P. F. Dessauer and D. W. Harvey, "An Historical Resource Study of the Valdez Creek Mining District," typescript report for Bureau of Land Management (Anchorage: 1980), 35-37.

4. This overview of Denali region mining derived from early USGS Bulletins and other descriptive sources. See, e.g., Stephen R. Capps, *Geology of the Alaska Railroad Region*, USGS Bulletin 907 (Washington: GPO, 1940), 180-188, for summary descriptions of these districts and references to specific USGS Bulletins on each of them.

5. Ibid.; Edward H. Cobb, *Placer Deposits of Alaska*, USGS Bulletin 1374 (Washington: GPO, 1973); Henry C. Berg and Edward H. Cobb, *Metalliferous Lode Deposits of Alaska*, USGS Bulletin 1246 (Washington: GPO, 1967).

6. Claus M. Naske and Don M. Triplehorn, "The Fedral Government and Alaska's Coal," *The Northern Engineer*, Vol. 12, No. 3 (Fall 1980), 20-21; Capps, *Geology of the Alaska Railroad Region*, 193-196.

7. Rolfe Buzzell's "Overview of Mining in the Kantishna District, 1903-1968," MS study on file at NPS Regional Office in Anchorage (1989), is the principal source for this section. Also see Thomas K. Bundtzen,"A History of Mining in the Kantishna Hills," *The Alaska Journal*, Vol. 8, No. 2 (Spring 1978), 151-161.

8. L. M. Prindle, "The Bonnifield and Kantishna Regions," in *Progress of Investigations of Mineral Resources of Alaska in 1906*, USGS Bulletin 314 (Washington: GPO, 1907), 213.

9. L. M. Prindle, Field Notebook 133-A, Kantishna District, USGS Technical Data File, Menlo Park, Calif., 30.

10. Prindle, "The Bonnifield and Kantishna Regions," 213.

11. Stephen R. Capps, *The Kantishna Region, Alaska*, USGS Bulletin 687 (Washington: GPO, 1919), 75-76.

12. Ibid., 76.

13. Dunn, *Shameless Diary*, 295.

14. Cook, *Top of the Continent*, 125.

15. This backtrail phase of Belmore Browne's adventures appeared in "Hitting the Home Trail from Mount McKinley," *Outing*, Vol. 62, No. 4 (July 1913), 387-404; quotations were from pages 395-396 and 399.

16. Lee R. Dice, "Interior Alaska in 1911 and 1912: Observations by a Naturalist," MS in Dice Collection, University of Alaska, Fairbanks, Archives, 69.

17. Ibid., 80.

18. Buzzell, "Overview of Kantishna District," 4-7; Bundtzen, "History of Mining in Kantishna Hills," 154-155.

19. Dessauer and Harvey, "Valdez Creek Mining District," 55.

20. William Schneider, "On the Back Slough," in Jean S. Aigner, et. al., *Interior Alaska, A Journey Through Time* (Anchorage: The Alaska Geographic Society, 1986) , 162.

21. A vast literature on cultural confrontation exists. A convenient summary is found in Chapter 7 of James W. Vanstone's *Athapaskan Adaptations, Hunters and Fishermen of the Subarctic Forests* (Arlington Heights, Ill.: AHM Publishing Corp., 1974).

Dall Sheep Ram. From the Denali National Park and Preserve Archive.

Caribou bull with misshapen antler. From the Denali National Park and Preserve Archive. NPS photo by Rick McIntyre.

C H A P T E R 5

Charles Sheldon and the
Mount McKinley Park Movement

A native of Vermont, where as a youth his interest in natural history could flourish, Charles Sheldon went on to Yale and bright prospects in the profession of law. Then the family business supporting this progression collapsed. But with a good start and his own talent and determination Sheldon became a success in the railroad business. He served as general manager of a railroad in Mexico from 1898 to 1902. During this time his investments in Mexican mining allowed him to retire from active business in 1903 at age 35. From that time on his avocation as a hunter-naturalist would become his public-service vocation in a life dedicated to preserving North American game animals.[1]

It was in Mexico that Sheldon's particular interest in the mountain sheep of North America first took hold. Learning that Dr. Edward W. Nelson of the U.S. Biological Survey (forerunner of the U.S. Fish and Wildlife Service) had done biological studies in Mexico, Sheldon contacted him in 1904. Sheldon's association with Doctor Nelson and his equally distinguished colleague Dr. C. Hart Merriam became a moving force in Sheldon's life. He decided to devote his natural history interests to furthering the work of the Biological Survey, especially as it related to the preservation of game animals and their habitats. Nelson and Merriam became his mentors in the mammology and specimen-collection work that eventually brought him to the Denali region in 1906 to study the white Dall sheep of the North.[2]

From all accounts and from original documents that trace his altruistic career Charles Sheldon emerges as a loyal, dependable, and friendly man. In his scientific work his search for facts was indefatigable. As a seasoned man of affairs he was astute in the ways of politics and could spot a rascal at a distance. He did not suffer fools, but friends he never forgot—no matter their station in life. He was indeed of the Eastern elite, but he was no elitist, as his enduring friendships with and favors from and to Alaskan friends demonstrate.

Physically Sheldon was a sturdy 5 feet 10 inches tall, weighing a hard 170 pounds. He was inured to hardship as the price of the wilderness adventures he savored and followed to the day of his death in 1928 at age 60. Harry Karstens and others of his Alaskan associates admired Sheldon as a fellow woodsman, a man to be trusted on any trail no matter how long and tough it might be. This was a compliment bestowed rarely on people from the Outside.

T E D D Y   R O O S E V E L T   O N   S H E L D O N

Teddy Roosevelt, the archetype of the strenuous life in the turn-of-the-century era when Sheldon rose to prominence, had this to say about his fellow hunter-naturalist in a review of Sheldon's book *The Wilderness of the Upper Yukon* (1911):

Mr. Sheldon is not only a first-class hunter and naturalist but passionately devoted to all that is beautiful in nature, and he has the literary taste and ability to etch his landscapes into his narratives, so they give to the reader something of the feeling that he must have had when he saw them—and that this is no mean feat is evident to everyone who realizes how uncommonly dreary most writing about landscape is, for the average writer either treats the matter with utter barrenness, or, what is worse, indulges at much length in "fine writing" of the abhorrently florid and prolix type.

Mr. Sheldon hunted in the tremendous Northern wilderness of snow-field and torrent, of scalped mountain and frowning pine forest; and in all the world there is no scenery grander in its lonely desolation than that which he portrays. He is no holiday hunter. Like Stewart Edward White, he is as skillful and self-reliant a woodsman and a mountaineer as an old-time trapper, and he always hunts alone. The chase of the Northern mountain sheep, followed in such manner, means a test of every real hunter's quality—marksmanship, hardihood and endurance, nerve and skill as a cragsman, keen eyesight, and high ability as still hunter and stalker. Mr. Sheldon possesses them all. Leaving camp by himself, with a couple of crackers and a piece of chocolate and perhaps a little tea in his pocket, he would climb the mountains until at last he saw his game, and then might have to spend twenty-four hours in the approach, sleeping out over-night and not returning to camp until late the following evening, when he would stagger downhill through the long sub-arctic dusk with the head, hide, and some of the meat of his game on his back. . . .

But the most important part of Mr. Sheldon's book is that which relates not to hunting but to natural history. No professional biologist has worked out the problems connected with these Northern mountain sheep as he has done. He shows that they are of one species; a showing that would have been most unexpected a few years ago, for at one extreme this species becomes the black so-called Stone's sheep, and at the other the pure white, so-called Dall's sheep. Yet as Mr. Sheldon shows in his maps, his description, and his figures, the two kinds grade into one another without a break, the form midway between having already been described as Fannin's sheep. The working out of this fact is a matter of note. But still more notable is his description of the life history of the sheep from the standpoint of its relations with its foes—the wolf, lynx, wolverine, and war eagle.[3]

On Conservation

Sheldon was not only a hunter-naturalist and gifted writer, he was also a man of broad philosophical perspective. The preservation of wild places and the wildlife inhabiting them, to which he devoted the specific actions of his public life, had a much broader objective. He believed that "the continued vigor and moral strength of the American people," would, in a closing America, be maintained only if the Nation's "forests, mountains, waterways, parks, roadways, and other open spaces" continued to provide opportunities for both energetic and contemplative outdoor recreation. Every generation of Americans, he asserted, must have these opportunities. They were part of the character-forming American heritage. It was incumbent on the federal government, through the various agencies that manage such landscapes, to aggressively provide for the health and welfare of the people through a national recreation policy that would foster and coordinate this critical public service, ramifying its benefits through all jurisdictions from federal to state to local. The particular points of this policy, as he sketched it about 1920, included a comprehensive recreation plan encompassing the great national parks and forests and wildlife preserves, as well as smaller regional and near-urban spaces for easy access for all; educational programs to guide the conservation of these open spaces; and the exclusion of economic development in the National Parks.[4]

In taking this stance, Sheldon joined the national debate then raging in American conservation policy. He was too practical a man and too politically attuned to espouse an extreme preservation position. At the same time, he differed from the prevalent utilitarian notion that all natural resources should be developed for economic ends. He believed that chosen landscapes should be maintained in pristine condition as reminders and places of generational reliving of the frontier experience

Grizzly on gravel bar. From the Denali National Park and Preserve Archive. NPS photo by Rick McIntyre.

that had driven America's history. His was a balanced concept that paired the Progressive conservation movement, organized around the "wise-use" ideas of Gifford Pinchot, with the older ideas of George Perkins Marsh and John Muir, which asserted man's obligations to the natural environment and the intangible benefits to be derived from Nature's unaltered works. In such balance would be found both the Nation's economic health and its spiritual salvation.[5]

SHELDON AND KARSTENS — 1906

Teddy Roosevelt's description of Charles Sheldon's field work on the Upper Yukon suffices for understanding his mode of operation at Denali. During his first visit in the summer of 1906, he and Harry Karstens, along with packer Jack Haydon of Dawson, traveled almost continuously with packhorses, living largely off the game that they hunted. Their rudimentary equipage and provisions allowed them to set up and fold camp with minimum effort. Typically, when a campsite was chosen after a day of travel, Sheldon took off alone while the men performed camp duties. He hiked over the ridges and into the lower elevations of the mountains noting everything he saw— game trails and other signs, and the animals themselves. He killed as necessary for meat. They entered the Denali piedmont and valley via Eureka ("about twenty tents and a few cabins"). At the head of Moose Creek they reached the crest of the outer hills overlooking lower Muldrow Glacier and McKinley River. Here ". . . Denali and the Alaska Range suddenly burst into view ahead, apparently very near."

I can never forget my sensations at the sight. No description could convey any suggestion of it. I have seen the mountain panoramas of the Alaska coast and the Yukon Territory. In the opinion of many able judges the St. Elias range is one of the most glorious masses of mountain scenery in the world. I had viewed St. Elias and the adjacent mountains the previous year, but compared with the view now before my eyes they seemed almost insignificant.

Three miles below lay the glacial bar of the Muldrow Branch of the McKinley Fork, fringed on both sides by narrow lines of timber, its swift torrents rushing through many channels. Beyond, along the north side of the main Alaska Range, is a belt of bare rolling hills ten or twelve miles wide, forming a vast piedmont plateau dotted with exquisite little lakes. The foothill mountains, 6,000 or 7,000 feet in altitude and now free from snow, extend in a series of five or six ranges parallel to the main snow-covered range on the south. Carved by glaciers, eroded by the elements, furrowed by canyons and ravines, hollowed by cirques, and rich in contrasting colors, they form an appropriate foreground to the main range.

Denali—a majestic dome which from some points of view seems to present an unbroken skyline—rises to an altitude of 20,300 feet, with a mantle of snow and ice reaching down for 14,000 feet. Towering above all others, in its stupendous immensity it dominates the picture. Nearby on the west stands Mount Foraker, more than 17,000 feet in altitude, flanked on both sides by peaks of 10,000 to 13,000 feet that extend in a ragged snowy line as far as the eye can see.[6]

Sheldon began his survey for sheep at the foot of the Peters Glacier moraine. Several days there produced no results, so the party got ready to move northeasterly along the piedmont, paralleling the range. The mountain loomed directly above the Peters Glacier camp, and Sheldon could not resist it. He had found old camps left by Judge Wickersham and Doctor Cook, so he must try at least the lower reaches of the mountain. On July 27 he climbed up the spur that curved around the east side of the glacier, then zigzagged upwards through soft snow to a point several thousand feet above the plain where the walls became vertical:

. . . As the clouds lifted, leaving the vast snow-mantled mountain clear, I seated myself and gazed for more than an hour on the sublime panorama. There was not a breath of wind, and no sound except the faint murmur of the creek far below, and the cannonading and crashing roar of avalanches thundering down the mountain walls.

Great masses of ice kept constantly breaking away from far up near the summit. Starting slowly at first, they increased in momentum and size, accumulating large bodies of snow and ice, some of which during the rapidity of the descent were ground into swirling clouds resembling the spray of cataracts. When the sliding material pitched off the glacier cap and struck the bare walls below, enormous fragments of rock were dislodged and carried along with the mass, which finally fell on the dumping ground of the moraine. Then, before the clouds of snow had disappeared from the path of the avalanche, the rumbling of the echoes died away and silence was again supreme. During the four hours that I was there, nineteen avalanches fell—some of them of enormous proportions. Eleven were near by and visible throughout their descent.

Behind me reared the tremendous glacier cap in all its immensity. To my left Peters Glacier filled the deep valley between the north face of the mountain and a high adjoining range; to my right was the northeast ridge of Denali; and, as far as I could see, on both sides of me were the spired crestlines of the outside ranges.

Directly below us was the newly formed moraine of Peters Glacier, the glacier itself appearing like a huge white reptile winding along the west side. Not yet smoothed by the elements, this moraine was one confused mass of drumlins, kettle holes, eskers and kames. Many miniature lakes glistened in the depressions; patches of green grass and dwarf willows along the water courses, with flowers and lichens, added a wealth of color to its desolate surface. Along the base of the mountain was the dumping ground of the avalanches—a wild disorder of debris.

Through bisected ranges of mountains I could see the rolling piedmont plateau, filled with hundreds of bright lakes, and still beyond could look over the vast wilderness of low relief all clothed in timber, until the vision was lost in the wavy outlines of rolling country merging into the horizon. Far to the northwest Lake Minchumina, reflecting the sun, fairly shone out of the dark timber-clad area surrounding it.

Alone in an unknown wilderness hundreds of miles from civilization and high on one of the world's most imposing mountains, I was deeply moved by the stupendous mass of the great upheaval, the vast extent of the wild areas below, the chaos of the unfinished surfaces still in process of moulding, and by the crash and roar of the mighty avalanches.

The sun was low; a dark shadowy mantle was cast over the wild desolate areas below; the skyline of the great mountain burned with a golden glow; distant snowy peaks glistened white above sombre-colored slopes not touched by the light of the sun, which still bathed the wide forested region of the north. A huge avalanche ploughed the mountainside not a hundred and fifty yards to my left, while clouds of snow swept about me.

Awakening to a realization that I had been and was still in a path of danger, I slowly made the descent.[7]

Frustrated by the lack of sheep, Sheldon and his men packed up and moved on, keeping close to the range. The ridges near the lower Muldrow were also barren of sheep. So they kept on toward the Toklat River headwaters. The plateau reminded Sheldon of "a well-stocked cattle ranch in the West, except that here cattle were replaced by caribou."[8]

A painful carbuncle on Sheldon's ankle forced a 3-day halt, even with Karstens' pocket-knife field surgery. Sheldon accepted this delay with equanimity, for the weather was perfect, and the layover gave him a chance to enjoy the smaller creatures:

The abundant ground squirrels amused us, marmots whistled on the moraine, Canada jays flew about, the tree sparrows and intermediate sparrows sang continually, and waxwings and northern shrikes were particularly plentiful. White-tailed ptarmigan with broods of chicks were near; the wing-beats of ravens passing overhead hissed through the air; Arctic terns flew gracefully over the meadows; and the golden eagles soared above the ridges. Old bear diggings were everywhere, but no large animal was seen except a big bull caribou which Haydon saw on the moraine. Our numerous traps failed to capture any mice, nor did we see any sign of these small mammals, always so interesting to the faunal naturalist.[9]

Finally, on August 5, with walking staff in hand, Sheldon and the others made their move for the Toklat headwaters. A nearby sheep trail and a white object in the distance cheered Sheldon, despite the pain of his affliction:

Sheep at last! I thought. But the field glasses revealed a grizzly bear walking along smelling the ground for squirrels or pawing a moment for a mouse. Under the bright sun its body color appeared to be pure white, its legs brown. It seemed utterly indifferent to the eagle, which again and again darted at it. Continuing, it often broke into a short run, pausing at times and throwing up its head to sniff the air—always searching for food.[10]

At last, at camp that night, Sheldon "looked toward the top of a mountain directly ahead and on a grassy space just below the summit saw twelve sheep, which the glasses showed to be ewes and lambs. This was my first sight of sheep in the Alaska Range; how elated I felt."[11]

Finding timber at the main forks of the Toklat, under the rise of Divide Mountain, the expedition set up its main camp. For 10 days Sheldon roamed the nearby crags finding sheep in numbers "more abundant than I had ever imagined." Groups of 60 or 70 ewes and lambs were not unusual. But even here, Sheldon's objects—to study the life history of these sheep and to collect representative specimens—could not be fulfilled, for not a ram did he find on the Toklat.

On August 16, with Sheldon's time running short for return to the Yukon and steamboat passage out, Sheldon and Haydon packed one horse and rode east toward the mountains of the Teklanika drainage. On that day of transit, with sheep on every mountain, Sheldon estimated that he saw at least 800 sheep, more likely 1,000. Excepting a band of young rams on the Toklat-Teklanika divide, they were all ewes and lambs. Disgusted, Sheldon sent Haydon back with the horses and, alone, made camp near Sable Pass.

Next day, on the north end of Cathedral Mountain, which he named as he scanned it, Sheldon saw a group of sheep high up. Getting closer and using the glasses, he saw that they were rams. Closer yet he could distinguish their big horns—these were old rams, nine of them with "strikingly big horns." Despite the day's long hike Sheldon instantly began the stalk, crawling across the flats visible to the sheep, crossing swollen glacial streams, and finally getting into the cover of the mountain flanks where he could climb rapidly. A squall of wind and rain heightened his sense of wild excitement in the magnificent mountain panorama. Low clouds made the crestlines seem suspended over a broken horizon.

The final hour and a half of the stalk required all of his patience, skill, and strategy—inching along when in view, moving only when the rams had their heads down feeding or were turned away, absolutely silent during his progress on knees and elbows over rough, loose rock. Finally he reached the brink of the canyon beyond which the rams were feeding. The rain had become a drizzle, but the strong wind still favored him:

Finding a slight depression at the edge I crept into it and lay on my back. Then slowly revolving to a position with my feet forward, I waited a few moments to steady my nerves. My two-hundred-yard sight had been pushed up, and watching my opportunity, I slowly rose to a sitting position, elbows on knees. Not a ram had seen or suspected me. I carefully aimed at a ram standing broadside near the edge of the canyon, realizing that the success of my long arduous trip would be determined the next moment. I pulled the trigger and as the shot echoed from the rocky walls, the ram fell and tried to rise, but could not. His back was broken. The others sprang into alert attitudes and looked in all directions. I fired at another standing on the brink, apparently looking directly at me. At the shot, he fell and rolled into the canyon. Then a ram with big massive wrinkled horns dashed out from the band and, heading in my direction, ran down into the canyon. The others immediately followed, but one paused at the brink and, as I fired, dropped and rolled below. Another turned and was running upward as I fired and missed him.

For a moment, after I had put a fresh clip of cartridges in the rifle and pushed down the sight, all was silence. I remained motionless. Then came a slight sound of falling rocks and the big ram appeared, rushing directly toward me—coming so fast that he crossed the slope to the brink of the canyon before I could get a bead on him. He dashed down the steep opposite side and came running up only twenty feet away, when I fired. He kept on, but fell at the edge of the canyon behind me. Two other big rams were following, but when I fired at him, they separated. One ran up the canyon and as he paused a moment, I killed him in his tracks. The other had gone below but at the sound of the shot, started back. When he reached the top I fired and he rolled down near the bottom. A smaller one ran up the slope near by, but I paid no attention to him.

Then another appeared on the edge of the canyon, where the first two had been shot. He had returned from the bottom of the canyon and seemed confused as to which way to run. Since his horns were large, I pushed up the two-hundred-yard sight, and brought him down. Another then came running out of the canyon directly toward me, and turned up the slope. As his horns were not very large, I let him go. The remaining three rams must have ascended through the bottom of the canyon for they were not seen again.

Seven fine rams had been killed with eight shots—and by one who is an indifferent marksman! My trip had quickly turned from disappointment to success.[12]

After dispatching the wounded animals Sheldon descended the mountain in darkness and reached camp about midnight. He made soup and tea and sat by the fire to dry his clothes—wet since the morning's first stream ford. Then he worked on his journal notes to record "the success of that memorable day." Now followed several days of intensive labor by Sheldon, still alone: butchering the sheep and hauling meat, skins, and skulls down the mountain; treating skins and skulls for specimen preservation; noting stomach contents, physical condition, and measurements. On the third night after the hunt, Karstens appeared with the horses, and next day the lot was hauled to the main camp. Sheldon's main work of the summer was done. He had tracked the Dall sheep in their Denali haunts and gathered specimens that could be analyzed by scientists and mounted for display in the American Museum of Natural History.

A flight of cranes winging south brought mixed emotions. Their urgency sparked his own not to miss the last steamboat before freezeup. At the same time, he knew that he had just begun to understand the Dall sheep and the larger world of the Denali region. Karstens had become a real companion—not only was he a master of all practical matters of camp life and travel in the wilderness, but also "brimful of good nature" and agreeably interested and helpful in the work that Sheldon was doing.[13] It would be hard to leave this life of freedom in a place that so fully requited Sheldon's spiritual, intellectual, and physical ideals.

But he would come back. The weeks of frustrating search for the big rams had become a symbol of all he did not know.

I realized that the life history [of the white sheep] could not be learned without a much longer stay among them and determined to return and devote a year to their study. With this in view I planned to revisit the region, build a substantial cabin just below my old camp on the Toklat, and remain there through the winter, summer, and early fall.[14]

The return trip through the nearly deserted camps of the Kantishna and down that river and the Tanana got him back to the Yukon in time. The Dawson-bound steamer *Lavelle Young*, crowded to bursting in that last-chance-out season, picked him up at Tanana Station, a cluster of saloons, gambling houses, and trading company warehouses, with an Indian village on one end and the Army's Fort Gibbon on the other. From Dawson another steamboat took him to Whitehorse, where he boarded the White Pass train to Skagway, whence he departed by ocean steamer on October 22.

A t D e n a l i — 1 9 0 7 - 1 9 0 8

Sheldon's year in residence in the lee of Denali, from about August 1, 1907, to June 11, 1908,[15] allowed systematic, season-by-season observation of the wildlife whose mysteries he had started to plumb the previous summer. From the home cabin that he and Karstens built at timberline on Toklat River, Sheldon ventured forth in good weather and bad. On long trips, say to the Teklanika Mountains, he and Karstens would set up camp and Sheldon, alone or sometimes with Karstens as hiking companion, would tramp the country noting the distribution and movements of the animals. He aimed to get a definitive picture of the life history of Dall sheep. During that pursuit he also gathered facts on other species, with a particular interest in the ever-shifting caribou, whose abundance in a given place one day and total absence the next intrigued him. In time he began to discern patterns that linked their seemingly random movements. He noted, too, the predictability of the sheep, whose pastures, changing with the seasons, largely defined his own rounds. Birds, bears, moose, foxes, and the multitudes of small creatures, including many species of field mice and voles, caught his attention, and their habits were noted as he tracked the sheep. The rutting behavior of caribou and sheep he described. Predation and flight, the antics of animals at play—all these he recorded.

For a man like Sheldon each season was another act in Nature's drama, each valley or ridge a setting, each event a scene. Winter landscapes, appearing to casual observation dim and lifeless, spoke strongly to Sheldon of life, of infinite adaptations by the many creatures that survived and found sustenance there despite deep cold and darkness only faintly relieved by a horizon-hovering sun. And then, of course, came spring: light, renewal, return of migrant birds, flowing waters, greening of plants, and then the short summer's surge to start the new generations.

The Wilderness of Denali—essentially Sheldon's field notes edited by Nelson and Merriam after his death[16]—captures the endless fascination of this naturalist's Shangri-La. In short, Sheldon fell in love with this country. The rush to accomplish too much that previous summer was replaced by a deliberate and contemplative energy. During this year he had time for people, and he became fast friends with Joe and Fanny Quigley. He got to know Tom Lloyd and his partners—Karstens' old comrades, the future Sourdough climbers—sharing with them his understanding of the mountain's topography. He met some market hunters, men he understood, but whose work worried him.

As Sheldon roamed the Denali wilderness another purpose—beyond the life history of the sheep—began to take form. He later confided to Madison Grant, fellow Boone and Crockett Club member and historian of the Mount McKinley Park movement, that it was the club's interest in establishing game refuges, particularly in Alaska, ". . . which inspired in him the thought of preserving this area after personally studying the situation in that land."[17] As long-term chairman of the club's Game Conservation Committee, Sheldon would help lead the club's evolution from the original ideal of a comradeship of riflemen and hunters toward a far-reaching ethic of conservation. This transformation matched the Nation's evolution from frontier to almost old-world conditions.[18] In Alaska, even then the Nation's last frontier, the Boone and Crockett Club, under Sheldon's leadership, would focus its new concerns on the establishment of a park-refuge that would preserve Denali's wildlife.

Except for the nascent idea, the park movement was still in the future when Karstens and Sheldon shared camp together. They did talk about market hunting: its potential impact as the surrounding country developed, and the waste entailed by the hunters feeding their dogs half or more of the meat taken before it could be delivered to the mining camps or Fairbanks.

As they roamed the country the idea of a park-refuge found embodiment in the landscapes occupied by the wandering animals. In a letter written on July 25, 1918, Karstens recalled his work with Sheldon beginning in 1906:

He was continually talking of the beauties of the country and of the variety of the game and wouldn't it make an ideal park and game preserve. . . . He came in the following July hunting for the Biological Survey and stayed a year, during that time . . . we had located the limits of the caribou run. We would talk over the possible boundaries of a park and preserve which we laid out practically the same as the present park boundaries.[19]

WORKING FOR PARK STATUS

With a sorrow he could not describe Sheldon left Denali and Alaska in the summer of 1908, never to return. But the idea of a "Denali National Park" (so named in his journal entry of January 12, 1908)[20] remained fresh in his mind. He envisioned accommodations and facilities for travel that would allow visitors the same enjoyment and inspiration that he had been privileged to experience. The essence of the park would be its heraldic display of wildlife posed against stupendous mountain scenery.

Upon his return to New York, Sheldon broached the park idea to his friends in the Boone and Crockett Club. He was heartened by their enthusiastic response. But all agreed that the time was not ripe for a public campaign. Congressional interests had

Wolf. From the Denali National Park and Preserve Archive.

turned from conservation issues, and the club, Sheldon included, had more urgent business to attend to. For the time being the prospective park's remoteness, paired with the decline in nearby mining activity, would have to suffice for its protection.[21]

Then in 1912, began a series of events that would vault the park proposal into the public arena. That year Congress passed Alaska's second organic act, providing for territorial status. To the existing offices of governor and non-voting delegate to Congress, the act added a territorial legislature. This body offered a political focus for working with the people of Alaska on the park proposal. Moreover, during the period of the park movement the delegate to Congress would be Judge James Wickersham, a friend of Sheldon's and an occasional dinner guest at Boone and Crockett Club affairs.

Tacked onto the organic act was a rider creating an Alaska Railroad Commission that would report on "the best and most available routes for railroads in Alaska which would develop the country and its resources."[22] President William Howard Taft appointed as chairman of this commission Alfred Hulse Brooks, another old friend of Sheldon's through their association in the Explorers Club. The commission quickly did its work and in early 1913 recommended two railroads to the Interior: one from Cordova to Fairbanks via the Copper and Tanana rivers, giving access to the Yukon Valley; the other from Seward via the Matanuska coalfield and Susitna River, then over the Alaska Range into the Kuskokwim Valley, opening up Alaska's second largest drainage system. After heated debates over the proposed routes and the socialistic implications of a government-built-and-operated railroad, a single compromise route to Fairbanks via the Susitna and Nenana rivers was chosen. This route would tap both the Matanuska and Nenana coal fields. And, through purchase, it would start off with 71 miles of privately built Alaska Northern Railroad track running from Seward to Turnagain Arm of Cook Inlet, and another 39 miles of the Tanana Valley line from Fairbanks.

Fears of socialism subsided in Congress as railroad entrepreneurs testified in favor of a government railroad to open up Alaska's Interior. They maintained that except for short mining-associated railroads, private efforts had failed to overcome Alaska's terrain, climate, and vast unpopulated spaces. A government railroad was essential if the Interior were to be opened to commerce, homesteading, and general progress of the sort that had followed railroad land grants and financial incentives in the Trans-Mississippi West. Finally the Alaska Railroad Act passed Congress and President Woodrow Wilson signed it into law on March 12, 1914.[23]

The Congressional focus on Alaska legislation (organic act, railroad, coal leasing, land-grant college);[24] the certainty of increased market hunting to supply railroad construction camps on the east side of the Denali region; and the prospects for gold-mining revival, coalfield development, and town-building along the rail line—all leading to yet more depredations on Denali's game—brought the park proposal to a head.

On September 21, 1915—with railroad construction already underway—the Boone and Crockett Club formally resolved to endorse the proposal for creation of a Mount McKinley National Park in Alaska. (Sheldon would continue to urge the name Denali, but Mount McKinley won out.) Sheldon and Madison Grant comprised a committee to carry the resolution into effect. Sheldon opened the campaign with letters to Delegate Wickersham and his old friend Doctor Nelson of the Biological Survey.[25]

Sheldon brought Wickersham in by seeking his views on the park proposal and how it might be received in Alaska, to which Wickersham promised careful consideration. But the letter to Nelson was a detailed statement of strategy. After noting that the time was now ripe for pushing the proposal and sketching boundaries that would "include a wide area of the best sheep, caribou, and moose country," Sheldon confided to Nelson:

Before doing anything about it, I wish to go to Washington with the plan complete a· I wish to project it and win over Wickersham, the delegate from Alaska. He was once a strong friend of mine and I have been careful to say nothing publicly against him [in debates over the proposed Alaska Game Law], always with a view to winning him to this project at the opportune time. After I get him and the Secretary of the Interior and a few influential senators and congressmen, I shall start the campaign by a B. and C. [Boone and Crockett Club] dinner in Washington composed of congressmen and senators and others specially with a view to this plan. I shall try to win over the Alaska people first. You should say nothing about this yet, since I want to make Wickersham feel he is the leading spirit of it etc. etc. . . . After the plan is well underway then my successor on the Game Committee will have a definite object to work for. I believe that the creating of a demand for this in Alaska will be the key to the whole problem and perhaps I can assist in establishing this. . . . It is absolutely necessary that it should not get out in any detail until I see Wickersham and so arrange things that he will get the credit for the idea which the B. and C. Club will stand behind and support.

The railroad which will reach that part of the country in two or three years makes a good reason for the Park, if the game is to be preserved as a reserve for that part of the country which is somewhat far for market hunters of Fairbanks. This letter to you marks the date when the idea is launched. . . .[26]

Sheldon's calculated approach was not frivolous intrigue. During the park proposal's gestation the Boone and Crockett Club and other big game groups had been working with the Biological Survey and Congress to strengthen the Alaska game code. A law of 1908, passed over Alaskan objections, had set bag limits to reduce the wholesale slaughter of bears and other species, and it had established a system of game wardens, game-guide registration, regulations, and permits to be administered by the territorial governor under the technical guidance of the Biological Survey. This law and the system it begat, including the inevitable "bureaucratic absurdities" (e.g., a late waterfowl season that postdated southerly migrations from northern Alaska), aroused Alaskan ire. The argument that Alaska's game was part of the Nation's public domain immediately polarized national versus local interests. Those who subsisted on game, those who hunted for the town and camp markets—remote places where beef could not be raised and cost a fortune when imported, and those who routinely killed bears wherever found because they were "savage beasts" had no patience with Eastern Establishment and federal interference. Successive territorial governors and the territorial legislature after 1912 reflected overwhelming Alaskan sentiment when they called for home rule over Alaska's wild creatures. "Arrogant cheechako" (i.e., greenhorn, especially of the Eastern variety) battled "local bar-room bear hunter" over the fate of Alaska's wildlife, in a frame of argumentation little changed to the present day.

The onset of World War I—which among other things caused inflation and diverted shipping from Alaskan waters, further stressing tenuous supply lines—exacerbated the struggle between stateside conservationists and Alaskans. The latter called for a ban on all hunting restrictions so they would not starve or be bankrupted by "the beef monopoly."[27]

The first hints of this wartime game preservation battle—which would become nationwide—registered in Alaska even before the United States entered the war in April 1917. This was partly a result of vastly increased U.S. ship-borne trade with the Allies centered on food and war material.

In this heated atmosphere Sheldon and Doctor Nelson would advocate a middle course toward market hunting that recognized Alaskan difficulties but would yet avert lasting damage to Alaskan wildlife (e.g., game shot legally could be sold). But other conservationists stood firm on the main tenet of game preservation in this country: no commercial hunting.[28]

Thus, from the inception of the park idea to its enactment, the Mount McKinley park-refuge proposal had to dodge and weave through a political minefield of strenuous opposition in Alaska. In addition, the conservation community itself would split over compromises on hunting that were the price paid for critical Alaskan support for both realistic hunting controls and a Mount McKinley National Park. The adamant and inflexible William T. Hornaday of the New York Zoo and the Permanent Wildlife Fund would brook no bending of the ban on commercial hunting. Sheldon and Doctor Nelson viewed him as intemperate, a potential derailer of those moderate game- and park-law provisions essential for *any* controls over Alaska's game. All those who understood the situation in Alaska knew that absolute solutions would fail in the vast territory with its mere handful of game wardens.[29]

In this context of larger affairs—international, national, and territorial—political acumen was essential to the life of the park movement and its successful conclusion. Proponents had to play both ends against the middle with perfect timing. For example, the respected Stephen Capps of the U.S. Geological Survey reported that market hunters were taking 1500 to 2000 Dall sheep from Denali's Toklat and Teklanika basins each year. This disturbing news, published in the *National Geographic Magazine* in January 1917, helped push the park bill through Congress the very next month.

PARK MOMENTUM

As there were dangers, there were also opportunities when the Mount McKinley park movement began in 1915. That same year conservation-minded Secretary of the Interior Franklin K. Lane invited his former college classmate Stephen T. Mather to come down to Washington and run the national parks himself if he didn't like the way others were doing it, as Mather had complained in a letter.

Dall Sheep Ram. From the Denali National Park and Preserve Archive.

Indeed, administration of the 13 existing national parks, plus several national monuments and other units, left much to be desired. No system as such existed. Rules varied from park to park. Superintendents and custodians were a mix of military and civilian personnel. Some of the latter, being local political appointees, made up their own rules as they went along. Loose guidance from successive Secretaries of the Interior meant that nobody was really in charge. The parks were orphans of the federal government.[30] Secretary Lane, reflecting the aggressive executive-branch philosophy of the Wilson administration, wanted to change this.

Mather came to the department from a background of successful business and newspaper experience. He was 47, dynamic, and financially independent—ready to perform public service for the wildlands he loved. As Lane's assistant for National Parks Mather teamed up with Horace M. Albright—a young research assistant who had been studying the condition of the parks for Lane. Their joint objective was to get Congressional sanction for a National Park Service that would manage the parks and monuments as a system. This reform became reality in August 1916 with passage of the National Park Service Act. Mather became Director and Albright Assistant Director of the new bureau.[31]

Into this activist and expansionist camp came Sheldon's proposal for a new national park in Alaska. As it turned out, Mount McKinley would become the first national park admitted to the system after creation of the National Park Service.

Sheldon wrote to Mather on December 15, 1915, using the Boone and Crockett Club's Game Preservation Committee letterhead, which listed such conservation luminaries as Sheldon himself (chairman), Charles H. Townsend, E. W. Nelson, and George Bird Grinnell. Sheldon described his visits to the Denali region, his love of its wilderness and wildlife attributes. He said that on this continent only the Grand Canyon could compare to the "region of the Alaska Range for the grandeur of the scenery and the topographical interest . . ." From his first visit, Sheldon related, he had "believed that someday this region must be made a national park." The imminence of railroad construction made this time "peculiarly auspicious" for legislation because the proposed park's "vast reservoir of game" would otherwise be destroyed to supply meat for the construction camps. The park's status as a game reservation would have to be made explicit in any bill. Interests of miners on the fringes of the park would have to be protected. But the boundaries Sheldon had recommended should exclude significant areas of mineralization from the park. It was essential that Delegate Wickersham be assured that his local constituents would be protected. Only then would Wickersham introduce the park bill, giving it Alaska's stamp of approval. The Boone and Crockett Club would stand behind the effort and assist in its passage through Congress. Sheldon then proposed a meeting with Mather to be followed by presentation of the proposal to Secretary Lane. The letter ended with a note of urgency: Postponement of action on Mount McKinley National Park could lead to destruction of its wildlife values, the key reason for designating such a park in the remote Alaska wilderness.[32] This letter defined the substance of the struggle for park legislation and the counterpoint arguments of the opposition. Mather endorsed the proposal without quibble, accepted associate membership in the Boone and Crockett Club, and on January 6, 1916, addressed the club's members in terms of his and Secretary Lane's full support for Sheldon's plan.[33]

The park idea soon captured the imagination of a significant part of the Eastern elite, including government leaders and scientists in the conservation and wildlife preservation fields. It was a simpler time, those early years of the century. The excessive layerings of today's government did not exist. Movers and shakers in business and government interlocked through their schools, career paths, and clubs. Phone calls and hastily scribbled notes sufficed to align key people when a change of course or a tactical diversion was necessary to steer a piece of legislation, as the McKinley park proposal would demonstrate.

Coincidentally, as the park movement got underway, Belmore Browne of the Camp Fire Club of America independently evolved a similar plan for the Denali region's preservation. When he presented his proposal in Washington he was surprised to find the Boone and Crockett Club and his friend Charles Sheldon already in the field. Quickly the two clubs joined forces and brought into the fold the American Game Protective and Propagation Association, whose president, John B. Burnham, would become overall coordinator of the legislative effort.

Alaska delegate Wickersham—always conscious of the needs of his Alaskan constituency—saw the advantages of the park in bringing visitors to Alaska from around the world. He would introduce the park bill in the House in the spring of 1916. Thomas B. Riggs of the Alaska Engineering Commission (and later governor of Alaska) saw the park as an aid to the fledgling Alaska Railroad, whose 400-mile wilderness route from Anchorage to Fairbanks would benefit from tourist traffic. He would, with Sheldon and Browne, draft the park bill, using Sheldon's recommended boundaries. With remarkable speed the teamwork of the three clubs and the inside help of Lane and Mather at Interior propelled the park bill into the hands of receptive legislators and onto the legislative docket. Wickersham's bill in the House, introduced April 16, 1916, was matched by an identical companion bill introduced by Senator Key Pittman of Nevada.

Then momentum slowed as amendments unacceptable to Wickersham and other members of Congress jammed progress. These difficulties would be overcome, finally. But yet another hitch doomed the House bill in 1916. The House Committee on Public Lands, following an informal rule, would report favorably on no more than two national park bills in a single session. Just as the McKinley bill got close, two other park bills were reported, so the House delayed action. Pittman's Senate bill, however, passed unanimously.

MOUNT McKINLEY BECOMES A NATIONAL PARK — 1917

When Congress resumed in January 1917 the park-bill proponents were ready. Their work during the Congressional recess resulted in piles of letters and editorials favoring creation of the park. Dr. Stephen Capps' supportive article in the January 1917 *National Geographic Magazine* also greeted the returning Congressmen. It stressed the urgency of stopping market hunting before Mount McKinley's wildlife was killed off. Several legislators attended the first National Park Conference, staged largely for their benefit, hearing pleas for the Mount McKinley legislation by Sheldon, Browne, and Mather, among others. Earlier committee hearings on the bill had given proponents another forum. The bill passed on February 19. And—in recognition of his park idea and tireless efforts to bring it to fruition—Charles Sheldon was delegated to deliver the act personally to President Wilson, who signed it on February 26, 1917, and gave the pen to Sheldon.[34]

Many years later Horace Albright recalled a footnote to this triumph: Sheldon had moved from Vermont to Washington to shepherd the park bill through. During the climax of the legislative process he had haunted the halls of the Capitol and mobilized his cohorts for the final push. Finally, he took a day off, and that was the day the bill passed. Next day, Albright, acting as Park Service director at the time, saw

Bull moose lying in the snow. From the Denali National Park and Preserve Archive. NPS photo by Bill Ruth.

Sheldon approaching his office, jumped up, grabbed his hand, and congratulated him for leading the creation of this great park. For his part, Sheldon stood aghast. Unaware of the bill's passage he had dropped by simply to check progress. His day off made him miss the vote. "He kicked himself the rest of his life that that was the one day he didn't go up there."[35]

The Mount McKinley National Park Act reserved some 2,200 square miles laid out in a rough parallelogram nearly 100 miles long and averaging 25 miles wide, running from the southwest to the northeast. At its upper end it expanded to the north to include the mountainous sheep and caribou country of the Toklat and Teklanika drainages. The boundaries excluded the Kantishna mining district and the forested moose country to the northwest where many miners wintered and hunted. The park captured the ridgeline of the Alaska Range, which backdropped the bordering piedmont plateau, the great valley of the Denali Fault, and the north-side outer ranges crossed by the north-flowing Toklat and Teklanika rivers.

As Sheldon himself described the park, it was a country *mostly above timberline, and yet with tongues of timber extending up the rivers. Outside of the rough ranges are gently rolling hills, hundreds of little straggling lakes, a region which, when roads are once established there, and conveniences for tourists, you can ride all over it with horses. It is accessible in every part, and the game of the region will be constantly in sight, a thing which is not true of most of the regions of our other national parks.*[36]

The price of this idyllic vision had been compromise. Delegate Wickersham had promised to protect his constituents in Alaska, and he did so. In addition to the Kantishna and northerly hunting-ground exclusions (which cut into the extended ranges of Denali wildlife), the law provided that prospectors and miners could locate new mining claims within the park. They could also "take and kill game therein for their actual necessities when short of food," but not for sale or wantonly.[37]

Amendments proposed by some conservationists to give the Interior Secretary greater regulatory control over these mining-related provisions had proved inimical to the bill's passage. Wickersham dug in his heels and was suspected of pushing the

House Committee to render favorable reports on two other national park proposals, thus using up its first session quota and killing the McKinley bill in 1916. But the pragmatism of Sheldon, Burnham, and Grinnell, among others, led to withdrawal of such amendments, and the bill proceeded to passage in the second session. These and other maneuvers lend a chess-game intricacy to the trail of correspondence during this period, much of it in the Mount McKinley Correspondence File (1916-24) in the National Archives.

The practical views of the chief sponsors, plus the urgency of protecting Mount McKinley's splendid assemblage of wildlife from the construction and development impacts of the railroad, had pushed the Mount McKinley proposal to enactment. Without that urgency—given plausibility by the repute of the chief sponsors, and by earlier revelations of wanton slaughter during the Alaska game code hearings—it is doubtful that the bill would have gone through. Alaska was a remote wilderness territory except along the coast and the major rivers. What need for a park designation in the mountainous Interior? Certainly the high mountains—girt by sub-ranges, vast gorges, and immense glaciers—needed no protection. So it boiled down to the wildlife, as the Congressional-hearings testimony amply demonstrates.[38]

Visitors would view that wildlife, which, with the mountains, composed that living landscape that had so moved Sheldon and shaped his vision. The utility of a great, unhunted game refuge in Alaska's center lent practicality to a proposal esthetic at its core. Here would be a reservoir of animals, which, upon overflow to surrounding regions, would supply the staunch miners and pioneers at frontier's edge. Thus would development of the country proceed apace, aided by visitors to the park whose locally expended funds would fuel progress, and whose enchantment with the country might lead to their own or others settlement there.[39]

On paper, all of this seemed certain to come about. But having created the park, Congress then rested. Minuscule appropriations proposed by the National Park Service and the Interior Department failed of passage. The war and immediate postwar turmoil had much to do with this. Whatever the causes, the park would suffer from this neglect.

Within a day of two of the President's signing of the park act, Sheldon had dashed off a note to Mr. Grinnell: ". . . I have been working to have included in the Sundry Acct. appropriations bill 10,000.00 for protection of the park and surveying the East North South and West line so that the game areas will be known."[40] But as Sheldon feared, the confusion of the last days of the session sidetracked this minor bit of business. The park would remain vacant of protectors, unmarked on the ground, and prey to poachers for more than 4 years.

During this interval, letters to Sheldon from his Alaska friends reported that poaching in Mount McKinley Park was on the increase. Railroad construction and the towns that sprang from its camps pushed on the park. So did the mining camps rejuvenated by the railroad. The National Park Service, frustrated by failure of its funding requests, arranged with the Governor of Alaska to have his wardens visit the park occasionally, but these rare inspections yielded nothing of protection, only evidence of the need for it.

In a resolution of January 10, 1919, the Boone and Crockett Club respectfully urged that Congress appropriate not less than $10,000 for a ranger force, with proper quarters and equipment, to protect the wild animals of the park, with a final paragraph that chided the Congress for its 2-year delay.[41] Five days later the Camp Fire Club of America issued a similar resolution.[42]

Territorial Governor Thomas Riggs, upon receipt of a copy of the Camp Fire Club resolution, wrote to the Interior Department requesting aid for the park so that its function as a game reservoir for the surrounding country, and its wildlife attraction for tourists, would be protected. Interior's Assistant Secretary John Hallowell responded to Governor Riggs with assurances that the Department had consistently pressed for appropriations for the park. He quoted Park Service Director Mather's memorandum in response to the governor's plea: ". . . ever since the creation of the park, we have each fall submitted, with our other park estimates, one for Mount McKinley, to the amount of $10,000, the limitation placed in the organic act." Hallowell concluded his letter to Riggs with the hope that the House Appropriations Committee would see the light in the coming year, but warned that the war-debt problem was making many useful projects postponable.[43] Still there was no result.

More than a year later, on November 17, 1920, Sheldon wrote to Grinnell:

. . . to me the worst news is that the game, particularly the sheep, in the McKinley Park are rapidly being killed off by the market hunters. . . [and the new influx of miners to the Kantishna]. Unless all the clubs in N.Y. and Burnham get together and make a drive for an appropriation this winter, there is serious danger to the game, particularly as the railroad will reach there soon.[44]

A month later, in a letter to the House Committee on Appropriations, Sheldon cited all of the above, including fears that renewed mining activity in the Kantishna might cause a full-scale rush that would "add to the slaughter already going on there." He concluded with the information that "plans for a wagon road to this region have been completed."[45]

The conservationists' bombardment and the desperate efforts of Steve Mather and Horace Albright finally jolted Congress to action. An $8,000 appropriation was passed for 1921. The park's pioneer era would soon begin.

❉

NOTES: CHAPTER 5

1. William G. Sheldon, "Biographical Notes on Charles Sheldon," 9-page MS in Sheldon Papers, University of Alaska, Fairbanks, Archives, Box 4:59, 1; E. W. Nelson, "Charles Sheldon," *American Forests* (November 1928), 659-660.
2. Ibid., 659; C. Hart Merriam, "Introduction," in C. Sheldon, *The Wilderness of Denali*, ix-xi; George Bird Grinell, "Charles Sheldon," 5-page MS biographical sketch in personal collection of William Sheldon, copied from research files of Gail Evans.
3. Theodore Roosevelt, "The American Hunter-Naturalist," *The Outlook*, Vol. 99, No. 15 (December 9, 1911), 854-856; quotation on page 856.
4. Untitled draft paper by Charles Sheldon, ca. 1920, 4-page MS in personal collection of William Sheldon, copied from research file of Gail Evans.
5. For a summary of the ideas and people that framed this debate see Grant McConnell, "The Conservation Movement—Past and Present," *Western Political Quarterly*, Vol. 7, No. 1 (September 1954), 463-478. Sheldon's significant contributions to the shaping of the nation's policies of wildlife/habitat conservation and management are described in James B. Trefethen, *An American Crusade for Wildlife* (Alexandria, Va.: Boone and Crockett Club, 1975), 190-194.
6. Sheldon, *Wilderness of Denali*, 8-9.
7. Ibid., 14-16.
8. Ibid., 21.
9. Ibid., 22.
10. Ibid., 24-25.
11. Ibid., 26-27.
12. Ibid., 51-52.
13. Ibid., 65.
14. Ibid., 103.
15. Charles Sheldon, "List of Birds Observed on the Upper Toklat River Near Mount McKinley, Alaska," *Auk*, Vol. 26 (January 1909), 66.
16. G. B. Grinnell, "Charles Sheldon," 5-page MS from William Sheldon personal collection, copy on file, Denali National Park and Preserve, 4.

17. Madison Grant, "The Establishment of Mount McKinley National Park," in G. B. Grinnell and Charles Sheldon, eds., *Hunting and Conservation: The Book of the Boone and Crockett Club* (New Haven: Yale University Press, 1925), 438.

18. Ibid.

19. Harry Karstens letter of 7/25/18 to Horace Albright, National Archives, Record Group 79, Entry 6, Mount McKinley corres., Box 382.

20. Sheldon, *Wilderness of Denali*, 272.

21. James B. Trefethen, *Crusade for Wildlife* (Harrisburg, Penn.: Stackpole Co., 1961), 185-186.

22. Quoted in Ernest Gruening, *The State of Alaska* (New York: Random House, 1954), 178.

23. Ibid., 175-187; Maj.-Gen. A. W. Greeley, *Handbook of Alaska: Its Resources, Products and Attractions in 1924* (Port Washington, N.Y.: Kennikat Press edition, 1970), 45-46.

24. Gruening, *State of Alaska*, 187-190.

25. Trefethen, *Crusade for Wildlife*, 187.

26. Charles Sheldon letter of 10/10/15 to E. W. Nelson, Sheldon Papers, Box 1:6, University of Alaska, Fairbanks, Archives.

27. Morgan Sherwood, *Big Game in Alaska: A History of Wildlife and People* (New Haven: Yale University Press, 1961), 30-34.

28. Ibid., 34.

29. Ibid., 34-35.

30. Horace M. Albright, *"Oh, Ranger!" A Book About the National Parks* (New York: Dodd, Mead & Co., 1947 edition), 185.

31. Barry Mackintosh, *The National Parks: Shaping the System* (Washington: National Park Service, 1985), 18-19.

32. Charles Sheldon letter of 12/15/15 to Stephen T. Mather, National Archives, Record Group 79, Entry 6, Corres. Mount McKinley, Box 383.

33. Trefethen, *Crusade for Wildlife*, 189.

34. James B. Trefethen's chapter on the establishment of Mount McKinley National Park in *Crusade for Wildlife*, 179-191, is a convenient synopsis of the park movement and the legislative process, much relied on in this narrative; see also Grant Madison's history in *Hunting and Conservation*, and anon., "The Mount McKinley National Park," *Field and Stream* (April 1917), 171.

35. Interview with Horace Albright, December 1986, in *Boone and Crockett News*, Vol. 4, No. 2 (Spring 1987), 4.

36. NPS, *Proceedings of the National Park Conference* (1917), 194.

37. U.S. Congress, House. Mount McKinley National Park, Alaska. Report No. 1273, 64th Cong., 2nd Sess. (January 10, 1917), 2.

38. U.S. Congress, Senate. Committee on Territories. Hearing on the Establishment of Mount McKinley National Park, 64th Cong., 1st Sess., May 5, 1916; U.S. Congress, House. Subcommittee of the Committee on Public Lands. Hearing on a Bill to Establish Mount McKinley National Park, 64th Cong., 1st Sess., May 4, 1916.

39. See NPS, *Proceedings of the Conference on National Parks* (1917), 193-242, for development of these themes by Sheldon, Burnham, Nelson, Browne, and Capps.

40. Undated letter from Sheldon to George Bird Grinnell, Denali National Park and Preserve Archive.

41. Draft resolution in Sheldon Papers, University of Alaska, Fairbanks, Archives, Box 4:46.

42. Attached to William B. Greeley letter of 1/17/19 to Territorial Governor Thomas Riggs, in Alaska State Archives, Record Group 101, Box 172:42.

43. Riggs-Hallowell corres. of 10/2 and 10/20/19, Alaska State Archives, Record Group 101, Box 172: 42.

44. Sheldon letter of 11/17/20 to Grinnell, Sheldon Papers, University of Alaska, Fairbanks, Archives, Box 1:6.

45. Sheldon letter of 12/15/20, Record Group 79, Entry 6, Box 479, National Archives.

The first McKinley Park Station, in 1922, was a converted Tanana Valley Railroad car. R. T. Nichols, the first station agent and postmaster, is shown at right. Courtesy of the Aalska Railroad Collection, AMHA.

C H A P T E R   6
Conditions in Alaska in the World War I and Postwar Periods

THE NEED FOR SELF-GOVERNANCE

The new park made its debut in an Alaska that still considered itself an abused colony. From the northerners' viewpoint the limited powers of their territorial government put them at the mercy of competing bureaucracies in faroff Washington, D.C. The bureaucrats' conflicting controls stifled Alaska's development. Isolated by distance and high-latitude climate from the usual amenities and choices of economic pursuit, Alaskans depended almost exclusively on the raw products of land and sea: minerals, timber, fish, furs, and game. From these products they derived both sustenance and the cash income for imported necessities that their limited frontier economy could not produce. Yet these were the very resources, along with the land itself, controlled by the distant bureaucrats.

In an address before the Annual Meeting of the American Mining Congress in 1921, Falcon Joslin of Katalla, Alaska, described the lack of progress and the loss of population in Alaska. He attributed the decline in commerce and the ghost-town atmosphere of such cities as Fairbanks to misgovernment and the mismanagement of Alaska's resources. Critical was the lack of efficient access to freeholds on the federally owned landbase. Alaska's pioneers had to depend on leaseholds or permit titles, which could be and often enough were taken away by the agents of government. Under this uncertain regime the true pioneer lost hope, leaving the land to the rapacious. Thus did the federal government's misguided conservation policies lead to perverse result: the true conservator, the freeholder, gave way to the freebooter who cared only for quick fortune at whatever cost to the land and the animals he destroyed. The weak territorial legislature, excluded entirely from such crucial concerns as land and fish-and-game laws, could only plea and pass protest enactments against the veto powers vested in Washington. As Joslin saw it, on a foundation of laws and regulations born of hearsay and inaccurate reports from visiting firemen, the Washington bureaucrats fought amongst themselves to retain powers and jurisdictions. The shadow commissions and bureaus established by the territorial governor and legislature lacked authority to rectify and coordinate administration.

Joslin concluded his essay on Alaska's governance with these words: "Naturally, this form of government is sufficient to devastate a province. It is certainly returning the Territory to the bears."[1]

Joslin's remedy for this sad state of affairs was home rule. People involved and knowledgeable in Alaskan conditions and affairs could solve the problems of transportation, revive sagging industries, open new ones, and coordinate administration of land and resources. True representation by accountable agents of government would attract solid citizens and open Alaska to development and progress commensurate with its vast resources.[2]

Joslin's analysis and prescriptions were not without merit. And they certainly reflected the sentiments of most Alaskans. More than 30 years later Territorial Governor Ernest Gruening would say essentially the same things in his book, *The State of Alaska* (1954), whose title reflected an objective still 5 years from attainment.

Sternwheeler pushing a barge at Nenana, 1918. Courtesy of the Stephen Foster Collection, UAF.

But in the World War I and postwar periods Alaska was far from statehood. Its remoteness, its small population, and the fluctuating prices of extracted products—often more economically available elsewhere—held Alaska down. (Excepting such bonanzas as the Prudhoe Bay oil discovery, these factors still moderate Alaska's economy.) In addition, outside monied interests—the syndicates and trusts that controlled much of Alaska's extractive and transportation industry—found comfort and profit in playing off competing Congressional committees and government bureaus in Washington; they minded not at all a weak territorial government that lacked power and means to regulate their activities. Similarly, home-grown Alaskan boomers wanted the benefits of government assistance but not the controls that went with it.

Beginning in 1913 the Wilson Administration had spoken strongly to Alaska's concerns. The President himself urged a comprehensive development policy for Alaska. He wanted complete coastal surveys and charting to reduce ship losses on Alaska's long and dangerous coastline; such action would help reduce shipping rates, which had been inflated by exorbitant marine insurance. In support of this initiative Wilson's Secretary of Commerce remarked on the "peculiar habits of surveying up there . . . [whereby] we have found many rocks by running merchant ships upon them . . . ."[3]

In 1914 a friend of Alaska, Interior Secretary Franklin K. Lane, had analyzed the governance of the territory in words that foreshadowed Joslin's later remarks. Lane proposed consolidation of federal functions in Alaska under a development board that would streamline administration and give Alaskans a single governmental authority for conducting business.[4]

Pieces of the Wilson Administration program did get enacted: coal lands opened to limited entry; school lands made available; chartering of an Agricultural College and School of Mines (later the University of Alaska); and authorization and appropriation of $35 million for construction and operation of the Alaska Railroad, which would open coal and community development along the railbelt into the Interior.[5]

But then the war came. Federal energies and attention, both in the executive departments and in Congress, turned from Alaska to the national emergency. Alaska's population, depleted by the war effort, would decline from 64,000 in 1910 to 55,000 in 1920, including a significant reduction of one-third of the non-Native population. In 1920 Alaska had fewer people by 12 percent than in 1900; during the same decades the national population had grown by 38 percent. Except for a wartime surge of copper mining, Alaska's economy grew shakier, dependent largely on Outside money for its major export industries: fisheries and mining. At war's end depression and stagnation gripped the territory: lack of development, lack of jobs, lack of people.[6]

In the 1920s the U.S. Congress pursued conservation measures to protect Alaska's fish and wildlife. But continuing stagnation led to closure of many federal facilities, including mining and agricultural experiment stations and military installations (including Fort Gibbon at Tanana). Not until the Depression Era and its New Deal programs under President Franklin D. Roosevelt would Alaska feel fresh infusions from the federal government.[7]

T H E   R A I L R O A D

Fortunately for their health and survival, specific people in specific places resist the logic of trends and general conditions. Bottomless energy and optimism distinguished the pioneers of isolated Alaska. Those who penetrated the remote Denali region possessed surpluses of both. Despite a subsistence lifestyle focused on mining and trapping, sustained by hunting and gardening, these hardy folks maintained the vision of a bountiful future. They continued their clamor for transportation relief. Access to the mineral wealth of the region—coal, gold, and other metals—would spur development, bringing progress and new communities. As water brought the rose's bloom to the desert, so would roads, trails, and rails bring "industrial advancement" to this new land.[8]

Books, petitions, tracts, and screeds of all sorts carried this theme across the country to the halls of Congress. The history of the new park and its surrounding region would largely be determined by development of a federally funded transportation system comprising the railroad and the roads and trails it spawned.

By the summer of 1922, when the first tourists came to Mount McKinley National Park, the railroad from Seward to Fairbanks lacked only one link, the bridge across the Tanana River at Nenana. A ferry in summer and rails over river ice in winter made temporary connection pending the bridge's completion in early 1923. It was

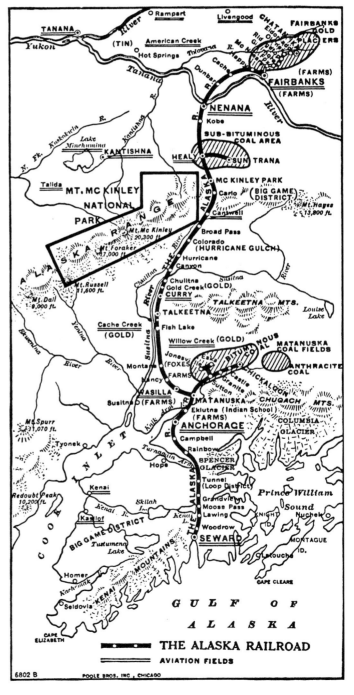

The Alaska Railroad during the 1930s. From The Alaska Railroad in Pictures, *Prince, 591.*

99

McKinley Park Depot in 1939. Courtesy of the Denali National Park and Preserve Archive. NPS photo by Grant Pearson.

now possible to make the Horseshoe Tour of Interior Alaska from the port city of Seward to the park and on to Fairbanks by rail; then by automobile on the Military Highway from Fairbanks to the ports of Valdez or Cordova.[9]

With variations as the road net proliferated and connected with the coastal city of Anchorage, this tour system based on the arterial railroad would last for 50 years. With few exceptions throughout that period people arrived at the park by railroad. There they would be met by the park's concessioner and conveyed into the park. Not until the summer of 1972 would the new state highway from Anchorage to Fairbanks allow automobile visitors to reach the park in significant numbers. This controlled railroad and concessioner access—at peak numbering only a few hundred visitors per day—would in turn control the park's planning, development, and operations.

As feared by park managers and planners alike, beginning in the 1960s as plans for the state highway matured, the rather cozy, old-style railroad park with its 1920s-30s facilities would be vaulted headlong into the mass mobility of the late twentieth century. The stories of resultant stresses and strains upon the old facilities, especially the pressures upon the designedly primitive park road (completed in 1938); the frustrations of visitors and park people alike; and the tug-of-war between resource (especially wildlife) protection and catch-up development schemes (both within the park and on its borders) properly belong in later chapters. But because the railroad-park syndrome and the radical changes wrought by the state highway have had such structuring effect upon the park's history—from the beginning to today—this fore-shadowing provides a course setting for much that follows.

Construction of the Alaska Railroad was a major engineering and logistical feat. All of the classic Alaskan conditions of remoteness, terrain, and climate opposed, obstructed, and only grudgingly surrendered to the small army that surveyed, sup-plied, and built the railroad.

Beginning in 1915, the Alaska Engineering Commission (AEC), an Interior Depart-ment agency run by U.S. Army engineers, deployed the men and material for the giant task. From construction headquarters at the tent city that became Anchorage, the line pushed northward to tap Matanuska Valley coal, which would fuel the railroad locomotives and machinery. Along the line two different kinds of crews did the work:

AEC-hired laborers built bridges and laid track; contract "station gangs" did the preliminary clearing, grading, and excavation.[10] The crews, working toward each other from Anchorage and the northern construction headquarters at Nenana, used every mode of frontier transportation: dogs and sleds, horse-drawn double-ender sledges and wagons, pack animals, and boats. Once track was laid trains shuttled supplies for the next increment.[11]

People flocked to the construction camps for work. Quickly built (and as soon abandoned) roadhouses, offering amenities unavailable at the camps, sprang up

Park Ranger Darrell Coe with 7-dog team about six miles from park headquarters. View NE from road. Snow Trac vehicle at right. Courtesy of the Denali National Park and Preserve Archive. NPS photo by Verde Watson.

Curry Hotel, on the Alaska Railroad near Talkeetna. From the Herbert Heller Collection, UAF.

Alaska Railroad engine crossing the Tanana River on the ice at Nenana, just prior to completion of the railroad. Courtesy of the Frederick C. Mears Collection, UAF.

along the way as workers and camp followers progressed with the railroad. Towns established at major river crossings (e.g., Nenana, Talkeetna), at division or section points (Curry, Cantwell), and at coal mining centers (Healy) would survive the construction era.

By late 1920 the gap between north and south ends of steel—between Healy and the Susitna River crossing—still stretched nearly 100 miles.[12] Centered on the Broad Pass area, this was the part of the railroad route that passed through what geologist George Eldridge had earlier described as "one of the grandest ranges on the North American Continent." Here, too, was some of the most difficult construction on the line.

These miles contain Hurricane Gulch and Riley Creek—deep incisions that required great steel bridges (still in use today). At Moody on the park's northeastern corner, a sliding mountain would require constant stabilization and periodic grade reconstruction. The 5 miles between Moody and Healy traversed the Nenana River Gorge, a place of tunnels and cliff-perched track overlooking turbulent waters that tear at the walls of the entrenched glacial river.

In spring 1921, the AEC's chief engineer Col. Frederick Mears decided to close the gap in the line with day-and-night track-laying and trestle construction. Hurricane Gulch (Mile 284 on the railroad), Riley Creek (Mile 347), and the Nenana River Gorge south of Healy (Mile 358) posed the greatest hurdles.[13]

Standard gauge track laid southward from Nenana connected that river supply point and the large construction base camp at Healy. Now the crews forced the heavy rock work in the canyon, carving platforms for track from the cliffs, penetrating rock buttresses with tunnels. Other crews continued grading south—beyond the gorge and past the park entrance at Riley Creek to Mile 335.[14]

When winter came the Nenana River's ice made a highway for transport of heavy equipment through the gorge. Horse-drawn rolling stock, draglines, and camp equipment and supplies speeded track laying from the upper end of the canyon to the north bank of Riley Creek at Mile 347. In describing the hard push through the gorge, AEC engineer E.J. Cronin asserted, "The Pharaohs of Egypt, in building the pyramids, faced no greater difficulties and hardships than did the crews under Superintendent of Construction Bill Packer in completing this project."[15]

No less difficult had been the bridge across Hurricane Gulch, fabricated and erected for the AEC by the American Bridge Company. This single-track bridge had to span a chasm more than 900 feet across and 300 feet deep. A great arch 384 feet long provided the central support, with 120-foot riveted-truss deck spans at either end, extended at the north end by a 240-foot-long steel viaduct. Using the cantilever method, the arch was started at both ends, each end held to the shore by steel backstays. Since track and material approached Hurricane Gulch from the south, the builders had to transfer the north-end materials across the gorge by two methods: 1) cableway transfer, and 2) erecting cranes on each end of the advancing arch to lower and pick up materials from the gulch floor. An ingenious system of telescopic backstays, shims, and hydraulic jacks allowed fine adjustments so the two halves of the arch could be fitted and closed into permanent position, which occurred without a hitch. Earlier a specially made steel tape, corrected for temperature, had been stretched between the approach spans under a tension of 50 pounds to get the precise 384-foot arch-length measurement. Erection of the bridge started in early June 1921. Sixty working days later the first train passed over the structure and track laying commenced north of the gulch.[16]

Completion of the huge bridge across the Tanana River at Nenana would wait until February 1923. But train ferries and tracks across river ice had already made the Tanana crossing operational. By late December 1921 only one gap remained to prevent trains from traveling the entire 470 miles between Seward and Fairbanks. That gap was Riley Creek at the entrance to Mount McKinley National Park. Crews from north and south had brought their respective ends of steel to the embankments flanking this deep-cut stream, but more than 900 feet separated them. The bridging of Riley Creek with a structure part steel viaduct and part timber-frame trestle focused the construction energies of the AEC, for this was the final operational link. The big construction camp on the south bank of Riley Creek overflowed with laborers and engineers. In about a month they finished the bridge and laid the last rails, thus achieving, as the New York Times of February 3, 1922, would proclaim, "the practical completion of one of the most difficult engineering projects undertaken by the United States Government."[17]

In fact, much remained to be done. Hasty construction, inadequate ballasting, and replacement of temporary wood trestles with steel would force the equivalent of reconstruction over many sections of the line. Severe maintenance and repair problems caused by snow avalanches, earthquakes and slides, frost-heave, and other Alaska dynamics would always drain the railroad's budget. From earliest operations, deficits between income and outgo would invite critical Congressional reviews. But the government owned-and-operated Alaska Railroad did what it was intended to do. It connected Alaska's vast Interior with Seward's ice-free port, and, by ocean ships, with Seattle and the rest of the world. In conjunction with spur wagon roads and trails, it stimulated mining in isolated districts. With its low-cost freighting capacity it made possible vast, long-term dredging operations for reworking the Fairbanks placer fields. It spawned towns and agricultural enterprise. It revolutionized Interior river transportation, making Nenana the queen city of Yukon-drainage steamboating. Few informed persons expected more, and such persons wrote off the road's deficits as a debt owed to a neglected frontier, the price paid to generate social and industrial productivity in a remote and detached province. Twenty years later the railroad would become a strategic link in the winning of World War II, aiding in the repulse of Japanese invaders and hauling fuel for the aircraft ferry operations across Alaska and Siberia to the Russo-German front.[18]

The railroad provided a north-south transportation backbone from tidewater to the Yukon. In the Denali region's upland country, far from deep-river ports, its effect would be multiplied by a feeder rail spur to the Healy coal mines, and wagon roads and trails that extended like ribs to east and west. This effect was intended and planned.

ARC AND AEC COLLABORATION

Col. James Steese of the Alaska Road Commission (ARC) and Col. Frederick Mears of the AEC had corresponded on this matter during the railroad's construction. In anticipation of the laying of steel the ARC conducted road-and-trail surveys and requested appropriations for their construction.

This was a mutually beneficial collaboration between the two territorial agencies, one (AEC) lodged in the Interior Department, the other (ARC) in the War Department, both run by Army engineers. The ARC had been charged by Congress at its founding in 1905 to provide transportation relief to the isolated sections of the territory, particularly those mining districts beyond easy reach of steamboat freighting. The AEC had been charged with construction and profitable operation of a railroad that would connect three small towns (Seward, Anchorage, Fairbanks) over nearly 500 miles of commercially unpopulated wilderness—with potential, but only if made accessible.

The mutual interests of the two agencies were conveniently summarized in a 1921 letter from the AEC's engineer-in-charge at Anchorage to AEC Chairman Colonel Mears:

I have read with considerable interest your exchange of communications with Colonel Steese

McKinley Park station and display booth, August 3, 1930. Courtesy of the Alaska Railroad Collection, AMHA.

of the Alaska Road Commission, *regarding the construction of wagon roads and trails in Alaska, more particularly those roads and trails which may be considered as feeders to the new Government Railroad.*

It goes without question that a main line passing through a more or less barren country, even though it may join populous sections, is working at a very great disadvantage. It, in a measure, resembles a bridge across a large stream from which there is little or no revenue and there is always considerable expense against it for operation. This, in fact, is the character of our road between Anchorage and Nenana, or shall I say, perhaps between Wasilla and Nenana. Through this intermediate section there are vast latent pos-

Teams hauling the mail, and a locomotive, through the Nenana River canyon in February 1921. Courtesy of the Alaska Railroad Collection, AMHA.

sibilities in the way of mines and agriculture which will produce little or no interest in the way of revenue to our road until joined to it by some means of transportation.

Engineer F. D. Browne continued with a discussion of the advantages to the railroad of tapping lode-mining districts, which had to ship bulk quartz ore to smelters:

Such a region is the Kantishna mining district, situated westerly from Mile 350 on the Government Railroad. A portion of the McKinley Park is traversed in reaching the Kantishna center of activity and a road in there, from whatever point may be selected on the railroad as a junction, will undoubtedly be one of the most favorable for the creation of an early tonnage for the road. All who have examined this territory declare that there is immense tonnage of valuable ore in sight. Even though this were not made available for some little time, it is no less important that McKinley Park be made available to the public and that a start be made in opening up the country adjacent to the head waters of the Iditarod and Kuskokwim Rivers via a route which shall pass near Lake Minchumina. Such a through line would be accessory to the proposed route through Rainy Pass to McGrath and Ophir and need in nowise conflict as two immense territories would be opened by the two different routes. This road into, and perhaps to be extended beyond, the Kantishna district, I believe, is the first and most important one that should be undertaken by the Alaska Road Commission.

I believe that every effort should be made to induce Congress to appropriate funds for the extension of the railroad, and even under the assumption that this is promptly and willingly granted, that no less importance be given the necessity of improving and extending all wagon roads and trails adjacent to the railroad that they may be producing tonnage and make the railroad what it should be, i.e., a unit in the development of Alaska.[19]

This letter's explicit reference to McKinley Park tourist access would produce a three-way collaboration between the AEC, the ARC, and the National Park Service (NPS). All three agencies would requite their distinct objectives from the park road that connected the railroad with the Kantishna district: bulk-haul and tourist-traffic revenue for the AEC, provision of miners' transportation relief by ARC, and visitor access into the park for the NPS, which would set the standards for the road through the park and provide appropriated funds for its construction by the ARC.

Other roads and trails based on the railroad would include the road west from Talkeetna to the Cache Creek-Yentna district, a bobsled trail east from Cantwell to the Valdez Creek district, a trail from Kobe to the Bonnifield district, and various feeders off the old mail trail between Fairbanks-Nenana and McGrath, including the Lignite-

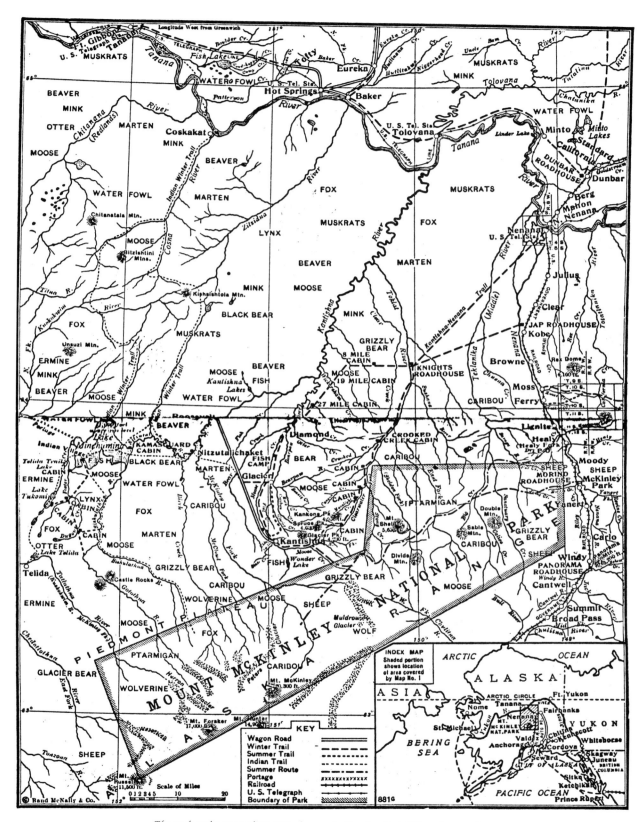

The park and surrounding area, drawn shortly after the 1922 park expansion.
From Rand McNally Guide to Alaska and Yukon, *Rand McNally, 8-9.*

Kantishna trail and the Kobe-Knight's Roadhouse trail.[20]

In September 1920 ARC engineer Hawley Sterling made a reconnaissance for a wagon road from the railroad to Kantishna. His purpose was to select the best route from a number suggested by miners in the district. Petitioners included Charles A. Trundy, U.S. Commissioner at Kantishna; K. E. Casperis, engineer for Mt. McKinley Gold Placers; and, according to ARC's Colonel Steese, "the most substantial operators in the Kantishna District," Joe Dalton, Joe Quigley, and Ed Brooker.[21]

In a 1921 letter to James Wickersham, Colonel Steese stated the objectives of ARC regarding transportation relief for the Kantishna miners: Interim relief would continue to be provided by keeping the winter dog trails open from the rail line to Kantishna, and by improving the wagon road from the Kantishna River's head of navigation at Roosevelt. The ultimate relief depended on construction of a first-class wagon road from the railroad to Kantishna. Steese noted "very violent advocacy" for various routes all along the rail corridor from Talkeetna to Nenana. (One petition called for a

Top photo: Early automobile ferry, probably the Big Delta Ferry *crossing the Tanana River. From the Fanny Quigley Collection, UAF.*

Bottom photo: Crane work at Nenana, circa 1921. Courtesy of the Stephen Foster Collection, UAF.

wagon road across main-range icefields!). With severely limited funds ARC could not indulge all these interests, but would have to choose only one best route.[22]

As it turned out, the 1920 survey and report by Hawley Sterling forced the decision on that one best route. Sterling tested two tracks. He went out by the "lower route" from Lignite to Toklat River and on to Kantishna via Clearwater Fork and Canyon, Caribou, Glacier, and Moose Creeks.

He returned by the Riley Creek or "upper route" through the high passes traversed by today's park road, coming out at what would soon be McKinley Station on the railroad.

In reporting the pros and cons of the two routes (the lower route at 2200 feet average elevation; the upper at 2800 feet) he contrasted the swamps and glacial muck over 50 percent of the lower route with the drier, harder ground of the upper route. Much better timber on the upper route would aid in bridge-building over streamcourses. Despite the lower route being shorter, construction and maintenance costs would be higher, for sidehill stretches across glacial-muck slopes would require constant gravelling and reconstruction in places where gravel sources were far distant. Because of extensive dry and naturally gravelled reaches along the upper route (and better gravel sources for wet-ground base material) the initial wagon road could be easily improved for automobile and truck traffic. The lower route could never be more than a mediocre wagon road.

Railroad bridge and sternwheelers at Nenana, during the 1947 break-up season. Courtesy of the Alaska Railroad Collection, AMHA.

Upper-route stream crossings would be fewer and shorter. Better grades, generally, and less steep cutbanks at stream crossings would allow a smaller work force, for most of the work could be done with teams and graders. This was an important consideration in labor-poor Alaska.

Finally, the upper route offered a natural gateway into Mount McKinley National Park. This would benefit the railroad through tourist-traffic income. And it offered the possibility of funding assistance from the National Park Service, thus stretching ARC's limited dollars.[23]

It would be difficult to overestimate the importance for regional and park history of Hawley Sterling's report. It forged into one the three distinct interests of the ARC, the AEC, and the NPS, leading directly to the 1922 NPS-ARC road-construction agreement, which was aided and abetted by the AEC. By selecting the upper route through the park for the transportation artery between the railroad and the Kantishna district, Sterling's report produced a kind of shotgun wedding between the miners and the NPS, one that over the years demonstrated the stresses of such forced alliances.

Because it was a long and difficult project—dragged out further by skimpy funding—construction of the park road consumed ARC energies on the north flank of the Denali region. Steese's original intent to push the road southwesterly into the Kuskokwim drainage was never realized. Alternate routes, such as through Rainy Pass, never got beyond primitive trails. Moreover, upon completion and upgrading of the park road for auto and truck traffic (plus the increased reliance on airplanes in the

'30s) even river transport and winter trails in the Kantishna area faded except for occasional hauls of ore with tractors.

Thus the park road emerged as the *only* significant surface connection between the railroad and mining and other interests beyond the park's northwest boundary. This circumstance inevitably produced conflict between the park and these economic interests.

The eventual 90 miles of park road, bought and paid for by NPS appropriations, was from the NPS viewpoint primarily a visitor access road. Only incidentally, in that view, was it a link in an industrial transportation system, whose other links were a railroad loading platform at McKinley Station and a 6-mile spur road to Kantishna beyond the park boundary. From other viewpoints, particularly the miners', the primacy of the road's industrial function was self evident. In their view NPS restrictions to preserve the scenic and wildlife-viewing function for visitors created red tape and bottlenecks.

Thus a mutually beneficial and fiscally efficient interagency agreement of 1922 built a dual-purpose road whose built-in conflicts have haunted park management up to the present day. From the time of its completion in 1938, the park road has been pressed into plans and schemes to equalize its park and economic functions, and—because the road remains the only surface access to this part of the country—to proliferate its functions at Kantishna and beyond.

Today's conservation concerns over the fate of the park road can be neatly summarized: The growing momentum of added economic purposes threatens the fragile balance that allows visitors to view the park's wildlife against its mountain scenery. Given the park founders' charge to preserve this scenery/wildlife combination the NPS has had to stand in opposition to these schemes. This historical progression, with all its present portents, had its origins in Hawley Sterling's 1920 report to the road commissioners.

Despite some disgruntlement at Kantishna (particularly the protests of Charles Trundy and K. E. Casparis) over choice of the upper or park route for the main road, that decision would stand. In a letter to Trundy, responding to his advocacy of the Lignite-Toklat route, the ARC declined responsibility for that trail and the old miners' cabins on it that travelers used for shelter. ARC stated that pending completion of the main road through the park, ARC would maintain only the Roosevelt-Kantishna wagon road and the sled road and shelter cabins from Kobi to Kantishna via Knights Roadhouse, Diamond City, and Glacier.[24]

THE RENEWAL OF MINING

In the early 1920s mining activity began to pick up at Kantishna,[25] thus the pressure on the ARC for this route or that route, depending on the future road's proximity to the particular miner's claims. As time would prove, the old-style gold placer methods—open cuts, shoveling in, and ground sluicing—would continue until the late '30s to be the district's mainstay. But a brief excitement came in the years 1920-24, product of new thinking and new money—some of it from Outside. Two outfits—McKinley Gold Placers, Inc., on lower Caribou Creek and Glacier Creek, and Kantishna Hydraulic Mining Co. on Moose Creek—put in major developments for large-scale hydraulic mining of bench deposits. Volume of processed material would make up for the sparse gold in the gravel—so ran the theory. But costs of transportation wrecked that notion and the big companies soon folded. New management and local partnerships took over the hydraulic operations for a season or two, but they could not make a profit either.

Improvements in ground-sluicing techniques—using automatic boomer dams to uncover paydirt—extended the lives of some placer claims and opened up a few new ones, including a revival of Joe Dalton's old claims on Crooked Creek at the north end of the district. All of these were small operations typically employing two to four men.

The legacy of these '20s and '30s placer operations includes the remnants of the system (dam, ditch, and siphon) that brought water from Wonder Lake to the Moose Creek hydraulicking site (opposite the mouth of Eureka Creek); the camp buildings, equipment, and workings on Caribou and Glacier creeks; and remains of boomer dams and subsequent small-scale hydraulicking at places like Twenty-Two Gulch.

As the placers flattened toward subsistence levels, lode prospects became more attractive. Joe Quigley worked and leased claims on the ridge that bears his name. The Humbolt prospect near Glacier Peak and the Alpha prospect high on Eldorado were also active. Silver-lead ore paid handsomely after World War I, which stimulated more lode prospecting throughout the district. Again, costs of transportation—particularly painful for lode miners, who had to ship their bulk ore to Outside smelters—made losers of mines that elsewhere would have shown profit. Lode gold mines, suffering the same problems, kept a few miners supplied with staples but made no fortunes. Joe Quigley, for example, grossed only $5,000 from his Red Top claim in the period 1920-24. Charles Trundy fared no better.

In 1920 Joe and Fanny Quigley found promising copper-zinc deposits at Copper Mountain (now Mount Eielson) within the park. Hundreds of claimants staked this and nearby mineralized zones, including Slippery Creek in the Mount McKinley foothills. But commercial values eluded the miners, and most of these claims—often after years of hopeful assessment work—were abandoned and lapsed.

By early depression days the population of the Kantishna district and surrounding mining areas had dwindled to less than 20 souls. In 1930 only two miners wintered over at Eureka. One trader and one trapper lived at Diamond. This was a far cry from the distant days of stampede—a cabin or two with smoke in the pipe, the rest falling and smothered with alders.

Quigley's serious injury, in a 1931 tunnel cave-in, ended his underground mining career. But his prospect there would pay handsomely in a few years.

By the mid-'30s low metal prices—tagged on to high transportation, equipment, and labor costs—had just about whipped mining enterprise in the Kantishna and surrounding districts.

Then came a series of breaks that produced the Golden Years of Kantishna mining, 1937-42. President Roosevelt raised the price of gold to $35 an ounce. The park road reached Kantishna. And the depression's duration had spawned a roving army of cheap labor.

Kantishna's resurgence in the late '30s and early '40s broke all production records for gold mining, indeed surpassing district totals of all the years preceding. Central to this revival was the Red Top Mining Company's 1935-38 development of the Banjo Mine under option from the Quigleys. When production started in 1939 the plant included road, airstrip, mill, assay shop, bunkhouses, blacksmith shop, and other facilities to tap the commercial-grade gold ore in the Banjo vein. Never before had commercial-scale milling of lode gold been attempted in this district. Banjo became the fourth largest lode mine in the Yukon Basin, producing in the years 1939-41 more than 6,000 ounces of gold and 7,000 of silver. As World War II approached the Banjo's success raised hopes that the district's marginal days had ended.

Lode-mining excitement extended to the antimony deposit at Stampede Creek, discovered long before but latent until the approaching war boosted prices for this critical metal. By 1941, 2,400 tons of ore yielding 1,300 tons of metallic antimony had been shipped from Stampede, making it Alaska's prime producer of this metal and one of the largest in the country. Earl Pilgrim, operator and eventual owner of the Stampede Mine, would be a continuing force in the Denali region's history, as will be demonstrated in Chapter 8. Placer mining, too, resurged in this period. Reworking of previously mined creeks with new methods—notably the Caribou Mines Co. work with dragline and other mechanized equipment—gave a foretaste of modern mining procedures that would become standard in Alaska placer fields after World War II. These techniques allowed enormous increases in production. Kantishna's aggregate placer-gold return of $139,000 in 1940 broke all previous records. The district's three all-time high production mines operated during this period.

Then, again, came a war. Transportation, manpower, fuel, supplies, and equipment all funnelled to the war effort, effectively crippling the boom. It died with the wartime order that banned gold mining as non-essential. A few small operations not covered by the ban limped along through the war years. Limited production, using bulldozers, loaders, and small-scale hydraulic outfits resumed in the late '40s. But the golden years were over.

Even the strategic-metal antimony mines on Stampede and Slate creeks—at first stimulated by the war—suffered from wartime transportation and manpower limitations. The drop in demand for strategic metals after the war would dampen further the marginal interest in Kantishna's remote antimony mines. The small tonnage of ores and concentrates these mines managed to ship meant little in the general mining collapse, which reached nadir in the '50s and '60s.

It would be 30 years before the Kantishna would know another boom, and that really a boomlet. In the mid-'70s, after abandonment of the gold standard the price of gold would soar to unimagined heights and the trek to the Kantishna Hills would again pick up its pace.

Other mining districts in the isolated Denali region experienced similar though locally varied histories in the years between the wars. As at Kantishna, the continuity of small-outfit mining bridged the lean years between short-lived and usually disappointing excitements.

Life in the Kantishna carried on despite the somber progressions of history. Two fresh-eyed visitors in the early '20s left verbal snapshots of day-to-day events that otherwise would have gone unrecorded. One, Mary Lee Davis, was the first woman to reach the camp via the yet unmarked park-road route over the high passes. She accompanied her mining-engineer husband on a business trip that, for her, was a pilgrimage to the land of The Most High. At the request of a prospector, the couple veered from course so John Davis could assess the man's claim. Mary wrote of long travel into the headwaters of a remote creek, "up the blackest gulch I think I ever saw, cracked open into the heart of barren hills that grew more eerie and more shadowed the further we reached into them. The 'cabin' was a mere hole blasted from the face of a mountain, and our 'bed' was a mere ledge, down which rock water dripped all night."[26]

Again en route they passed a cold night on spruce boughs and woke to a celestial sunrise that revealed the "unutterable majesty," the "patient stillness" of Mount McKinley. "A streamer of cloud, the hallmark of the very loftiest summits, drifted above like alder smoke. One seemed to see the very gate of heaven thrust open . . .

with golden and crimson light draping this highest altar."[27]

Mary spent most of her Kantishna time with Fanny Quigley—and most of that time tramping the hills with pack dogs, for, said Fanny, "I can't be shut up in a cage." Her conversation ranged the spectrum of a frontier woman's life, from hauling logs for firewood to hunting, one of her favorite pursuits:

One hunter is better than two when you're after big game, because you have to be changing your mind all the time. You'll change a whole day's hunting plan in a second, while one foot is in the air just ready to put down—if your eyes or ears tell you something new. And you can't be bothering to explain to the other fellow all about it. When Joe and I hunt together, we hunt separate. And you don't want to waste shots. It costs too high, in lots of ways. I'd be ashamed not to fetch in a hundred pounds of meat to a cartridge. A 30-30 is big enough artillery for black bear or moose, but a 30-40 is a heap sight better. And caribou, though they aren't large-bodied, will walk off with a load of lead. That's serious when your rifle means eighty per cent of your grub-stake, and you have to make every shot count. Quick death means clean butchering; and that counts, too, when you've got a carcass to handle alone, like I do. Heart, brain, or spinal cord is the mark. One well-put bullet is enough—or should be! A shot in the guts means a messy job of butchering, if you're out for meat, and a flank shot ruins a good hide if you're out for fur. You may be thinking of the mercy of it—that's open. I'm thinking about grub-stake.[28]

Years later, after Joe's crippling mine accident, while Fannie carried the whole load with the help of her dogs, she would write to Mary: "Went down six miles for some meat I killed. Then I have about fifteen cords of wood to haul, so you see when night comes I am tired."[29]

In 1922-23 Ed Brooker, Jr., took time off from his senior year in high school Outside to join his parents in Kantishna, where Ed Brooker, Sr., was U.S. Commissioner and Postmaster.[30] After riding the train from Seward young Ed was greeted by his mother at McKinley Station where she had been working as a cook at Morino's Roadhouse. Together they travelled by pack train through the park to Kantishna.

As Kantishna's commissioner, the elder Brooker was judge, chief law officer, mining claim recorder, and, generally, "the Government" as it existed in bush Alaska in those early days. He had just finished leading a posse that subdued and shipped out a deranged German miner who had been shooting up the Glen Creek camp. When young Ed and his mother arrived unexpectedly at Brooker's tent on Friday Creek at midnight, the youngster shook the tent frame without saying a word, wanting to surprise his dad. Still jittery from the ordeal with the German, Brooker cried out, "Who's there?" Ed didn't answer, but shook the tent again, whereupon he heard: "Tell me who you are or I'm coming out shooting!" "Needless to say," Ed recalls, "I spoke up. We had a happy reunion."

That summer of 1922 Ed and his dad built a log cabin on Friday Creek, on the flat where it breaks out of the hills. They made it eight logs high so they would not have to stoop when they moved around inside. Frank Ten Eyck, who also lived at the foot of the hill, helped them saw lumber for the roof, which they tarpapered and sodded.

Father and son climbed Monument Dome often that summer, so called because of the USGS survey marker on top. It is now called Brooker Mountain after Ed's dad. Ed accompanied Joe Quigley and "Dirty" Pete Pemberton on a trip out to the railroad and Fairbanks so he could visit old school friends. "Joe was a regular mountain goat in hiking, and Pete and I were dragged out at the end of each day. We went light and ate light. This was the way Joe traveled." Joe stayed on in Fairbanks so Ed and Pete traveled back without him over the still unmarked trail through the park. They carried a rifle for bear protection but didn't need it. "We saw all manner of wild game which was a thrill."

During winter keeping body and soul together was the main activity at Kantishna.

When weather allowed, the miners used the frozen, snow-covered ground as a highway to ship out silver ore for the Tacoma smelter. Hawley Sterling, who would later supervise ARC construction of the park road, was one of the miners; Little Johnny Busia (Boo-SHAY), a Croat who had come over from Europe some years before, was another.

One time Jim O'Brien and Mace Farrar left Copper Mountain by dog team, bound for Kantishna in minus 40 degree weather. In camp on the McKinley River Mace chopped his lower leg to the bone when his axe glanced off a frozen cottonwood. He quickly smeared sugar on the wound to stop the bleeding. Then O'Brien loaded him in the dog sled and drove him non-stop more than 100 miles to get medical help. "Mace was OK again in a few weeks."

Ed clerked for his dad in the latter's role of recorder for the mining district. Ed's description of the recording procedure shows how miners established their claims:

When one stakes land and calls it either a lode or placer claim, a location notice is placed on a stake at the point of discovery. Usually, this piece of paper was put in a Prince Albert tobacco can fastened upside down on the discovery stake (protection against the weather). To be binding and legal, it was (and is) necessary to take the location notice to a recording office where a typed or hand written copy is made and filed in a recorder's book.

Ed notes that these books were legal size and loose leaf, so notices could be typed and inserted. He used his dad's old portable Royal, commenting that the typewriter under his management at age 16 made many mistakes. Miners had to perform at least $100 dollars worth of work each year on each claim to retain their rights, then had to so swear by affidavit, which was also copied and filed in the recorder's book. Many recorders could not type, so wrote their entries; among them were calligraphers who produced "real works of art."

The isolation of the winter camp—125 miles by winter trail from Nenana—forced the miners to hunt wild meat for subsistence. Besides, Ed comments, "Canned corned willie gets a bit tiresome." Spurred by the need for fresh meat Ed and John Bowman, who also lived on Friday Creek, set out with dogs for Copper Mountain to get a sheep. Mace Farrar and Fred Jungst—grubstaked by Ed's mother to prospect that mountain—had a tent below it in the Thorofare Basin. There the hunters aimed, planning to use the tent as a base camp. A sudden blizzard caused white-out conditions, and after miles of zero visibility, guiding themselves by contours and wind direction, the half-frozen nimrods luckily stumbled onto the tent. It was 10 miles from nearest timber, but the absent owners had left dry wood and shavings by the stove for quick fire and warmup, as demanded by the Code of the North. Next day they began climbing to the wind swept ridges, where the sheep could dig down to forage through the shallow snow. The constant wind had packed Copper Mountain's snow slopes, forcing the hunters to kick steps in the plaster-like crust. After a day of futile labor, and another night in the tent, they returned to Friday Creek empty handed.

John Bowman was used to failure. After making a small fortune in the Klondike, he lost it in the saloons of Dawson. Subsequent mining in the Koyukuk district, 400 miles north of Denali, and in the Kantishna, had not improved his finances. But somehow he always got enough booze. Ed recalls a Bowman birthday party in mid-winter. One of his cronies on Slate Creek constructed a wooden birthday cake, then covered it with tasty frosting. Following a convivial dinner, Bowman tried to cut the cake, finally giving up with the comment, "It musht be froshen."

Commissioner Brooker had finally married Joe and Fanny Quigley after they had consorted for many years without benefit of nuptials. It was rumored in camp that the commissioner, lacking a Bible, sealed the sacrament with a Montgomery Ward catalogue. Upon recordation in the commissioner's ledger, however, all was legal and binding.

Personal feuds and friendships tempered neighborliness at Kantishna, as elsewhere. In 1954 Johnny Busia told Ed Brooker that around 1950 only Johnny, Joe Dalton, and Pete Anderson wintered in Kantishna. Dalton had given Johnny trouble over mining claims. So when Dalton died, Johnny—in his words—"wrapped him in a blanket and put him in a shallow hole with an old board to mark his grave." Later, Johnny found his friend Pete Anderson dead in his bunk: "I made a good box, put Pete in carefully, dug a good hole, buried Pete and put a good fence around the grave and put up a good marker."

Ed's mother told him of the flu epidemic that spread from Fairbanks to Nenana in March 1920 when "bigshots" traveled through by train and broke quarantine. His mother closed her restaurant to serve as a volunteer nurse. Whiskey, used by some as a cure, proved negative. The Nenana Indians were nearly wiped out. "Wooden boxes (rather than coffins) could not be built fast enough. Several bodies were put in a single box."

When Ed went into Nenana, he attended Joe Burns' movie house, where Vic Durand provided music to accompany the silent film on the screen, "playing the piano with his feet, playing the mouth organ from a rack over his shoulders, and playing a violin with his hands." Fanny Quigley got into Nenana about once a year to see a film. "Fanny, with a dress on top of her overalls would, in a loud voice, explain what the movie was all about and what was going to happen next. No one had the nerve to ask her to keep quiet."

About midway through the 1922-23 winter, Ed Brooker departed to resume his schooling:

Dad and I loaded back packs with grub and blankets and started walking to the Alaska Railroad and Nenana from which I could go outside. We elected to go out with the carrier of the U.S. mail who made the 125 mile trip about once a month using a single horse and a type of sled called a double ender. This was a flat bed job about three feet wide and approximately 14 ft. long. The winter trail led north a few miles beyond the Kantishna foothills and east to Healy station on the railroad. I'm guessing that we made about 20 miles each day and had cabins of one sort or another to stay in at night. One stop for the night was at Knight's Roadhouse on the Toklat River. A Mr. and Mrs. Knight with one son had lived here for a number of years. In summer they saw no one because the terrain both east and west of them was swamp, and mosquitoes, almost impassable. They were self sufficient with their garden, their game and perhaps some fish, though the Toklat River is muddy.

Their place stands out because it was the only stop we made where the cabin was warm when we arrived and we did not have to cook our own grub. In passing, I have heard that the Knight family stayed on for a number of years till both Mr. and Mrs. Knight passed away and were buried by their son. I have lost the story of the son.

In due time we arrived at Nenana, Dad put me on a train bound for Seward (on the coast) where I boarded a salt water ship for Seattle. Again, there was a long tedious train trip from Seattle to Palo Alto, but this time, I had a bit more experience behind me. Dad went back to Friday Gulch where Mother and he spent the winter.

Recent correspondence with Ed Brooker, in his eighties a man of sharp recall, has helped resolve the construction date of the two-story log structure known locally as the Kantishna Roadhouse. According to Ed, coincident with the post-World War I mining boomlet, spurred partly by a pegged price for silver, a man named Wilson along with his wife and child, came to Eureka (the early name for Kantishna) about 1919 or 1920 and built the two-story log cabin for his family. Wilson preceded Ed's dad as Postmaster and U.S. Commissioner in the Kantishna.[31] These remembrances are independently supported by a telegram dated March 29, 1921, to Col. James Steese requesting ARC's completion of the Roosevelt-Kantishna road, and listing concerned citizens of Kantishna and Nenana as signatories. Joined with familiar names such as Joe Dalton, the Quigleys and the Hamiltons is the name and title: C HERBERT WILSON COMMISSIONER.[32] A USGS photograph by geologist P.S. Smith in 1922 shows the two-story structure at the Eureka townsite surrounded by tents and small cabins. Another informant, Art Schmuck (presently of Nenana but formerly a Kantishna miner) recalled to this author the structure's door-lintel date of 1919 when he first saw it in 1955. The carved date on the lintel (no longer in place) reflected traditional practice for noting a cabin's construction date. The carved 1919 stuck in Art's memory because that was the year of his birth. With all of this evidence assembled we can state with certainty that the cabin was in place by summer 1922 (from the photo). And, by way of the Brooker and Schmuck remembrances, plus the supporting wire, we can assign with reasonable certainty a 1919 or 1920 construction date. The contextual occurrence of the 1920-1924 mining boomlet, which attracted professional "boomers," including Ed's dad, is also supportive of construction during this period. The building's ongoing roles as post office (Johnny Busia always called it "the post office"), as informal roadhouse (a place where visitors not otherwise accommodated could spread their bedding), and as community meeting place lends substantive significance to "the Roadhouse."

Ed Brooker's life spans the revolution from nineteenth century to the twenty-first. In his reflections on those long-ago days at Kantishna he wrote a simple profundity that riveted this writer: "One thought in this account is that, never again, will children be born and grow in an environment without cars and airplanes, but rather with horses, dogs and their own two feet."

THE NEW TOWNS

Distinct from the older mining camps, the railroad created new towns that began as construction camps and persisted as trading and transportation centers. Nenana, Cantwell, and the revived Talkeetna illustrate this progression. Healy, just north of the park, also got its start as a town with arrival of the railroad builders. Its continuing history would rest on a combination of railroad operations and mining of the great coal deposits bordering Healy and Lignite creeks, which opened up with the advent of railroad transportation.

Healy's early settlers came in the train of strikes at the Bonnifield and Kantishna fields. Soon appeared a roadhouse and a store, a moonshiner's still, a cafe, and the cabin of a commercial meat hunter named Colvin who also trapped and guided. As more trappers and prospectors came into the camp, they settled near Colvin's cabin on the Nenana River bluff opposite the mouth of Healy Creek. The AEC's Construction Camp 358 (from the railroad milepost) suddenly picked up the settlement's pace. Flanking Camp Creek was a big camp of 120 people, a construction headquarters designed to push the rails through the Nenana Canyon. By 1920 the AEC had built dormitory, mess hall, hospital, store, warehouse, barn, and blacksmith shop. Thus the straggling settlement transformed into a railroad "company town." The imminence of the railroad's completion spurred development of a succession of coal mines: up Lignite Creek, in the Nenana River terrace underlying the railroad camp and townsite, and about 4 miles up Healy Creek at Suntrana. The greater Healy-Suntrana community was evolving into a dual company town as a railroad and coal-mining center.

Nenana during the 1920s. Courtesy of the D. F. Sherrif Collection, ASL.

Once the line was completed freight trains overnighted at Healy. Passenger trains overnighted at Curry to the south, but stopped for lunch at Healy, where as many as 200 passengers filed daily into the new railroad-hotel dining room. Singleton's private roadhouse-hotel deferred to this modern accommodation, becoming a store where railroad workers swapped yarns with Healy's old-timers around the pot-bellied stove.

At the end of World War II the railroad reestablished Healy's center about one-half mile north of the old depot and town, which had suffered a fire that destroyed the hotel. More urgently, the settlement, perched on the eroding river bluff, was sliding into the water. What was left of the old town was torn down and scattered, except for Colvin's cabin, which was tied to its precarious overhang for sentimental reasons.

Railroad cutbacks of recent years led to the operational demise of the second-generation railroad depot, hotel, and utility functions. Except for the concrete-block engine house the buildings were auctioned off and moved. Today, trains pass through but seldom stop. With opening of the Parks Highway in 1972, Healy began its second relocation, now centering on the highway 1 1/2 miles west of the river.[33]

In 1922, mining engineer John A. Davis (the same who in 1921 journeyed to the Kantishna with his wife Mary) documented the shift in the nature of Denali region coal mining—from small-scale local to big-scale export—with the coming of the railroad. He reported that the Healy River Coal Company mine at Suntrana was the sole producer of coal in the Nenana fields. A 4-mile-long railroad spur line, completed that year, now connected the mine with the mainline of the railroad, and bulk shipments could begin. The earlier hauling of coal from mine to railroad—by horse-drawn sleds in winter and tractor-drawn wagons in summer—could meet local AEC and domestic needs. But it took the mine-mouth railroad to establish the bulk market in Fairbanks.[34]

Once that market was established—for Fairbanks' power and domestic uses, and for dredge and dragline placer operations in surrounding gold fields—the underground Suntrana mine would weather Alaska's boom-and-bust economy for 40 years. (World War II increased the demand for coal, and soldiers helped man the mine and the railroad.)

Today, the successor Usibelli Coal Company employs a giant dragline to strip-mine the vast deposits between Lignite and Healy creeks (the underground mine at Suntrana flooded in the early '60s). Long trains load at a slow roll through a modern tipple opposite Lignite Creek, whence the coal is transported to Seward, then loaded in ocean ships bound for Korea.

Community history at Healy and Suntrana included founding of one-room schools in 1937 (Healy) and 1942 (Suntrana). Before then children studied by correspondence, as was (and still is) typical in isolated bush communities.

The poor road between Suntrana and Healy and lack of an automobile bridge across the Nenana encouraged motive innovations. In the late '30s one boy ice-skated the frozen creek from Suntrana to Healy for his classes. The Healy River Coal Company rigged an old truck with railroad wheels to shuttle local residents across the railroad bridge. This conveyance, called the Doodlebug, also took ladies of the evening to the Goat Ranch near Suntrana on payday weekends. "Goat Mary" Thompson had opened a beer parlor there in 1935. Her establishment converted to a brothel when payday came. One informant told local historian Beverly Mitchell that

Tanana and Fort Gibbon, at the junction of the Tanana and Yukon rivers, in 1919. Courtesy of the Stephen Foster Collection, UAF.

her first husband went up to the goat ranch one night "to settle a disturbance." When he failed to return she went up herself and shot the place up with a shotgun, whereupon several customers in various states of undress cleared the premises.

More typical of community recreation were the practical pastimes of hunting, gardening, and berry-picking. The self-sufficient residents of these isolated communities filled evening hours with readings, dramatic presentations, cards, and dancing. Summer holidays were observed with baseball games and community picnics.[35]

To provide a base for railroad construction, the AEC laid out the Nenana townsite and built the yards, government structures, and a hospital. The new town joined the Indian village of Tortella and St. Mark's Episcopal Mission (est. 1907) at the confluence of the Nenana and Tanana rivers. By 1920 what had started as the railroad's northern construction headquarters had grown to an Alaskan metropolis of more than 600 people.

Private businesses served and supplied the AEC and its workers. Other entrepre-

The Tanana River bridge, at Nenana, under construction. Courtesy of the Alaska Railroad Collection, AMHA.

neurs laid the groundwork for river transportation systems, which, upon completion of the railroad from Seward, would make Nenana the chief port of the Yukon-Tanana drainage. Known as the Hub City of Interior Alaska, this crossroads of rail and riverine transport gave access to the world's products, brought first by ocean ships to the railroad's southern terminus at Seward.

For the isolated camps and settlements of the northern Denali region—their own industry limited to frontier blacksmithing—the crated machinery in Nenana warehouses meant a future of progress and prosperity. Here, too, shined bright lights that illuminated the trappings of civilization: hotels, taverns, restaurants, and a high-class billiard hall. Groceries, hardware, clothing, and modern domestic fixtures filled the racks and floors of Nenana's stores. During the early history of Mount McKinley National Park—its orientation northward as dictated by the Alaska Range—Nenana's goods and services provided a mercantile Mecca, a chance to get out of the bush and meet old friends, and get medical help unavailable on the far creeks.[36]

Some of the men on the far creeks—the lone or partnered trappers—looked to the trading centers only for bare necessities: ammunition, steel traps, and a few staples. They were going backwards in time, trying to find in Alaska a last resort for the mountain-man life that had ended in the Rockies a century earlier. One of these, Fabian Carey of the Minchumina area, described in later years the rewards of this historic lifeway: "Only a handful of us live to fulfill our boyhood dream of following the far trails and seeking lost horizons. . . . My blazes are weathering at many a remote campsite and along many an unmapped stream and mountain glade. . . . I am well content."[37]

Perhaps less romantic, less conscious of reliving a past era was the austere Hjalmar "Slim" Carlson. One story about him shows the difference between his kind of loner and the camp and community people—who, though on civilization's edge, formed a loose society that sought progress and its benefits. It seems that Joe Quigley went over to see Slim at one of his cabins on Birch or Slippery Creek, taking some coffee as a treat. As the two men sat down to a meal of wild meat Joe offered a steaming cup to Slim. He refused, saying that he could not afford coffee or tea, so didn't want to taste it and then be unhappy about not having it later. His usual hot drink was Hudson Bay tea brewed from the leaves of a local plant.[38]

A Native of Sweden, Carlson had immigrated to the United States as a youth and made his way across the country to the Northwest where he worked in logging camps. He came to Alaska in 1914 for railroad work, and in 1918 crossed over Anderson Pass to the sheep hills and McKinley River country north of Mount McKinley. For several years he prospected and worked as a mine laborer in the Kantishna, but finally decided against them as uncertain and not worth the effort, given camp prices. So he settled into hunting and trapping. Establishment of the park would force him northward to the Castle Rocks area. Later he trapped along Birch and Slippery Creeks. Cabin remains and place names within the old and expanded park trace the course of his wanderings.[39]

Carlson was a practical man. Once he walked up Muldrow Glacier with an old dog, thinking he might climb the mountain. Near the head of the glacier he contemplated the distance yet to go:

I said, my goodness, what the dickens, I got nothing up there. Why should I go up there? I decided, I'm going to go back again, there's no use for me to go up there, but to look around . . . . Well then I went down to my camp again. Took it easy and stayed home a few days.

Slim got his meat in the fall ("caribou as thick as buffalo on the plains"), trapped until it got too cold, then hibernated in the cabin until it warmed up a little in February. He took his furs to trade for supplies in Nenana: "nothing but flour and sugar and a little salt . . . . That was just about all I could afford to buy. I almost lived on the country. I made my own clothes out of caribou and moose skin."

Carlson was hard and strong. Cold didn't seem to bother him while on the trail. One time he met some Indians while driving his sled "with no hat or cap on me, no coat, and plenty warm." The Indians were freezing and told him that he must be a tough man. "And I probably was."

Once while sheep hunting near McGonagall Pass, Slim found some boxes of tea left by early mountaineers. That night he cooked up some sheep and brewed a big pot of tea. Next morning he had terrible diarrhea ("thought I was going to die"). Was it caused by the sheep meat or the old tea? Carlson's friend Slim Avery was expected at the hunting camp the next day. Avery drank tea morning, noon, and night. So before Carlson took off to hunt, he left the tea out. Avery arrived and helped himself to a kettle-full. When Slim got back he observed that Avery seemed to be feeling fine, then told him about the diarrhea. Avery laughed at the joke on him—Carlson's testing the tea on him. Then, applying the logical process of elimination, they blamed the sheep meat and brewed another batch.

Trapping right under the mountain did not pay. Slim got only a few mink and wolverines. About that time, too, in the early '20s, the park rangers began cruising into his territory. So he moved north to the woods, beyond the park boundary. There he hunted black bear, rendered their fat ("just as clear as the regular lard you buy") and sold what he didn't need to the families at Kantishna for 40 cents a pound.

It was about 1924 that Carlson left his cabin on Clearwater Creek in the park. He first built a cabin at Castle Rock, then bought out Gus Johnson's productive trapline on Birch Creek, where he built a fine home cabin. Yet later, the overflow and flooding on Birch Creek impelled him to shift over to Slippery Creek where he built another big cabin. This was rich country and he "made it pretty good after that."

Slim liked this independent life with nobody to argue with or tell him what to do. He left prospecting and wage labor behind to trap exclusively. Shortly he mastered the trapper's art, devising his own techniques after exhausting the arcane scent and set formulas published in trappers' books and magazines. Fur prices were high in the '20s: $80 for a red fox, $45 to $60 for a lynx. Marten were closed then, but sometimes one wandered into a trap. "Of course you were supposed to turn them into the territory, and I guess most of the trappers did." With good trapping, high fur prices, and plenty of caribou it was a good life.

When caribou declined in the '30s, particularly in the park in the vicinity of his old Clearwater cabin, Slim rejected the theory that wolves were to blame. "There was very few wolves up there." He figured that wolves had got a bad name, and he did not favor the bounty for their control. He speculated that the caribou had just migrated out, shifted their range.

In those days a good salmon run came up Birch Creek. Slim trapped enough fish to feed his dogs, so he didn't need to kill deer for them.

Living by himself, and with only 3 or 4 other trappers scattered in the flats north of the park, Slim seldom saw anyone except during town visits. People in Nenana wondered how he stood it, why he didn't go crazy. "But it didn't interfere with me at all. I had no trouble there . . . . I never thought of it."

But one thing, I always was busy, always had something to do. In the summer when the mosquitoes was so thick, well I didn't rush out and cut no trail or make no cabins then, but so soon as they thinned down a little I was on the trail and went out the trap lines and scouted over the country and looked around all the time. Always busy.

Slim remembered that mosquitoes seemed more vicious then. And no one came up with any dope that worked. In fact the bugs homed in on the various mixes of lard and Creolin and other ingredients that people tried. The dogs suffered horribly. When Slim put mixtures on them, though, they just licked them off. Nets, hats, gloves, and the thickest underwear you could get were the only protection.

Once in a while something happened that made him blue (like when he axed his thumb off and nearly bled to death) and he wished he could talk to someone to shake it. But usually he just worked harder and the blues went away. Sure he talked to himself, but he didn't come back with feisty answers. Slim said *that* was the time to get out, a sure sign that a man had got "bushed." The secret was a nice disposition and not being the worrying kind.

Slim's adventures included scrapes with bears, but mainly he tried to get along with them as fellow travelers in the woods. One September he killed several caribou, then went back for his dogs to pack in the harvest. Meanwhile, a big grizzly had taken over his kills. Slim didn't want to mess with the bear, but he did want his meat. So he loosed the dogs, which got into a running, dodging battle with the bear. While this went on Slim built a temporary 12-foot-high cache in the trees. There he put his meat to freeze and be retrieved later.

Once Slim caught a handsome black wolf in a trap. He was caught by two toes and couldn't get away. "So I sat and talked to him for a while, and he wagged his tail to me and kind of whined . . . . I talk to him just like a big man. I got to kill you, that's all there is to it." He had tried to release the wolf, but it grabbed his leg in its jaws, not breaking the skin. That scared Slim, so there was nothing else to do, though "I hated like the dickens to kill him."

Slim got on well with the Indians. He was glad to see them when they came by ("because I never seed no body else") and he always laid a big spread for them. If he had something they needed he gave it to them, if he could, and accepted no pay even though they offered. He respected them and what they did; they respected him and his trapping territory.

Slim Carlson died in 1975. His life in the country had spanned nearly the entire history of the park. Fittingly, friends at Minchumina—where he spent his last years—buried his ashes near a lake called Lonely, under the shadow of Mount McKinley.

THE INDIANS OF DENALI

As the modern world moved into the Denali region, the environment of the Native people underwent drastic change. These shifting conditions, many of them devastating to the lifeways of traditional people, called for radical adaptive responses. Change and movement had distinguished Native culture long before white men came into the country. But the acceleration of change brought by the newcomers, and the breakdown of protective isolation—both physical and cultural—severely distorted the patterns of Indian life.

Even in the remote region north of the Alaska Range disease had early wreaked havoc with the Kolchan, Koyukon, and Tanana bands. Smallpox brought by nineteenth century Russian and Yankee traders and travelers had spread into the Interior along the rivers, reaching remote places by intermediate Native traders. By the turn of the century the Kuskokwim-Tanana Lowlands had suffered significant population losses and relocations. Hudson Stuck noted in 1911 that the Minchumina people were a weak band of survivors, most of them destroyed by measles in 1900 and

Tanana Mission at Tanana, 1934. Courtesy of the J. B. Mertie, Jr., Collection, USGS.

diphtheria in 1906. Influenza in the 1920s and 1930s, along with hideous forms of tuberculosis, further depleted the region's Native population.[40]

Bands and families regrouped and consolidated. Some went to Nenana or villages on the Yukon. Others grouped together at Telida and Nikolai on the upper Kuskokwim. Once populous seasonal camps such as Bearpaw, Birch Creek, and Toklat now numbered only one or two families comprising the survivors of many families. Nearby cemeteries held the relatives who made up entire family trees, now reduced to only a few living representatives.

For the survivors, the influx of gold miners, explorers, mountaineers, and other travelers on the Nenana-Kantishna-McGrath trail had brought temporary economic opportunity. The services rendered by the Indians in transport, accommodations, and provision of meat made them functional in the evolving economy. Cash earned from these services buttressed their basic economy of trapping, hunting, and fishing.

But growing dependence on the cash economy had its downside. Time on the land for family hunting and fishing—and for training young people in these arts and skills—decreased. Individualized hunting with rifles replaced communal hunting patterns, which weakened the social elements of the hunt: ceremonials, family integration through participation, joint processing of the harvest of the hunt, and the sharing of products amongst all members of the society.

Trapping itself, though a land-based activity, accentuated dependence on cash income. Trapping took time from hunting and fishing, thus forcing more dependence on trading-post foods. Money spent for store food was wasted. Native food offered better nutrition—physically, socially, and spiritually.

In time fixed villages replaced the seasonal rounds and camps of semi-nomadic tradition. The family stayed home while the hunter-trapper roamed. The domestic functions of settled life were different from those of the nomadic family. Old social roles and integrative divisions of labor—necessary when the whole family moved from camp to camp—ceased to apply.

From the fixed villages, fast travel (as distinct from deliberate seasonal migration) was required to get to hunting places, to run extensive traplines, and to visit towns for trading. This style required more dogs, more dependence on fish to feed them, less time for the season-long hunts in the upland caribou ranges. Lacking game meat, the family itself depended more on fish as the staple food. The adoption of fishwheels about 1918 contributed to removal of families and bands toward the big rivers where these large contraptions could be used. These movements took the people farther away from the highlands bordering the range. Thus, even before World War II, except for a few families pursuing more traditional patterns in the Minchumina and near-rivers area, the Indian population of the northern Denali region had largely evacuated to its fringes.

A few hunters and trappers still made seasonal forays in the northside highlands. They came from Minchumina, Nenana, and Telida. Men from Nikolai still hunted sheep in the mountains north of Rainy Pass. But the old rounds that had long led whole bands of hunters to the very foot of the Denali massif were essentially over by the time the new park became operational in the early '20s.

Both north and south of the range, white miners had occupied the near foothills bordering the future park. Some of these stampeders, cursed with barren claims, shifted to full-scale market hunting to supply their luckier fellows. When the early rushes ended, the remaining miners turned to a combined mining and subsistence lifestyle, with hunting and trapping critical elements. Their influence thus spread to the fringing hills and lowlands where game and furs were plentiful. Coincidentally, the number of full-time white trappers was gradually increasing. Some of these hunters and trappers, knowing the country well, began guiding Outside trophy hunters. Among them were rich clients who could spend weeks killing animals whose meat was only selectively used.

Depopulation, relocation, and competition from newcomers on the land had worked together to severely reduce the Indian presence in the central Denali region. Transportation innovations played a strong part in this transition. On the northside, the introduction of airplanes for transportation and hauling of mail and freight had by 1930 made obsolete the old trail systems, roadhouses, and supply services that for awhile gave the Indians a functional role in the new economy. Contributing to this demise, the park road, even before its completion, siphoned transportation through the park and away from the old trails.

The airplane also opened up the most remote regions with amazing rapidity. Prospectors, hunters, trappers, scientists, and others suddenly showed up at places where distance and terrain had once held the map blank, where logistics had blocked all but the most temporary traverse. There were no longer refugia where Native people could pursue their own ways in isolation. To the south and east the railroad transformed the Susitna-Nenana corridor into a string of transportation and supply centers catering to the mining camps and towns along the way. Indian life at places like Talkeetna, Cantwell, and Nenana was overwhelmed by wage-work opportunities and the flood of non-Native people and activities. Here the Natives' integration into the cheap labor phase of the transportation and mining economy was nearly complete. For many of these people, hunting, fishing, and trapping became adjuncts to wage work instead of the other way around as in more isolated places.[41]

As ties to traditional territories and activities attenuated, and as relocation to permanent villages accelerated, schools—both mission and government—exerted ever stronger influence on Indian life. St. Mark's Mission and School at Nenana, founded by the Episcopal Church in 1907, offered benign assistance to many Indian children, including health care, education, and spiritual instruction. Given the tragedies of mass death by disease and the orphanage of many Indian children, the mission is remembered by students of those days as an oasis of order in a disordered world. This memory was enhanced by the school's philosophy, which was shaped by Archdeacon Hudson Stuck's knowledge of bush life. He knew that Indian students must not be torn whole from traditional ways, that they must apprentice in the wilderness arts and skills employed by their elders. The schools under his jurisdiction were instructed to give the young people time on the land with their Native guardians to get that training. Otherwise, he maintained, they would become disfunctional in their own societies, unable to support their families in adulthood.

Stuck feared that the government would impose compulsory education on the Natives, with a philosophy that would deprecate and suppress traditional ways. And indeed this happened. As a result, remaining traditional families had to leave the woods and live in towns or school villages, or they had to board their children at distant schools. Thus the organic, participatory education of the traditional society ceased to function. Young people in these inhospitable schools heard constant criticism of their parents' mores and customs, were forbidden under threat of punishment to use their own language. They came back from school confused, ignorant of the woods, lacking respect for their elders. In this way, too, the traditional social fabric was rent, and recruits to carry on the old customs and crafts were lost. Individually, students caught between two worlds lost self esteem. Many could not function well in their own society. And their rudimentary schooling—stacked against prevailing biases and lack of opportunity in all but the lowest stations of the white world—gave little chance for real assimilation into that world. Tragically, assimilation had been the rationale for this destructive educational regime. In the upshot, traditional families and societies were sacrificed to educate children for a life they rejected or could not attain. They had been forced along the path of directed change by a dominant society secure in its own dogmatic beliefs.

Only in recent times has the value of cultural diversity been recognized, and the rich knowledge of indigenous peoples appreciated in school programs for Native children. Amazingly, after all these hurts and hindrances, many young people—now middle-aged and with their own grandchildren—went back to school in the woods with their elders and today function as tradition-bearers in their own right. The way continues long and difficult, however, toward a balanced education that makes possible productive lives in both Native and white cultures.[42]

A few old cabins and cemeteries provide reminders of recent Native history in

Denali National Park and Preserve. Aside from ancient lithic scatters and the rare stone tool, few other material remains can be found, short of archeological excavation to document the long span of Native occupation here. During the prehistoric and early historic period uncounted shelters, drying racks, caches, and other temporary camp structures briefly marked the landscape. Made of wood, skin, or earth, they have long since faded back into Nature's scene. Selected place names along with natural landmarks and rock shelters are still recalled by the few elders yet alive who lived through the transitions described above.[43]

Historical developments in the Denali region during the years around 1920 shaped the context of the new park. This was the world that first Superintendent Harry Karstens would deal with beginning in 1921. As important, certain key themes proved so persistent over the years that Karstens' successors still deal with them. Many of these themes stem directly from the railroad-park road connection, which dominated the development of the park, the experiences of visitors, and the logistics of its northside neighbors for 50 years.

If anything, that dominance has been accentuated in the recent past, since opening of the Parks Highway. This is so because the railroad park of the 1920s through 1960s—its essential infrastructure completed in 1939—continues to function as the rickety stage upon which today's events transpire.

Remaining chapters of this history trace first, the pioneering of the park; second, the consolidation of the park to meet pre-World War II conditions; third, the hauling and tugging to meet the onset of the automobile, as illustrated by the development debates of the '60s; and finally, the attempt to consolidate the expanded park through environmental (and politically feasible) design to meet modern conditions. This last phase is still in progress, with the issue still in doubt.

Many other themes come into focus as the above structural sequence unfolds. One of these, the wolf-sheep controversy (ca. 1930 to 1950) forced the adoption of ecological management principles in this park well before such terminology became commonly understood, much less applied.

Paradoxically, because this park was until just yesterday so remote—so alone in its singularity, so spotlighted as the premier Alaskan symbol—it became a testing ground for the evolution of park policies that would ramify far beyond its boundaries.

✳

Notes: Chapter 6

1. Falcon Joslin, "The Needs of Alaska," reprint of address delivered at the Annual Meeting of the American Mining Congress, Chicago, October 17-21, 1921, in reprint file, University of Alaska, Fairbanks, Archives.
2. Ibid., 11-13.
3. Ernest Gruening, The State of Alaska (New York: Random House, 1954), 217-218.
4. Ibid., 201.
5. C. M. Brown, "American Alaska," in Writing Alaska's History, Vol. I (Anchorage: Alaska Historical Commission, 1974), 55.
6. Gruening, State of Alaska, 227-230.
7. C. M. Brown, "American Alaska," 55.
8. Alfred Hulse Brooks, quoted in Evans, From Myth to Reality, 116.
9. Col. J. G. Steese, "Across Alaska by Automobile," American Motorist (March 1923), 12.
10. C. M. Brown, "The Alaska Railroad: Probing the Interior," report for the History and Archeology Branch of the Alaska Division of Parks (Anchorage: October 1975), 31.
11. H. F. Dose, "Report on Trail from Nenana Watershed to End of Steel on Susitna River," Alaska Railroad Record, Vol. II, No. 14 (Feb. 12, 1918), 110-111.

12. C. M. Brown, "Alaska Railroad," 36-37.

13. C. M. Brown, "Alaska Railroad," 38-39; T. W. Secrist, "Alaska Railroad Surveys Through Broad Pass," *Engineering News-Record*, Vol. 86, No. 15 (April 14, 1921), 632.

14. Bernadine L. Prince, *The Alaska Railroad in Pictures*, 1914-1964 (Anchorage: Ken Wray Print Shop, 1964), 393.

15. Ibid., 449.

16. E. G. Amesbury, "Erection of Hurricane Arch Bridge in Alaska," *Engineering News-Record*, Vol. 88, No. 4, (Jan. 26, 1922), 144-146.

17. Quoted in C. M. Brown, "Alaska Railroad," 39.

18. Ibid., 39-42; Alaska Department of Transportation and Public Facilities, "Historical Profile of the Alaska Railroad," contract report of Sept. 1980, available at Alaska State Library, 8-10; anon., "The Alaska Government Railroad," *The Pathfinder*, Vol. 3, No. 3 (Jan. 1922), 1-6.

19. F. D. Brown letter of 12/8/21 to Col. F. Mears, in Frederick Mears Collection, University of Alaska, Fairbanks, Archives.

20. See ARC Annual Reports (1917, 1921, 1922) and Col. James Steese articles on Alaska roads and trails, including "Across Alaska by Automobile," *American Motorist* (March 1923), 12-13, 24; "Road Construction Under the Alaska Road Commission," *The Highway Magazine* (Jan. 1923), 11-12; and "Building Roads to Develop Alaska," *The Highway Magazine* (Dec. 1924), 13-15.

21. Steese letter of 11/14/21 to James Wickersham, Bruce Campbell Collection.

22. Ibid.

23. Hawley Sterling report of 11/16/20 to the Board of Road Commissioners for Alaska, 1-9, in Bruce Campbell Collection.

24. Lunsford Oliver (ARC engineer) letter of 10/31/24 to Charles Trundy; Steese letter of 11/14/21 to James Wickersham, both in Bruce Campbell Collection.

25. The following summary of Kantishna mining history (1920 through World War II) is based directly and almost exclusively on Historian Rolfe Buzzell's 1989 paper, "Overview of Mining in the Kantishna District, 1903-1968." Buzzell's excellent study for the National Park Service's Mining Compliance program occurred contemporaneously with the present author's Denali National Park and Preserve Historic Resource Study, which allowed a division of labor between the two authors, with Buzzell responsible for the mining history for which this author is indebted and grateful.

26. Mary Lee Davis, *We Are Alaskans* (Boston: W. A. Wilde Co., 1931), 183.

27. Ibid., 190.

28. Ibid., 204-205.

29. Ibid., 213.

30. The following account is based on a biography prepared some years ago by Edgar Brooker, Jr., for his family. Mr. Brooker kindly gave permission to use his story and his words for this history. All quotations are from pp. 32-39 of the biography, or from letters of Feb. and March 1984, and July 4, 1988, to this author.

31. Edgar Brooker letter of 7/4/88 to this author.

32. Signal Corps telegram of March 29, 1921, in Bruce Campbell Collection.

33. The foregoing account of Healy's history and evolution is heavily based on Beverly Mitchell's college term paper, "An Early History of the Healy Valley," (May 1989), 16pp. Ms. Mitchell and this author have shared sources and perceptions of Healy's history, and this author deeply appreciates her synthesis of documentary and oral-history data in her paper.

34. J. A. Davis, "Coal Mining in the Nenana Field, Alaska," in *Annual Report of the Mine Inspector to the Governor of Alaska* (Juneau: Territory of Alaska, 1922), 143-155.

35. Mitchell, "History of the Healy Valley," 9-10.

36. Anon., "Nenana, the Hub of Interior Alaska," *The Pathfinder*, Vol. 2, No. 5 (April 1921), 1-9.

37. Quoted by Charlie Mayse in "Scion of the mountain men," *The Alaska Journal*, A 1981 *Collection* (Anchorage: Alaska Northwest Publishing Co., 1981), 71.

38. Edgar Brooker biography, appended anecdotes.

39. Biographical data and the following narrative derived from transscript of Slim Carlson interviews in 1965 by Florence Collins and Diane Thiede, Minchumna residents. Tapes and transcript on file in the Oral History Archive, University of Alaska, Fairbanks.

40. William Schneider, Dianne Gudgel-Holmes, and John Dalle-Molle, *Land Use in the North Additions of Denali National Park and Preserve: An Historical Perspective*, National Park Service Research/Resources Management Report AR-9 (Anchorage: Alaska Regional Office, NPS, 1984), 18.

41. Ibid., 8-37; William Schneider, "On the Back Slough," in Jean S. Aigner, et al., *Interior Alaska, A Journey Through Time* (Anchorage: The Alaska Geographic Society, 1986), 167-194; Ronald T. Stanek, "Historical and Contemporary Trapping in the Western Susitna Basin," Technical Paper No. 134, Alaska Department of Fish and Game, Division of Subsistence, Anchorage, 1987, 63-66; David Charles Plaskett, "The Nenana River Gorge Site: A Late Prehistoric Athapaskan Campsite in Central Alaska," master's thesis, University of Alaska, Fairbanks, Dec. 1977, Chapter 8, Ethnohistoric Summary of the Lower-Middle Tanana and Nenana Rivers, 184-201; Dianne Gudgel-Holmes, "Kantishna Oral History Project—Interviews with Native Elders," typescript report of National Park Service, 1988.

42. Episcopal Church, "St. Mark's Mission, Nenana," *Alaskan Epiphany*, Vol. I, Nos. 1-3, 1980, 4-5, 8-9, 16-17; Moses Cruikshank, *The Life I've Been Living* (Fairbanks: University of Alaska, 1986), 18-25, 114-115; Mackenzie, *Wolf Smeller*, 8; Gary H. Holthaus and Raymond Collins, "Education in the North: Its Effect on Athapascan Culture," 12-page typescript paper, ca. 1971 in Denali NP Archive.

43. Dianne Gudgel-Holmes and C. E. Holmes, "Predictive Model of Aboriginal Site Types and Locations for a Catchment Basin along the Denali Park Road within Denali National Park and Preserve," typescript for National Park Service, Alaska Region, 1989, 29-33.

Riley Creek bridge construction camp, during the winter of 1921-1922. Courtesy of the Alaska Railroad Collection, AMHA.

The Pioneer Park

Recall that Congress had rested on its laurels after enactment of the park legislation in 1917. For more than four years McKinley was a park in name only—unfunded, unmanned, unprotected. Finally—after many petitions from conservationists, the Governor of Alaska, and Interior Department and NPS officials—Congress appropriated $8,000 for the fiscal year beginning July 1, 1921. Increased market hunting and poaching, paired with the threat posed by the approaching railroad, had jolted Congress to take the first step in carrying out its own statutory mandate: to preserve the park as a game refuge.

By then the name of Henry P. Karstens headed the list of those being considered for the job of park superintendent. Karstens had broached the subject in a 1918 letter to NPS Assistant Director Horace Albright. This was the letter, solicited by Albright, that established Charles Sheldon as the originator of the Mount McKinley National Park idea. In describing Sheldon's concept of a park that would protect Denali's game, Karstens stated: "One thing which brings it home to me is, Sheldon promised to assist me to get the Wardenship if it went through."[1]

In this same letter Karstens expressed irritation with Alaska Governor Thomas Riggs, who ". . . tried to tell me that he was the man that proposed the park." Not only did Riggs disbelieve Karstens as to Sheldon's role, he also tried to talk the Sourdough out of applying for the superintendent job. Karstens continued:

I was thinking it over for a day or so when I found out that Mr. Raybourn [W. B. Reaburn], one of Riggs' men [on the Alaska-Canadian Boundary Survey] had made a special trip out to Washington to put in his application. Raybourn is a fine man & if I cannot have the position I hope he gets it.

Almost 3 years later Governor Riggs still favored Reaburn for the job. At the request of NPS Director Stephen T. Mather, Riggs evaluated candidates for the superintendency, dismissing all but Reaburn and Karstens from consideration. His profile of Karstens was prophetic:

Harry Karstens is an excellent man and perhaps deserves consideration for the fact that he made possible the ascent of Mt. McKinley for the Stuck party. He is a good woodsman and thoroughly energetic. If it were not for Reaburn I should give serious consideration to Karstens. He is not, however, any where near the equal of Reaburn, as he is very independent and would be apt to tangle up with the authorities the first time there should come a little disagreement. In the appointment of Reaburn I know that you would make no mistake, whereas if Karstens should be appointed there might at times be friction not only with your office but with visitors to the park. I know that Charlie Sheldon will go to the mat for Karstens and if I were in Sheldon's place I would do the same thing.[2]

Mather noted with concern the governor's fears that the feisty Karstens would cause problems for the park and the Service. But Charles Sheldon's previous sponsorship of Karstens had already elicited Mather's all but unbreakable commitment to the Founding Father that "There is no question in my mind about Karstens being the man for the place. . . ."[3]

Henry P. (Harry) Karstens, first park superintendent, 1921-1928. Courtesy of the Charles Sheldon Collection, UAF.

Governor Riggs certainly suspected that such a commitment was already made, for Mather had earlier told him of Sheldon's high recommendation of Karstens for the pioneer superintendency.[4]

As Karstens' 7-year administration of the park progressed, Mather would have ample reason for rueful pondering of Riggs' warning. Karstens' superintendency would fall into two arenas: 1) the true pioneering of a wild and undeveloped park—in which he excelled, and 2) the bureaucratic and public-official aspect—in which Karstens' direct-action approach often produced conflict at the park and distress among his Washington Office mentors who were trying to coach him along the path of prudence.

In the early years, with the focus on dog-team patrols and the hewing and laying of logs for park buildings, Karstens' rough-and-ready manner fit the park's needs like a glove. Later, when the finesse skills of interagency cooperation, resolution of disputes with park neighbors, and fiscal and personnel management became the paramount needs, Karstens—despite his own earnest efforts and the sympathetic counseling of Assistant Director Arno B. Cammerer—could only partially make the transition.

Nor were Karstens' troubles entirely of his own making. There were some hard cases out there, people who practiced calculated provocation to bring out the old Sourdough in him. After an explosion, they would write letters to Juneau and Washington officials misconstruing events and exaggerating Karstens' responses to them.

In sum, Karstens would be a pioneering hero part of the time and a man who outlasted his greatest usefulness part of the time. But he did well the two most important tasks of his charge: he all but stopped the poaching that was eroding the park's vulnerable wildlife, and he completed, largely with his own hands, the park's first-stage development that made it an operating unit of the National Park System. On balance, his strengths as pioneer superintendent outweighed his flaws as prudent bureaucrat.

The First Superintendent

On April 12, 1921, Director Mather sent a 10-page letter of instructions to Harry Karstens, formalizing the multifaceted charge that Karstens took on with Mount McKinley's superintendency. Much of the letter shows the hand of Arno B. Cammerer, Mather's administrative right hand and patient mentor to Karstens. But aside from details about Karstens' interim appointment as ranger-at-large until funds came on July 1, accountability of funds, budget preparation, and the like, the letter's substance was pure Mather. Taking into account the mining and hunting compromises that burdened the park's establishment act, Mather noted that special regulations adjusted to these factors would soon follow. Karstens would apply general and specific NPS policies at Mount McKinley with " . . . tact, good judgment, firmness, fearlessness, and a cool head at all times." He would proceed gradually with enforcement—explaining and warning before charging and arresting. All persons, whether permanent on the land or visitors, would be treated with respect and courtesy. Violators of the law—poachers and trespassers—would be removed with only such "violence as may be necessary, with an admonition not to repeat the offense." Karstens would get to know park neighbors, officials in other agencies, the U.S. District Attorney in Fairbanks, and potential concession operators who could provide services to visitors. He would canvass local people to find a suitable man for assistant ranger. And he would report his work regularly to the Director.[5]

This would be a ticklish business. Karstens would stand alone in this huge and totally undeveloped wilderness park, itself nested in a vast surround of wildness. He would bring with him a public lands philosophy still new in the States and completely alien to Alaskan attitudes and experience. Likewise new and alien were the laws and regulations with which Karstens would apply and enforce that philosophy. Of local precedent and backup he had none. Steve Mather concluded his letter to Karstens with the promise of all possible support from Washington. Then he said with somber understatement, "The rest is up to you."[6]

The core of the Service's philosophy derived from the Yellowstone National Park Act of 1872 and the National Park Service Act of 1916. Horace Albright, with the aid of the Nation's leading conservationists, had translated these graven statutory tables into a letter setting forth the policy objectives and management principles that would govern the Service. On May 13, 1918, Interior Secretary Franklin K. Lane sent this letter to NPS Director Mather, thus formalizing the Service's charter.

The chief principle was that "Every activity of the Service is subordinate to the duties imposed upon it to faithfully preserve the parks for posterity in essentially their natural state." Only those commercial activities specifically authorized by law or permitted for the accommodation and pleasure of visitors would be allowed. In its own planning, development, and operations the Service would avoid the inroads of modern civilization so that unspoiled bits of native America could be experienced by present and future generations. Where improvements were necessary, they would be designed to harmonize with the landscape. Hunting, timbering, grazing, and other consumptive uses would be disallowed or phased out, consistent with law. Private inholdings, especially those seriously hampering the administration of these reservations, likewise would be phased out over time by purchase or donation.[7]

Armed with such notions, Karstens surely had his work cut out for him. Alaskans were accustomed to using at their pleasure the whole spread of the essentially unsupervised public domain, which constituted all but a few parcels of Alaska's huge territory. Now someone, albeit one of their own, would be telling them to "stop and git," and arresting them if they didn't. Karstens' first imperative was to protect the park's wildlife. This was policy. In the Director's Annual Report for 1919, Mather had informed the Secretary and the Congress that:

It will not be the policy of the National Park Service to immediately open this park to tourists; in fact, several years may elapse before any program for developing the scenic and recreational features of the park is adopted. We are interested now only in the preservation of the caribou, mountain sheep, and other animals that make this region their home. . . .[8]

To protect the park Karstens needed a base camp accessible to both the railroad—his line of access and supply—and the park itself. McKinley Station on the railroad near the Riley Creek-Nenana River junction had to be the location, for it was the topographically determined entrance to the park. The original configuration of the park placed its nearest boundary some 16 miles west of McKinley Station. Even after Congress extended the park to within 3 miles of the station on January 30, 1922, Karstens had to secure an administrative corridor to assure his unhampered access to the park and an entrance for "a main artery road through the upper passes," which Karstens cited in his June 1921 report to the Director as "the park's most urgent need."

Eventually, executive orders gave him the corridor and land upon which to build his base camp, but not before the expenditure of much blood and sweat over strategically placed homesteads that temporarily blocked his plans. From this base camp—with its cabins, barns, and kennels—Karstens and his men (when he got them) could range the boundaries and the choice hunting grounds, tracking, warning, and, if necessary, arresting wrongdoers.

After a summer 1921 swing into the park with pack horses—touching bases with his old Kantishna comrades and explaining the park and its regulations—Karstens began to scrounge, beg, and borrow tools and materials for the base camp. He made a deal with Pat Lynch, who agreed to relinquish his homestead on Riley Creek at the south end of the railroad bridge, so Karstens had a place to build. This site had been used by the AEC for its Riley Creek-bridge construction camp. From this and other abandoned camps, Karstens salvaged buildings and equipment for his own camp. This location in the creek bottom was Karstens' second choice. He wanted to be on the high ground on the same level as the railroad and the station. But Maurice Morino's homestead and roadhouse complex occupied all of that ground, and difficulties between the two men produced an impasse. The AEC, trying to secure its own right-of-way and administrative site on the Morino property, distanced itself from

Dan Kennedy was the park's first concessioner. Courtesy of AMHA.

Karstens during this time to preserve good relations with Morino. It was a pretty tangle that caused Karstens sleepless nights and provoked long letters to Washington officials and Charles Sheldon.

Karstens' *ad hoc* deals, his loan and salvage arrangements with the AEC, his commitments to Nenana storekeepers for essential supplies—all necessary acts to get the park going—threw the auditors in Washington into a tizzy; but Cammerer understood, calmed the auditors, and continued to coach Karstens on the procedures that would let him proceed, yet keep the accounts and administrative proprieties straight. The correspondence between the two men followed a cycle something like this:

Karstens: Wait 'til I tell you about this one.

Cammerer: Harry, I know you had to do it, but next time do it this way.

Karstens: Thanks, Mr. Cammerer, I sure won't do that again, and by the way, what do you think of this deal I just pulled off?[9]

Thus, by hook and by crook Karstens could report these accomplishments after a year on the ground:

A Superintendent and assistant were provided for. Two dog teams of five dogs each with harness, sleds and equipment for winter operations; also three horses, harness, bobsled, wagon, and horseshoeing, blacksmith and harness repair outfits with necessary equipment were acquired.

Base camp was established at McKinley Park Station on the Government railroad, where a portion of land one mile wide extending into the park was set aside for entrance and administrative purposes.

The superintendents dwelling and office were built at this point with barn, storehouse, workshop and necessary out buildings.[10]

Already the plan to protect first and do other things later had gone awry. Karstens had too many things to do all at once. He oversaw the park boundary survey and marked the line with boundary signs. Lands issues had obtruded, as had the building of the base camp, which was prerequisite to any substantial and steady in-park operation.

Getting supplies into the park and selecting tent or existing cabin sites for patrol shelters also had to be done first. Deploying the supplies, erecting tents, cutting and transporting wood fuel, repairing abandoned cabins (after checking with locals whether they were abandoned, or if the builders had any rights to them)—all these things, too, had to be done first, *if* ranger patrols were to be anything but easily eluded charades.

As a first step toward maintaining the NPS presence inside the park, Karstens and his assistant ranger pioneered a wagon road 12 miles along Hines and Jenny creeks to Savage River. On this rough track they conveyed a ton of supplies drawn by a four-horse team, then established a cache and supply point for interior-park patrols.[11]

The intent to deal with visitors later, after first things had been done, went against the old saying: Time and tide wait on no man. Imminent completion of the railroad forced the issue. Tourism promoters, shipping lines, railroad officials, and boomers and boosters in various Alaska towns were already advertising tours by ship, steamboat, auto, and railroad. Mount McKinley National Park ranked as the prime objective of this grand loop through the Interior.

Potential concessioners crowded Karstens' office with schemes for hotels and transportation systems into the park. Much correspondence ensued between the park and Washington to evaluate these proposals. And the concession candidates were less than loath to contact the Governor and the Delegate to Congress in their pursuit of monopoly rights within the park. This, too, required correspondence.

The proposed main road into the park, the one the ARC would build for the NPS, tied directly to the concession proposals. For, lacking the road, all but the hardiest visitors would be left standing and fuming at the station waiting for the next train.[12]

While Karstens labored to create a rudimentary park administration and operation, the ARC moved forward on park-road construction. Col. James Steese of the ARC had outlined the dual park and commercial road project in an April 1922 letter to Director Steve Mather, conditioned upon NPS provision of funds and design control.[13] Mather's acceptance sealed the agreement and spurred the ARC's route survey and erection of shelter tents and trail markers clear to Kantishna that summer. From 1923 to 1938, the ARC gnawed away at the road project: 2 miles in 1923, 5 or 10 miles each succeeding construction season, depending on terrain and funds available in the Service's park-road account. At each construction camp the ARC built a standard-plan

14-foot by 16-foot log cabin that served as cook house in summer and storage cache in winter. Work-crew tents clustered around the cabin, forming the season's home camp, which would move on westward with construction progress.[14] As camps were abandoned, the cabins could be used as ranger-patrol shelters. Several of these ARC cabins survive today as ranger stations along the road. Also still used are similar patrol cabins of the 1920s and '30s, built by the rangers at strategic points along the old park boundary.

By end-of-season 1924, the road was passable for buses and touring cars out to Savage River, 12 miles from McKinley Station.[15] The primitive concessioner tent-camp there, operated in 1923-24 by horse-packer Dan Kennedy, was taken over and improved by the Mt. McKinley Tourist and Transportation Company under Robert Sheldon's management (no relation to Charles Sheldon). The 1925 tourist season recorded the first significant visitation into the park, 206 persons versus only 62 in 1924. The company's 4 touring cars had trouble at times handling visitor traffic between McKinley Station and Savage Camp.

The camp itself became a "tent house colony" during the summer. Dining hall, social hall, and tent houses took care of some 60 people at a time. Barns, a corral, and utility buildings completed the camp, which was served by running water.

From this base, visitors could proceed on horseback, and later by Concord stages, on various loop trails into the Savage and Sanctuary rivers country. Spike camps allowed overnight wilderness experiences. More adventurous visitors could take guided pack-train trips into the park's farther hinterlands.

By 1928 the company had progressed westward along the ever extending road and beyond, on the grubbed out trail that marked its future course. Smaller camps at Igloo Creek, Polychrome Pass, Toklat River, and Copper Mountain (renamed Mount Eielson in 1930 for bush pilot Ben Eielson) hosted those who sought the more primeval spaces. By 1929, the company's 22 buses, 9 touring cars, 4 stages, 2 trucks, and a trailer were pressed to the limit to handle visitors and logistics. At that, with only 150 or 200 visitors in the park at a given time, this was the golden age of park touring: the festive train ride and arrival at McKinley Station, the lined up buses and touring cars, the scenic drive into the park, with welcoming arrival at various camps. Here amidst rustic but comfortable settings (and at Savage quite civilized dining and dancing) visitors could choose amongst many treks by horseback, packtrain, and stage that took them into Mount McKinley's wildlife and scenic splendors.[16]

But, as the Superintendent's Monthly Reports reveal, all was not rosy. Karstens spent inordinate time monitoring both road construction and concession operations. Disputes between him and the road engineers over clean-up of construction debris, micro-choices of route and design to meet the "park ideal," and management of NPS funds kept the air and the wires humming. Depending on the tourist-camp crew make-up, Karstens had some good years and some bad years. Once the proximity of game tempted nimrods on the crew to poach. Sometimes rates or food and sanitation standards departed from concession-contract terms. But all in all, the park had become a legitimate and much enjoyed objective for tourists.

Despite the increasing pace and strain of his work, and as a part of his charge to win the hearts and minds of Alaskans, Harry Karstens took every opportunity to express his poet's love of the park. On one of his business trips to Anchorage he addressed the Women's Club on the park's progress, ending with this peroration:

A natural park is being preserved in its naturalness for you and for me and for our children— unspoiled, unmarred. To enjoy this "pleasuring ground for the benefit and enjoyment of the people," its sublimity of beauty and grandeur, one must be in tune with these things. There is little to offer visitors who need attendants to make them comfortable, who think of walking in terms of cement and board paths, riding in terms of cushioned motor cars, who cannot appreciate a forest unless it is manicured or enjoy animals that have never felt the touch of the hand of man and do not wish it, who would be annoyed by noisy squirrels and gophers and whistling marmots and myriads of ptarmigan, hordes of rabbits, who would become hysterical about a few insects or faint and panic stricken if they missed a meal or two. Neither is there much consolation for the one who is prone to indulge in the pompous manner and the arrogant word.

But there is much to offer those who understand the language of the "great silent places," the "mighty mouthed hollows, plumb full of hush to the brim." To the hardy, venturesome ones there are heights to be scaled where bands of sheep and herds of caribou look with wonder and curiosity at the traveler. There are noisy mountain and glacier streams, noble crags and precipices, master pieces of nature's rugged architecture that have never yet been photographed. There are glaciers to cross. There are mountains to climb, from the easily ascended near-by domes to the dizzy peaks amid the everlasting snows. Eagles will be seen soaring about their breeding places among the pinnacles on the jagged sky-line.

Mount McKinley National Park has an abundance for each and everyone. Here will be found an indescribable calm; a place to just loaf; healing to the sick mind and body, beyond reach of the present day mental and nervous and moral strain.[17]

One of Karstens' most important acts as superintendent was relocation of the park headquarters in 1925. The base camp on Riley Creek below the railroad bridge was inconvenient, a second-choice location from the beginning determined by the Morino homestead, which occupied the best ground around McKinley Station. Moreover, in winter the frigid air sank into the creek bottoms making them 10 to 15 degrees Fahrenheit colder than nearby benchlands. The difference between -45 degrees and -60 degrees is profound and potentially lethal. Colonel Steese had helped Karstens out some by giving him office space in an ARC building at the station. But the families of Karstens and his staff, and the park's horses and dogs benefitted not at all from this partial solution.

In February 1924 Karstens wrote to the Director:

Owing to the survey and part construction of a road from the Alaska Railroad at McKinley Park station through the strip of land set aside by Executive Order for Park purposes, to the Eastern boundary of the Park, I believe it is time to take up the question of moving our headquarters from its present location to a point along this road. There is a beautiful spot, with ample room for expansion, one and two-third miles from the railroad, which is not within the boundary of the Park proper but is on the land temporarily set aside by Executive Order dated January 13, 1922.

I wish the Service would advise me if I could build headquarters on this land, and if I could expend Park funds (if available) on such work. My idea is to make this a permanent location, plotting out the site with a view to future development and adequate sanitation. Such buildings as we can construct will be built of logs, having an eye to their permanency and attractiveness, and also for warmth and comfort. Building headquarters at this point will simplify the work of checking persons entering the Park or leaving it. The present location is very unsatisfactory in this respect.[18]

After several exchanges of correspondence on the relocation Karstens' old friend, Acting Director Cammerer, ratified the new headquarters site and coached him to proceed promptly with construction of "temporary" buildings even before appropriated funds became available:

There has been one point that you have mentioned here and there in preceding correspondence and that is the possibility of establishing park headquarters farther on in the park, or near the park boundary. I am fully convinced that such a move is very desirable from an administrative standpoint and for other reasons, particularly now that the new road into the park is being developed. You should, therefore, bring with you to Seattle a map showing the proposed location of such new administrative headquarters, and you should include in your supplemental estimates an amount sufficient to construct a few permanent buildings, adequate in size and design for permanent construction. Of course, if headquarters is established before funds for such buildings will be available, as I expect will be the case, it will be necessary for you to establish in temporary living headquarters, such as you are now living in at McKinley Park Station, temporary structures.[19]

Karstens and his rangers moved rapidly. They dismantled several structures at the Riley Creek base camp and built, largely from the salvage, three one-room log cabins, a barn, and other utility shelters at the new headquarters site. This small, park-like plateau, girt by mountains, with a cover of white spruce and willow, lay in the angle between Rock and Hines creeks. At an elevation of 2,000 feet above sea level and 600 feet above McKinley Station, the headquarters benefitted from the warm-air inversion typical in winter. It offered a stunning view down the Hines Creek fault and across the Nenana River to the alpine peaks that rim the Yanert drainage.

In time, with the efforts of Karstens and his crew—and the work of successor superintendents Harry Liek, Frank Been, and Grant Pearson—the headquarters complex of the early '40s gave the park a first-class administrative, residential, and utility base, including stables and kennels for pack and patrol animals. Together with the patrol and boundary cabins (15 in all built by 1939), and the ARC cabins along the road, the park boasted an operational plant that, with a few additions in the 1950s, proved adequate until the advent of highway access in 1972.[20]

Karstens' headquarters locale would be challenged in 1929, when Chief Landscape Architect Thomas C. Vint visited the park to initiate the first professional planning effort. He thought the headquarters should be moved back to McKinley Station. But Director Horace Albright, knowledgeable about cold and wind from his Yellowstone superintendency days, vetoed any shift back to the low, exposed country along the railroad. When Albright visited the park in 1931 he said the clean and well laid-out headquarters area, with its sturdy and handsome log structures, compared favorably with any park headquarters in the States. He described it as ". . . a distinct credit to the Service, and an important asset, as it is seen by all tourists as they go down to visit . . . the dog kennels."[21]

Today the log buildings built by Karstens and his successors comprise a functional registered historic district still used for administrative and residence purposes by the Service. Visitors still enjoy this rustic period-piece as they wander through it on the way to the kennels and dog-sled demonstrations.

Despite plans for staging, things had happened "all at once" from the beginning at Mount McKinley National Park. Aside from setting up physically to manage the park, Karstens had to have a charter of authority, adapted to the statutory provisions that, among other things, protected valid mining claims, allowed new-claim entries under the mining laws, and gave prospectors and miners operating within the park the right to:

take and kill therein so much game or birds as may be needed for their actual necessities when short of food; but in no case shall animals or birds be killed in said park for sale or removal therefrom, or wantonly.[22]

These provisions, the price of getting the park bill through Congress, and particularly the hunting exception, caused immediate foreboding among the Founding Father conservationists, Washington officials of the Park Service, and Harry Karstens himself. John Burnham of the American Game Protective and Propagation Association, in late 1920, coordinated the efforts of his organization, the Boone & Crockett Club, and the Camp Fire Clubs to pay for weatherproof posters to be placed in the park quoting the Congressional proscriptions on hunting. Early in 1921 Burnham and his associates drafted suggested regulations for the park that emphasized the Interior Secretary's legal obligations under Section 5 of the park act to regulate the taking of game to assure its protection. The draft regulations would empower the park superintendent to confiscate game killed, along with the hunting outfits of violators of the Congressional proscriptions. They also provided for fines and imprisonment of those convicted.[23]

In April 1921 Assistant Director Cammerer sent to Karstens the Park Service draft regulations, which included much of the Burnham material, plus pen-and-ink comments solicited from Charles Sheldon, who wanted Karstens to review the regulations. All of Sheldon's suggestions concerned the hunting issue. Paramount was the need for a permit system that would enable the superintendent to distinguish real prospectors-miners from the poachers and market hunters who posed as such.

In forwarding the draft and comments to Karstens, Cammerer stated that the

act creating the park was particularly specific in giving miners and prospectors all possible leeway in pursuing their work, and I think they are permitted to go in without a permit; in other words, it would be difficult to enforce a permit clause if a miner decided not to apply for it.[24]

Cammerer sought Karstens' best thought on this issue, which came in a quick reply to the Director just before Karstens embarked from Seattle to start his new job at the park.[25] He strongly endorsed the idea of a permit system to control both hunting and timber cutting in the park. As an added benefit, the permit system would require face-to-face contact with permittees, giving Karstens a chance to explain the park rules to them. He said, "Alaskans as a general rule try to be law abiding in everything except hunting, and in that they think they have a perfect right to game—and wherever they want it." Karstens plugged for a regulation requiring prospectors and miners to keep a record of game killed so he could judge if they were hunting only when truly necessary, as Congress intended. He agreed with Sheldon that there should be no exception to confiscation of violators' game and outfits, for ". . .confiscation would have a tendency to keep wrongdoers out of the park." Differing from Sheldon, Karstens would allow miners to feed game meat to their dogs if the alternative were killing the dogs, for local fish were poor and supplies out of reach in hardship conditions. He believed that Toklat-Nenana Indians, who usually ran out of their dried and smoked fish by spring, had a special claim to survival hunting in the park up the Toklat's forks; and for the same reason, Birch Creek Indians of the upper Kuskokwim sometimes were forced to get a few caribou and moose in the park near Kantishna. (On the last, Cammerer in a letter of May 4, 1921, granted that this was a delicate issue and gave Karstens leeway to use his own judgment.)

As finally issued on June 21, 1921, the special regulations for Mount McKinley National Park avoided the permit issue, but required that prospectors and miners keep records of game killed, open to examination by the superintendent. Killing game principally for dog food could occur only on the condition of an advance permit from the superintendent, but excess meat left over from human food could be fed to dogs without a permit. Confiscation of violators' game and outfits was affirmed. Other provisions relating to miners and prospectors working in the park (e.g., carrying guns without a permit; using dogs for transportation and packing) reflected standard Alaska practice.[26]

The patchwork nature of these regulations, the ambiguities dictated by law, and the near impossibility of nailing down a prosecutable violation, especially in Alaska's social environment, are obvious. As park proponents feared, it was the hunting provision more that any other that would plague the park's administration and preservation. Letters of complaint about wanton killing of park game from conservation luminaries such as Dan Beard, Sr.,[27] vied with inquiries from the mining constituency, such as the interrogatory from J. A. Davis of the Bureau of Mines Experimental Station in Fairbanks.[28] Davis wanted clarification of the regulations to guarantee the miners' rights to work and hunt in the park in a way that would aid the mining enterprise—including use of timber, water rights, construction of ditches and dams, etc. But always the hunting provision and its abuse by some miners and a hard core group of dissembling poachers and market hunters grabbed the spotlight.

The latters' numbers increased under cover of the Kantishna mining excitement in the early '20s. This got the attention of the joint National Parks Committee of the Nation's leading conservation organizations. The minutes of the committee's meeting of April 17, 1923, quote a resolution urging the Secretary of the Interior and the National Park Service to take all necessary action to control hunting at McKinley, and calling on Congress to increase appropriations for wardens to enforce the controls.[29]

In his 1923 Annual Report to the President, Interior Secretary Hubert Work decried the miners' wanton killing of game in the park for themselves and their dogs. He asserted the need for amendatory legislation to repeal the hunting provision of the park act.[30]

Even the *Pathfinder of Alaska*, after isolating the renegade few from the majority of law-abiding prospectors and miners, conceded that if Mount McKinley's game was in fact being destroyed as reported by the Secretary, ". . . he is right in taking steps to put a stop to the practice," for the one place where plentiful wildlife "should be saved is in a National Park."[31]

The Secretary's idea of legislative repeal got locked in after he received his solicitor's opinion that—as Cammerer had earlier stated to Karstens—the park's legislative history did not support the Secretary's explicit regulation of hunting by prospectors and miners. The solicitor cited the settled rule of law, which states that if a right is granted by statute (in this case the park's establishment act) it cannot be abridged by the regulations of an executive department.[32]

The Service's Washington Office and the park tried all manner of expedients to restrict park hunting to actual necessity, as Congress intended. But these efforts fell far short. Reports of renegade trappers in the McKinley River drainage added to the concerns over wildlife destruction. Pleas to Congress for funds for more rangers went unheard.[33] In cooperation with the U.S. Biological Survey, by now in charge of Alaska Game Law enforcement, Alaska Game Wardens were appointed without pay as park rangers, and rangers were deputized as wardens.[34] Still, the park's vast spaces and the law's vast loophole defeated the objective of preserved wildlife.

In early 1924 biologist Olaus Murie of the Biological Survey, then studying caribou in the park, reported to his boss, Dr. E. W. Nelson, that the future of the park's game was really endangered.[35] About the same time Karstens wrote a long letter to the Director citing many hunting depredations—sled loads of meat being transported out of the park by men who maintained that everyone else was killing animals where and when they saw fit. It was impossible for Karstens, often away on public business, and his one assistant ranger to cover even the near hunting and exit sites, much less the far reaches of the park. He concluded:

My recommendation would be to close the park to all hunting. As long as prospectors are allowed to kill game, just as surely will the object of this park be defeated. Any townie can take a pick and pan and go into the park and call himself a prospector. This is often the case. Compromises will not do for compromises only leave loopholes for further abuse.[36]

Karstens' letter, along with the other reports that documented wholesale killing of park wildlife, inspired Washington officials to call together leading conservationists—Dr. Nelson and Olaus Murie of the Biological Survey, John Burnham of the Game Protective Association, and Charles Sheldon—to develop with the Service a strategy leading to repeal of the park-act hunting provision. During the course of this meeting Director Mather made the point that ". . . the United States was planning to put some $275,000 into new road work in Mount McKinley Park, and that any depletion of the wild life would be bound to have an adverse affect on the visitors, who, seeing the Mount McKinley National Park as the chief scenic asset of Alaska, would expect to see some of the wonderful caribou herds and flocks of sheep . . . ." He urged all present to make the point with Alaska Delegate to Congress Dan Sutherland that these visitors, potential settlers and investors, ". . . would do more toward developing Alaska's resources than any other possibilities to which Alaskans could point to build up their territory."[37]

Eventually, as a result of mounting conservation pressure and the perversion of the open-ended hunting provision that could not be regulated, Congress repealed it by an amendatory act approved May 21, 1928. The same act opened the way for more rangers by lifting the $10,000 annual appropriation limit imposed by the establishment act.[38]

In a related effort initiated by Director Albright, Congress in 1931 granted the Secretary explicit authority to regulate surface use of mineral land locations, and to require the registration of all prospectors and miners entering the park.[39] But not until 1976 were new-claim entries under the mining laws prohibited in McKinley Park.[40]

Slowly, structural changes and adjustments of law to make the park administrable were taking place. Meanwhile, Karstens and his rangers carried on their work—patrolling, stopping wrongdoers, making friends or enemies as occasion demanded, and, as a by-product, establishing an enduring Park Service tradition in Alaska.

As a Sourdough himself—Klondike stampeder, hunter, dog-driver, mountaineer—Karstens set the tone for that tradition. When Grant Pearson came to work for him as a buck ranger in 1926, Pearson knew he was in the presence of a living legend.[41] Pearson, who would become McKinley's superintendent and a legendary outdoorsman in his own right, never lost his affection and admiration for Karstens. Even after the troubles that drove Karstens from the Service, Pearson held that the government ". . . couldn't have chosen a more competent man to pioneer the initial development" of the park.[42]

Pearson's recall of his testing days as a new ranger paint a picture of early park conditions and Karstens' demanding standards:

Superintendent Karstens certainly did not like government red tape, especially when he was of the opinion that it was necessary to discharge an employee. Quite often when some of the personnel became angry with him, he preferred to settle matters outside the office with their fists, rather than prefer official charges. That situation eventually led to his downfall in government work.

During the three years I worked under the supervision of Karstens, I found him to be very fair and considerate. I made several long trips into the back country of the Park with him and he taught me many original ways of getting along the trail.

On several occasions during the time I was at the park Karstens actually came to blows with some of the park personnel, and I never knew him to come out second best.

Considering that he was in a frontier area, he was a realistic administrator. Those were the days when a Ranger was not required to pass a Civil Service Examination. He had his own system, and considering the type of duties a Ranger was required to perform, his system certainly weeded out those *who were unfit for the job. When I talked to Karstens about a Ranger's job, he asked me a number of questions about my experience as a woodsman and wilderness man.*

I shall never forget that, when he got through asking questions, he said, "You're lacking in experience, but I think you can learn. I'll send you on a patrol trip alone. You will be gone a week. If you don't get back by then, I'll come looking for you, and you had better have plans made for a new job. Now this is what I want you to do." He then outlined a week's patrol trip cross-country through territory new to me. There were no blazed trails to follow. One could follow only the terrain cross-country. He also gave me a rough map and much valuable advice. No reliable maps of the Park were available in those days.

Karstens said, "This will be a trial trip, and real test for you. We can't use anyone on our Ranger force who can't take care of himself in the wilds.

The Ranger you are replacing was unfit for this service. We sent him out on the same patrol you are going to make and he returned in a most pitiful condition. He just staggered back, almost starved. The poor fellow was gone for three days and couldn't find the patrol cabin. He hadn't eaten a hot meal since he left. His reason was that he couldn't find any water that wasn't frozen to ice. The ground was covered with snow. He had a trail axe and could have cut some dry wood and melted ice or snow for water. Luckily the weather was warm, about zero and he didn't suffer any frostbite.

When this fellow took the job he said he had had plenty of experience out in the wilderness by himself. This trip you are making isn't too tough. However, it is the kind that separates the glamour boys from the type we can use in our work.[43]

Karstens never rested on his laurels. He got into the park whenever his administrative and public-relations duties allowed. And when he left town or office for the trail, he did more than tour. Often he traveled alone on long dog-team patrols, siwash camping (camping without tent or supplies) in the woods as in the days before cabins. Whenever he went out, he did something that set an example for his men, whether it was long hours tracking a violator or building a patrol cabin with his own hands. He did this, too, because out there, off the beaten path, he was the happiest of men.[44]

KARSTEN'S RANGERS

The rangers who survived Karstens' weeding process—stalwarts like Fritz Nyberg and Pearson, and the temporaries who helped them—built a rangering record that made Mount McKinley the Yellowstone of the North, the operational academy for Alaska park rangers. That this record required exertion in difficult social and physical environments comes through in early park reports, a few highlights of which follow:

The case against Jack Donnelly for killing and transporting game from the Park was considered a very good one, but the prosecution failed because of the reluctance of the people, as represented by an average jury in this instance, to convict anyone for illegal hunting. This general disinclination to punish illegal game killers is recognized by everybody, and the Park seems destined to suffer along with the rest of the territory as a consequence. It is very discouraging for those appointed to protect game and who feel responsible for results. Our only hope for adequate conservation lies in the obtaining of whole-hearted support by the people. Once we get enthusiastic sympathy for our aims—and no thinking, unselfish person denies that they are right—co-operation will follow. The process of swinging the attitude of these people to the point of recognizing the importance and value of conservation of wild life, as practiced by the national parks, promises to be a slow and tedious one, requiring much missionary work.

Superintendent's Monthly Report, February 1924.

May 1927

Ranger Swisher, Pearson and I left for Toklat River in early morning. Going over Thoroughfare (Pass) and down into Toklat, we got in snowslush up to our necks. Dogs could neither walk or swim—we had to pull them across. Got in early, changed clothes, spent the balance of the day cutting logs for cabin.

Chief Ranger Nyberg

November 1927

There was four inches of snow during the month making about ten inches on the level. About two thirds of the month was bitter cold being about thirty-five to forty below towards the last of the month. The winds in the canyons and passes were very penetrating. Streams were overflowing and glaciering up very rapidly. During the coldest weather the dogs had to travel through water which was very hard on the dog's feet during the cold weather. The relief tent at East Fork is all surrounded by overflow ice. The new cabin at Toklat and the dog-houses made this stretch of freighting much less disagreeable than heretofore. If there were several more of these cabins along the trails and along the boundary, patrol work could be carried out much more effectively. It is not fair to the rangers to ask them to patrol in the cold weather and get wet in the overflows and then have to spend the night out in the open under a spruce tree. Especially as they travel alone it is too dangerous to ask any man to do. This month Ranger Pearson was caught in a blizzard in the Copper Mountain basin with the nearest cabin or shelter of any kind 17 miles away. There was no timber in the basin for wood to make a fire and he had to double back 17 miles to the Toklat cabin, arriving late at night. It is important that there should be a cabin at Copper Mountain.

Chief Ranger Nyberg

December 1927

There are twelve trappers at least along the east boundary and seven white trappers and several natives trapping along the northern boundary between Healy and Toklat. There are five trappers between Toklat and Wonder Lake. There are at least four and probably more between Wonder Lake and the West end. Practically all of these trappers have dogs that are fed from caribou and sheep. With a ranger force of three and hardly any cabins along the boundary it is practically impossible to properly patrol this section. With present conditions the rangers are forced to make a hurried trip through, spending the nights beneath spruce trees. Along the 150 miles of boundary which is about two hundred miles the way we would have to travel, there are only four cabins. In cold or stormy weather it is too risky a proposition to send the rangers over this hard stretch with no cabins to stop in. The trappers are well acquainted with these conditions and make use of the knowledge.

Chief Ranger Nyberg

March 1928

Chief Ranger Nyberg and I left Kantishna station at three oclock the morning of the 29th. As the light snow that was falling made the trail unusually good we made the 35 miles to Toklat by nine oclock in the morning; and continued on to Igloo 20 miles farther.

There was game on the trail between Polychrome Pass and East Fork. The teams broke into a fast run, one of the dogs in my team went down and they dragged him a hundred feet before I could stop them. He was unable to rise and I found one of his front legs was broken close to the shoulder. The break was so bad there was no hope of recovery so I took the collar and harness off and shot him. The dogs were continually breaking through the ice on the creek; he was the slowest dog in the team and getting tired he must have stepped through the ice and was unable to pull his leg out soon enough.

Park Ranger Arthur Gardner

Ranger Gardner's evident distress at having to destroy one of his dogs testifies to the rangers' affection for and dependence on these often unruly and frustrating animals. Dog-team work can be the hardest imaginable for both man and beast. Breaking trail in deep snow with snowshoes, pulling the dogs as they wallow through it, holding the sled on line while floundering across sidehill slopes or sliding in a gale on glare ice, pushing and yelling encouragement as the dogs drag a loaded freight sled up a cut bank—all these standard problems of dog driving leave little time for leisurely sledding through the scenery. Straightening out tangled dogs and lines, deicing sled runners after traversing overflow, and breaking up dog fights that can maim or kill one's only transport in lethal weather and terrain do little to relieve the normal stresses.

Yet, for those who accept these travails to explore the crystalline landscapes of winter the dogs are a constant amazement. No matter how hard the previous day, they greet the morning with eager anticipation—another great day of bone-tiring labor lies ahead. When a good team responds to a good driver the power and energy they display in overcoming the most difficult conditions wrings the heart. For one alone on distant patrol, the dogs are the only companions. They become as family.

Functionally, particularly in the early days (and yet today in specialized tasks) the dogs alone gave access to the park's winter remoteness. Even after the advent of airplanes and snow-cats the dogs proved their worth. Temporarily banished from the park after World War II, they were brought back as dependable complements to the various machines powered by internal combustion engines, which proved fickle in deep cold and bad storm, and dysfunctional in many terrains.

Anyway, the training, driving, and upkeep of dogs has been too integral a part of McKinley-Denali rangering to be valued solely in practical terms. The sled dogs of Denali are both symbol and substance of that tradition that encourages rangers to actually range in the Alaskan wild. Their continuing use for specialized patrol and freighting of supplies, and their unfailing appeal to visitors through scheduled dog-sledding demonstrations, is recognized as one of the park's historic themes, represented structurally by the historic kennels complex and patrol cabins.[45]

In those pioneer years, getting the park going and giving it protection, along with public missionary work, took most of the park staff's time. But emergencies and new duties kept intervening. In July 1924 a major fire surrounded McKinley Station and the park's Riley Creek base camp. Strong winds fanned it along the first mile of the new park road toward the park proper. Summer camps around the station were abandoned. Park families left their quarters to huddle on a Riley Creek gravel bar. Night-and-day work and vigilance, and a change in the weather, ended the danger after 4 days. But the park entrance was a charred wasteland[46]—a contributing reason for Director Albright's veto of Landscape Architect Vint's 1929 recommendation to move the park headquarters back to McKinley Station.

As a result of the Prohibition Amendment and an earlier law prohibiting the manufacture and sale of alcoholic liquors in the Territory of Alaska, park rangers were drafted into the enforcement apparatus to destroy moonshine stills and close down dispensaries.[47] This thankless task exacerbated the park's relations with private landholders around McKinley Station. Both Morino's Roadhouse and Duke Stubb's store had become drinking hangouts for wintering miners, whose cabins had proliferated on the unwithdrawn lands between the park boundary and the Nenana River. Prohibition actions against these two dispensers, and neighboring moonshiners who supplied them, complicated an already strained situation. Particularly grating was Morino, whose strategically located homestead surrounded McKinley Station and the park-

Squatter's cabin near the park headquarters, circa 1930. Courtesy of the miscellaneous MOMC file, AMHA.

entrance corridor. The bitterness sown by these episodes would contribute to Karstens' downfall and create long-term problems when these people and their allies became inholders after the boundary extension of 1932.[48]

GETTING READY FOR TOURISTS

Nor would tourists and special visitors wait until everything was nicely organized. The NPS itself—at first to justify establishment of the park, then to get money for its protection and development—had constantly touted the park's potential for the territory's economy and development. The connection between park tourism and profitable operation of the Alaska Railroad had been exploited continuously since the first public announcement of the park idea in 1915. Little wonder, then, that the sequence of protection first and visitors later telescoped together.

By 1922 the *Rand McNally Guide to Alaska and Yukon* featured a detailed map of the park showing an established trail from McKinley Station to Wonder Lake and beyond to the very foot of the mountain.[49] At the time of this guide's printing the trail was not even marked.

About the same time a consortium of steamship lines, railroads, and other tourism interests formed an organization called Alaska Vacation Land. Its advertisements in prominent magazines such as *The New Yorker* and *Sunset* highlighted McKinley Park on a tour called The Golden Belt Line, which began at the port of Cordova, proceeded to Chitina on the Copper River and Northwestern Railroad, then up the Richardson Highway to Fairbanks, and back to the coast past the park on the Alaska Railroad.[50]

In a circular of July 1924, the Alaska Railroad reminded its agents "that here in Alaska is situated one of America's most wondrous playgrounds." They were exhorted to "boost Mt. McKinley Park whenever and wherever possible."[51] At the time this circular went out the first full-time ARC construction crew of about 90 men had just established their camps and grubbed out the first 4 miles of the road.[52]

A couple of months earlier Karstens had advised Dr. Frank Oastler of New York City that "All transportation, after leaving the railroad, must be by saddle and pack train." He should be prepared for a 2-week outing if he planned a round trip to the foot of the mountain.[53]

Colonel Steese, temporarily heading both the Alaska Railroad and the ARC, warned Assistant Director Cammerer in July 1924 that "we shall do our best to hold people off this year," but unless the NPS could coax more substantial road funds from

Congress, the park faced a deluge of disappointed visitors. For every trekker who enjoyed the "very meager and rough camping facilities" and transportation currently available, there would be a crowd at the station to whom "the National Park Service will have to do a lot of explaining."[54]

Karstens, viewing with alarm the visitors' force-fed expectations versus the park's actual state of staffing and development, had earlier written this plaint to the Director:

The establishing of transportation to the park will add to the many other duties of the superinten-dent and his one ranger. We will do our best, and are eager to cope with any situation that may develop, but is it fair to the Park?[55]

Opening of the railroad from Seward to Fairbanks in 1923 brought a series of VIP tours past the park. Their ceremonial stops at McKinley Station publicized the park's grandeur and beauty. Their frustration at being unable to enter a National Park effectively blockaded by lack of roads and accommodations spurred public clamor. These events helped move Congress to the first significant appropriations for road construction.

On June 7 a Congressional party numbering 65 persons spent an hour and a half at the station. Superintendent Karstens addressed the group, citing the park's urgent need for a road and increased appropriations.[56] Chairman Steese of the Alaska Railroad and ARC wrote to Karstens a few days later to relay "the many pleasant comments we have received concerning your address . . . , I believe we may safely count upon receiving increased consideration at the hands of Congress next winter."[57]

Next, on July 8-9 came the Brooklyn Eagle Party of 70 persons. For several years the *Brooklyn Daily Eagle* newspaper had sponsored western park tours with the cooperation of the Interior Department and the NPS. Each year they officially dedicated a National Park. This year it would be Mount McKinley.

As originally planned, the 40 or 50 hardier members of the party would be transported over the rough trail to partake of a caribou barbecue at concessioner Dan Kennedy's Savage River camp. But tight train schedules and Kennedy's inability to set up for such a throng at the opening of his first season cancelled that event. Karstens

The Mt. McKinley Tourist and Transportation Company took over from Dan Kennedy in 1925. It retained park concession rights until the eve of World War II. Courtesy of AMHA.

The Brooklyn Eagle party at the park's dedication ceremony,
June 1923. Courtesy of the Fanny Quigley Collection, UAF.

had worked like a dervish to pull this off and, as usual, he would not be defeated. He dragooned everyone in sight to transport and set up the barbecue at McKinley Station. He called in the Biological Survey's caribou man, Olaus Murie, to hunt sheep for barbecue meat. Except for the usual disappointment at being unable to get into the park, the barbecue and dedication came off splendidly.[58]

By now Karstens' plaint about extra duties when the railroad brought visitors to the park had the ring of understatement. And it was not over. But cope he did.

Less than a week later, on July 15, President Warren G. Harding's party of 70 persons showed up. After an overnight layover at Broad Pass (the train simply pulled into a siding because the Curry Hotel, the later overnight stop, was under construction), the Presidential Special steamed into McKinley Station. For about 20 minutes the President mingled and shared refreshments with the crowd that greeted him there. Superintendent Karstens accepted the invitation to join the President's party for the Golden Spike driving at the north end of the newly completed Tanana River bridge—the symbolic signal of the railroad's completion. During the train ride to Fairbanks Karstens worked the President's men with stories of the park and a catalogue of its needs.[59]

Shortly after his visit the President authored an encomium to Mount McKinley that concluded with these words: "Somehow Mount McKinley is distinctly typical of Alaska, so mighty, measureless and magnificent, resourceful and remote, with some great purpose yet unrevealed to challenge human genius."[60]

While in San Francisco on his return from Alaska, President Harding died of an embolism. Interior Secretary Work would state in his 1923 Annual Report to new President Calvin Coolidge that "The official visit of the President and his Cabinet has unquestionably done more to direct attention to Alaska than any previous event."

Not all special visits were so pleasant. Famous outdoors writer and film-maker William N. Beach set up a visit to the park in 1922, writing ahead to Karstens and getting his enthusiastic response and offer of help. Beach said he wanted to shoot McKinley's sheep with a camera, but, unstated to Karstens, he wanted to shoot them with a rifle, too. Using his connections he tried to get a special permit for sheep hunting. The Biological Survey helped the territory to manage Alaska game, so Beach approached its chief, Dr. E. W. Nelson. Beach started with a statement to him by Alaska Governor Riggs that he saw no reason why Beach couldn't get a special permit for hunting in the park. Beach then urged Nelson to intervene with the Park Service in his behalf. Nelson refused.

In a letter to Charles Sheldon, Nelson recounted this episode and said that he had written to Karstens to the effect that such special permits for famous people would wreck the park and enrage Alaskans. He went on to say that Karstens' careful enforcement of the park hunting ban would be for nought if any exceptions were allowed. He urged Sheldon to help him head Beach off from further pleas to the Interior Secretary by alerting Mather and Albright.[61]

In the upshot Beach did secretly shoot a sheep near his camp at Igloo Creek. On his return to New York he sent a new Mauser rifle to Karstens as a token of appreciation for courtesies extended. Shortly thereafter Beach attended a society dinner and told the gentlemen next to him that he had killed a sheep in Mount McKinley National Park. The man happened to the assistant field director for the National Park Service.

The Service then moved against Beach, obtaining a signed statement from him acknowledging the illegal kill. When informed of this by the Service, Karstens returned the rifle, which he never had a chance to fire.

Beach had also sent a Mauser to an Alaska Game Warden who had seen the sheep at the Igloo Camp when passing through. The warden kept quiet about the incident, but later admitted to Karstens that perhaps he had seen a sheep head at the camp. Beach was prosecuted before the U.S. District Attorney in Fairbanks in September 1923. He finally pled guilty, after citing a hungry camp as his excuse. He paid a $10 fine and court costs, assessed by a sympathetic U.S. Commissioner. But as Karstens remarked, any conviction for illegal hunting in Alaska was "quite a feat."

The positive results of this unsavory affair were public statements and articles supporting McKinley as a wildlife sanctuary from the new governor, Scott Bone, and delegate to Congress Dan Sutherland.[62]

Some "just plain folks" came into the park in those early days. One woman who had seen the mountain many times from a distance wrote an account of her 1927 back-pack trip, a few lines of which follow:

But it is only after one has seen Mt. McKinley from the nearer reaches and in such evident cool superiority to its rugged surroundings that he can realize its true fitness as the nucleus for one of the greatest and most attractively wild of all the national parks.

The sky was clear except for a few fluffy clouds floating in the direction of the range. Perhaps we would not see McKinley at all that day. But after a few more labored steps we reached the summit of the pass, and peeking out from the side of the hill on the left was what at first looked like a white cloud, the rugged top of the mountain. The clear outline of the two peaks, the sharpness of ridges on its surface, the unmarred purity of whiteness on perpendicular walls, the wind-swept smoothness of depressions all gave the impression of exultant height and aloofness.

This was my first near view of Mount McKinley, the white wonder of the range, the top of the continent.[63]

Completion of the Alaska Railroad keyed a boom in Interior tourism during the 1920s. Joined at Fairbanks by riverboat and auto-road links to the White Pass railroad out of Skagway and the Yukon, and the Copper River railroad out of Cordova, the new Alaska Railroad attracted significant numbers of tourists away from the previously favored coastal towns and cruise ships. Interior hotels and their rustic roadhouse cousins, restaurants, and gift shops featuring Native arts and crafts all benefitted from this shift.

In tune with Alaska's frontier character many accommodations provided only the basics of shelter, warmth, and meals. Tasty wild-meat stews, baked bread, and garden vegetables, served home style, catered to the healthy and hungry traveler. One guidebook warned the finicky: "No allowance is made for delicate or jaded appetites."[64]

The Depression hit Alaska tourism hard. But in the late '30s the well heeled headed north for fear of Europe's war threats. Then World War II, with Japanese invasion of the Aleutian Islands and the priorities of war mobilization, halted all tourism to the territory for the next several years.

Over much of Alaska the post-World War II revival of tourism followed new routes constructed and perfected during the war. A major development was the opening of direct commercial air travel from the Outside. The Army-built Alaska-Canada (Alcan) Highway allowed direct auto access to Fairbanks from the States. The Glenn Highway connected Anchorage with Fairbanks via the prewar Richardson Highway. Scores of secondary and emergency military airfields—turned over to the territory after the war—opened up remote areas to casual visitors.

But in the yet essentially roadless Denali region, the railroad's prewar-style travel and touring patterns would persist for another three decades. Given the already existing railroad, the military had skipped the Denali region when it built new elements of Alaska's wartime infrastructure. Thus the park continued to be isolated from the independent auto touring that had become commonplace in road-accessible parts of Alaska.[65]

EARLY SCIENCE IN THE PARK

In the early years scientific interest in McKinley Park centered on the large mammals. The park's special status as a game refuge offered scientists the unique opportunity to study the life histories of unhunted animal populations over a significantly large range of the subarctic.[66] Cooperation between the NPS and the U.S. Biological Survey in Alaska began when the latter's assistant biologist, Olaus J. Murie, conducted reconnaissance surveys in and around the park in the years 1920-22. Though his work occurred in the context of a long-term study of the caribou, his early notes and reports yielded meticulous descriptions of flora and fauna of all kinds, couched in the life-zone ecology of the time. Aside from Charles Sheldon's work in 1906-08, which concentrated on the white sheep, Murie's were the first scientific reports relating to the park's biology.

The Biological Survey's chief, Dr. E. W. Nelson, had commissioned Murie to travel all through Alaska on the caribou study. He was particularly concerned with the relationship between imported domestic reindeer—first brought to Alaska in 1892 to supplement Native food supplies—and the larger, sturdier wild caribou. When migrating caribou passed close to domestic herds of reindeer, some of the latter drifted off with the wild animals. Being of the same species, the animals interbred, to the detriment of the caribou. Nelson conceived the idea of improving the reindeer stock by controlled interbreeding with choice caribou bulls. This would not only improve the meat yield of the domestic animals but would also help protect the caribou by transmitting their sturdiness and disease immunities to the reindeer herds, thus making casual encounters less detrimental to caribou.[67]

As a result of Doctor Nelson's correspondence with Director Mather on this subject, Olaus Murie was given permission to capture some of the large bulls at the park for breeding with the reindeer. During the period July 4 to October 23, 1922, Olaus and, from early September, his younger brother Adolph ("Ade") Murie, worked to this end with Karsten's cooperation and a crew of hired hands from Fairbanks.

They made camp on the upper Savage River near its main forks, and built a caribou corral about a mile and a half up the Savage west fork. Murie had studied Indian drive and corral structures in the upper Yukon region and this one followed their design. It had two long wings about 600 yards long that funneled caribou along a well trod trail that came over the pass from Sanctuary River. The wings converged on a gate that opened into a corral about 60 yards in diameter. A small pen inside was used to hobble and dehorn bulls so they could be worked without lethal danger to the wranglers. Captured bulls were taken to the Biological Survey station at Fairbanks to consummate the breeding experiment.[68]

Olaus Murie continued to have intermittent contact with McKinley Park into the early '60s, with significant influence on the park's biological and wilderness management. But the younger brother, "Ade" Murie, remained a real fixture in the park into the '70s. His reports on McKinley mammals, birds, and ecological studies number in the scores, with many of them published in popular form. These, plus his periodic evaluation of the wolf-sheep status during the '30s and '40s, and his many letters and comments on the park's evolving development exerted a force both spiritual and scientific:

❋   in establishing an early version of ecosystem-management at the park;
❋   in averting a big-game management bias, which would have included mandatory wolf-control quotas;
❋   in moderating post-World War II development concepts that would have subjected wilderness and wildlife to undue intrusion; and
❋   in justifying recent northern boundary expansions to preserve extended wildlife habitat.

In sum, these contributions probably made Ade Murie the single most influential person in shaping the geography and the wildlife-wilderness policies of the modern park.

Ade Murie's alliance with the fate of this park did not happen in a vacuum. In 1926, George M. Wright and Joseph S. Dixon visited McKinley Park to study its "outstanding assemblage of animal life." George Wright was an independent biologist who, at first with his own money, hired or contracted colleagues to form the Service's first wildlife division. He believed that only science-based management could save the National Parks from the devastations of contextual and in-park exploitation and development. Joe Dixon was one of these colleagues, a professor of mammalogy at the University of California. As a first step, they envisioned a series of faunal surveys for each of the great National Parks. They shared the premise that protection of wildlife and their habitats,

far from being the magic touch which healed all wounds, was unconsciously just the first step on a long road winding through years of endeavor toward a goal too far to reach, yet always shining ahead as a magnificent ideal. This objective is to restore and perpetuate the fauna in its pristine state by combating the harmful effects of human influence. . . . The vital significance of wild life to the whole national-park idea emphasizes the necessity for prompt action.[69]

Their accounting for the dynamics and relations of flora, fauna, and geography gave their methodology the cast of modern ecology.[70]

Recognizing the superlative natural laboratory and unique wildlife gathering offered by McKinley Park, Wright and Dixon launched their investigations there, with advice and assistance from the NPS, the Biological Survey, the University of California Museum of Vertebrate Zoology, and the United States National Museum. Their work constituted the first comprehensive, ecologically based survey of the park. The many specific research tasks they proposed continue to enlarge the park's massive scientific bibliography.

Their evaluation of McKinley Park's unique significance in the early years can be read today as a pronouncement on the values of Alaska's expanded park, refuge, and Biosphere Reserve systems developed over the years since their pioneer work:

[Mount McKinley], *because of its remote location, favorable climatic conditions, and large size, is the only park today that contains an adequate and abundant breeding stock both of wild game and of large carnivorous animals. Too, the natural association and interrelation of certain typical and vanishing examples of North American mammals, such as grizzly bear, wolverine, timber wolf, caribou, and Alaska mountain sheep, can probably be maintained by reason of the adequate room and the suitable forage conditions.*[71]

END OF THE KARSTENS ERA

As these precedent-setting events paced the park's early history, Harry Karstens' superintendency fell on hard times. Despite his continuing accomplishments in the realm of park protection and pioneer development, his volatile personal relations with other officials, park neighbors, the park concessioner, and park employees created an atmosphere of siege. Many episodes were innocent of all but quick temper, even if beyond condoning. Many others were the result of calculated conspiracy and baiting by persons whose interests lay in discrediting the superintendent. But in aggregate, the result was turmoil and publically registered displeasure with the incumbent.

In an attempt to clear the air Director Mather and Assistant Director Cammerer commissioned investigations of Karstens in 1924 and 1925. Cammerer's informant, A. F. Stowe, was a personal acquaintance of the assistant director and a local man who knew the histories of many of Karstens' accusers. At home in the local environment, he quietly observed the individuals and dynamics of the various disputes. In a letter to Cammerer in early 1925 he cited chapter and verse of the origins and motivations of the disputes and parties thereto. He had found attempts to crowd Karstens' legitimate jurisdiction over the park, along with all manner of personal spite, revenge, and envy. He concluded his letter with these words: "I believe today the same as I have always believed that in the present incumbent you fortunately selected the best qualified man living in Alaska for the Superintendency of the Park."[72]

Mather, through the Secretary of the Interior, requested that U.S. Post Office investigators detail every aspect of the charges against Karstens, and solicit opinions as to his competence and stability from such distinguished persons as James Steese, Governor Scott Bone, and newly appointed Governor George Parks. The investigators' report of June 29, 1925, represented 2 months' work carried out in Seattle, Juneau, Anchorage, Fairbanks, and the park and vicinity. With attached exhibits, the 13-page report, whose substance was an indictment, provides a saddening glimpse into the subsurface labyrinth of Karstens' personal conflicts as superintendent.

The complainants charged Karstens with an arrogant and violent temperament, lack of executive ability, and petty forms of annoyance directed toward any person who differed from him or showed him up. Governors Bone and Parks felt that though Karstens may have been too direct in some of his methods and personal responses, he had probably been unfairly incited by smaller men, whose aims regarding the park crossed Karstens' duty to protect it. He should, they believed, be transferred to another park where his genuine attributes could be properly channeled and supervised. Colonel Steese came to essentially the same conclusions, but dwelt at length on Karstens' suspicions that everyone was out to get him. Steese further stated that he should be removed immediately so that his presence would not hinder the road project. Other correspondents, as well as the investigators, said about the same: that

Mountain Climber with sled. From the Denali National Park and Preserve Archive.

despite Karstens' many excellent qualities as a pioneer he lacked the poise and balance for public administration.[73]

In the upshot, Mather, Albright, and even old friend Cammerer were forced regretfully but realistically to share that opinion.[74]

During the remaining 3 years of his superintendency Karstens struggled mightily to complete the park's first stage of development and operations. His energies were eroded by many who, aware of the investigation, sensed his vulnerability and capitalized upon his coming demise. Many letters from job applicants found their way to Washington. Karstens' growing belief that his mentors in Washington had lost faith in him did little to relieve his anxiety.

The worst part of the wind-down of Karstens' NPS career still lay ahead when Director Mather visited the park in August 1926. Karstens set up an 8-day saddle-and-pack-horse trip through the park, visiting many of the sites, including the Toklat cabin, that Charles Sheldon had described to the director in Washington. Together Karstens and Mather explored the headwaters of Stony and Moose creeks, then proceeded on through the passes to Copper Mountain and near views of Mount McKinley. As always in the outdoors world that he loved Karstens proved a gracious host, an impressive man in his element. Grant Pearson wrote that Karstens' guidance through the park gave the Director—the first Washington Office official to visit it—a lasting impression of its wilderness and wildlife values.[75]

By 1928 the park road extended 40 miles into the park. Appropriations were up to $22,000. The much enhanced concession operation hosted close to 1,000 visitors with facilities and activities that combined comfort, entertainment, and challenge in balances attuned to visitor tastes. The park headquarters and supporting administrative facilities made possible reasonable park operations. A small but barely adequate ranger staff patrolled and protected the park from all but the most remote incursions. Much work remained to be done. But much had already been done.[76] This accomplishment had been wrought largely by the fallible but dedicated man who entered the park alone on a borrowed horse in 1921.

Karsten's resignation in October 1928 combined frustration over his continuing battles with ill-disposed people, disgust with the complex administrative demands of a maturing park, and his conviction that he could no longer command the respect and affection of his superiors in Washington. Even his friend, advisor, and faithful supporter, Charles Sheldon, had died. Grant Pearson, perhaps to soften these grim motivations, invoked another cause: the park had become too tame for a pioneer like Karstens. So he went to Fairbanks and resumed his transportation business.[77]

Director Mather, felled by a stroke, resigned in January 1929. His successor, Horace Albright, visited McKinley Park in 1931. He was greeted by Harry Liek, Albright's choice to replace the departed Karstens. Albright suffered an attack of appendicitis while in the park and was flown to Fairbanks for hospitalization. While he was there, Karstens and his family repeatedly visited Albright, showing great kindness, bringing flowers, and loaning books about McKinley from their personal library. Karstens said he wanted to go back to work at the park, even as a subordinate ranger. But Albright talked him out of it, for Karstens would not be happy or useful in such a position. Albright tried without success to change Karstens' view that Director Mather had been against him ever since the 1926 visit. In a memorandum from his hospital bed to the Washington Office, Albright recounted these things. He expressed his enduring admiration for the man in his pioneer role, sympathy for his troubles in later years. But he was firm in his conviction that Karstens could not fit back into the Service.

Perhaps if he were just starting out; but not now, not with all those unresolved resentments. He concluded:

I hope the Service will always have Karstens' good will, and I told him we wanted him to feel that he had a great many friends in the Service, and that we wished him well. He promised to help us, and Supt. Liek especially, as opportunity afforded him a chance.[78]

❄

NOTES: CHAPTER 7

1. Harry Karstens letter to Horace Albright of 7/25/18, National Archives, Record Group 79, Entry 6, Mount McKinley Corres., Box 382.
2. Gov. Riggs letter to Director Mather of 2/19/21, Alaska State Archives, Juneau, Record Group 101, Ser. 130, Box 195.
3. Mather letter to Sheldon of 1/27/21, University of Alaska, Fairbanks, Archives, Sheldon Collection, Box 2.
4. Mather letter to Riggs of 2/5/21, Alaska State Archives, Juneau, Record Group 101, Ser. 130, Box 195.
5. Mather letter to Karstens of 4/12/21, National Archives, Record Group 79, Entry 6, Box 381.
6. Ibid.
7. Horace Albright, *The Birth of the National Park Service: The Founding Years*, 1913-33 (Salt Lake City: Howe Brothers, 1985), 68-73; see also the Service's 1925 "comprehensive policy" update issued as a press release by the Department of the Interior on March 13, 1925, Alaska State Archives, Record Group 101, Box 246.
8. National Park Service, *Director's Annual Report*, 1919 (Washington: GPO, 1920), 109.
9. This summary impression derived from Karstens letter and report files in National Archives, Record Group 79, Entry 6, Boxes 369, 379, and 382, and from his letters to Charles Sheldon in Sheldon Collection, University of Alaska, Fairbanks, Archives, Box 1. Lands Records from the Denali NP&P Archives give details on Morino and Lynch homesteads and administrative determinations thereon.
10. Karsten's report to the Governor of Alaska, July 22, 1922, copy in National Archives, Record Group 79, Entry 6, Box 384.
11. Ibid.
12. The Superintendent's Monthly Reports record the building pressures on the new park.
13. Steese letter to Mather of 4/20/22, Denali NP&P Archives.
14. Gail Evans, "From Myth to Reality," 242-243.
15. ARC Annual Reports, 1924-1925.
16. George S. Stroud, "History of the Consession at Denali National Park (formerly Mount McKinley National Park)," typescript report for the National Park Service (Anchorage: 1985), 1-6.
17. Address to Women's Club of Anchorage, July 24, National Archives, Record Group 79, Entry 6, Box 384.
18. Karstens letter to Director of 2/15/24, National Archives, Record Group 79, Entry 6, Box 384.
19. Cammerer letter to Karstens of 2/5/25, National Archives, Record Group 79, Entry 6, Box 381.
20. Grant H. Pearson, "A History of Mount McKinley National Park, Alaska," typescript administrative history prepared by the superintendent in 1953, 42-43; Mount McKinley NP "Building Inventory," prepared for the superintendent by Historical Architect Harold LaFleur, 9/16/75, in Denali NP&P archive; abstract of Mount McKinley NP "Headquarters Building Development," from Superintendent's Monthly Reports, 9/25 through 10/43, in Denali NP&P Archives; Dave Snow, Gail Evans, Robert Spude, and Paul Gleeson, *Historic Structure Report, Mt. McKinley Park Headquarters District & Wonder Lake*, 3 vols. (Anchorage: NPS, Alaska Regional Office, 1987).
21. Albright letter to Vint of 8/18/31, Denali NP&P Archives.
22. Mount McKinley National Park Act of 2/26/17 (39 Stat. 938), Sec. 6.
23. Burnham letter to Cammerer of 12/18/20, National Archives, Record Group 79, Entry 6, Box 384.
24. Cammerer letter to Karstens of 4/12/21, National Archives, Record Group 79, Entry 6, Box 384.
25. Karstens letter to Director of 4/23/21, National Archives, Record Group 79, Entry 6, Box 384.
26. Mount McKinley NP Rules and Regulations of 6/21/21, National Archives, Record Group 79, Entry 6, Box 384.
27. See Cammerer letter to Beard of 11/1/21, Natinal Archives, Record Group 79, Entry 6, Box 385.
28. Bureau of Mines corres. with Mather under cover of 10/15/21, National Archives, Record Group 79, Entry 6, Box 384.
29. National Parks Committee Minutes of 4/17/23, National Archives, Record Group 79, Entry 6, Box 384.
30. Secretary of the Interior, Annual Report of the Secretary of the Interior, 1923 (Washington: GPO, 1924), 82.
31. *The Pathfinder of Alaska*, Vol. 5, No. 3 (Jan. 1924), 13.
32. Interior Department Solicitor's opinion to Secretary of the Interior of 7/5/23, National Archives, Record Group 79, Entry 6, Box 384, 11-12.

33. See Cammerer letter to Congressman Cramton of 1/5/28, National Archives, Record Group 79, Entry 6,Box 370; Gov. of Alaska corres. with NPS, State Archives, Record Group 101, Boxes 277 and 291 (1927-1929).

34. See corres. in reference to Frank Dufrensne letter to H. W. Terhune of 11/9/27, National Archives, Record Group 79, Entry 6, Box 370.

35. Nelson letter to Acting Director Cammerer of 1/24/24, National Archives, Record Group 79, Entry 6, Box 370.

36. Karstens letter to Director of 1/4/24, National Archives, Record Group 79, Entry 6, Box 385.

37. Cammerer Memorandum for the Files of 2/6/24, National Archives, Record Group 79, Entry 6, Box 385.

38. U.S. Code, Title 16 (1982 edition), 198.

39. 46 Stat. 1043.

40. 90 Stat. 1342.

41. Grant Pearson, *My Life of High Adventure* (Englewood Cliffs, N.J.: Prentice Hall, Inc., 1962), 23.

42. Grant Pearson, "The Seventy Mile Kid" (Los Altos, Calif.: self-published, 1957), 7.

43. Ibid., 9.

44. Ibid., 10.

45. The importance of dogteam patrols and freighting permeates superintendent and ranger reports in the park archives, with Karstens' Nov. 1925 Monthly Report, setting up remote-area patrols a good example; see also the writings of Grant Pearson ("Seventy Mile Kid" and *My Life of High Adventure*), and the article by the late, lamented, McKinley ranger-interpreter Jim Shives, "The Sled Dogs of McKinley," *Alaska Magazine*, Vol. 44 (Oct. 1978), 6-8.46. Karstens telegram to Director of 7/17/24, National Archives, Record Group 79, Entry 6, Box 381.

47. Cammerer letter to Karstens of 7/1/25, National Archives, Record Group 79, Entry 6, Box 381.

48.Mount McKinley lands files in General Records, Alaska Regional Office; see particularly Morino and Stubbs files.

49. *Rand McNally Guide to Alaska and Yukon* (New York: Rand McNally Co., 1922), 8-9.

50. Alaska Steamship Company interview with Robert Rose (10/8/85), conducted by William Schneider, University of Alaska Oral History files.

51. ARR Circular Letter to All Agents of 7/12/24, National Archives, Record Group 79, Entry 6, Box 382.

52. Superintendent's Monthly Reports for May and June 1924.

53. Karstens letter to Oastler of 4/4/24, Denali NP&P Archives.

54. Steese letter to Cammerer of 7/12/24, National Archives, Record Group 79, Entry 6, Roads.

55. Superintendent's Monthly Report for May 1923.

56. Superintendent's monthly report for June 1923.

57. Steese letter to Karstens of 6/11/23, Denali NP&P Archives.

58. Brooklyn Eagle letter to Gov. of Alaska, State Archives, Record Group 101, Box 219; Superintendent's Monthly Report for July 1923; NPS Director's Annual Report for 1923, 167.

59. Alaska Railroad "Presidential Special" brochure, July 13-19, 1923, Denali NP&P Archives; National Park Service, Director's Annual Report for 1923 (Washington: GPO, 1924); Superintendent's Monthly Report for July 1923.

60. Alaska Railroad "McKinley Park Route" brochure, 1924, Denali NP&P Archives.

61. Karstens-Beach corres. of May-June 1922, Denali NP&P Archives; Nelson letter to Sheldon of 1/10/23, National Archives, Record Group 79, Entry 6, Box 385.

62. Cammerer letter to the Secretary of the Interior of 4/10/23, National Archives, Record Group 6, Box 385; Karstens letter to Director of 10/3/23, Denali NP&P Archives; Karstens letter to Gov. of Alaska of 2/5/24, National Archives, Record Group 79, Entry 6, Box 385; Dir. Mather letter to Del. Sutherland of 2/25/24, National Archives, Record Group 79, Entry 6, Box 385.

63. Leslie Marchand, "Mount McKinley," *Farthest-North Collegian*, Vol. 5, No. 1 (1927), 5-6, University of Alaska, Fairbanks, Archives.

64. Frank Norris, "Showing Off Alaska: The Northern Tourist Trade, 1878-1941," *Alaska History*, Vol. 2, No. 2, (Fall 1987), 8-9.

65. See Norris, Ibid.; Dorothy E. Haley, "The Steel Train into the Heart of Alaska," *The Pathfinder of Alaska*, Vol. 6, No. 6 (April 1924), 19-20; Roderick Nash, "Tourism, Parks and the Wilderness Idea in the History of Alaska," *Alaska in Perspective*, vol. 4, no. 1 (1981), 12-15; William H. Wilson, "The Alaska Railroad and Tourism, 1924–1941," *Alaska Journal*, vol. 7, no. 1 (Winter 1977), 18–24.

66. Olaus J. Murie, memorandum for Dr. Nelson of 12/11/25 in O. Murie Collection, University of Alaska, Fairbanks, Archives, Box 4; O. Murie field notes and draft reports re: Mount McKinlay work, 1920-1922, O. Murie Collection, Boxes 2, 4, and 7.

67. E. W. Nelson letter to Mather of 4/13/22, National Archives, Record Group 79, Entry 6, Box 385; associated corres. in this file records Karstens' assistance to Nelson in gathering various mammalian specimens for Biological Survey analysis beginning 1921.

68. O. Murie, Savage River Camp report, 5 pp., with map of upper Savage River camp and corral, O. Murie Collection, University of Alaska, Fairbanks, Archives, Box 2; O. Murie daily log, 6/26/22-10/24/22, O. Murie Collection, Box 7; Jule Loftus, "Corralling Carbou—A Wilder West Sport, "*Farthest-North Collegian*, Vol. 2, No. 1 (1924), 20-21.

69. George M. Wright, Joseph S. Dixon, Ben H. Thompson, *Fauna of the National Parks of the United States*, National Park Service Fauna Series, No. 1 (Washington: GPO, 1933), 4.

70. Ibid., 9-19.

71. Joseph S. Dixon, *Birds & Mammals of Mount McKinley National Park, Alaska*, National Park Service Fauna Series, No. 3 (Washington: GPO, 1938), ix.

72. Stowe letter to Cammerer of 3/23/25, National Archives, Record Group 79, Entry 6, Box 381.

73. Report on charges against Mr. H. P. Karstens to Chief Inspector, Post Office Department, of 6/29/25, National Archives, Record Group 79, Entry 6, Box 381.

74. See corres. re.: Karstens' resignation and replacement in National Archives, Record Group 79, Entry 6, Box 369.

75. Pearson, "Seventy Mile Kid," 10.

76. Superintendent's Monthly Reports, 1926-1928; various letters and memorandum reports to Director, including Karstens letter to Mather of 2/26/26, National Archives, Record Group 79, Entry 6, Box 369.

77. Pearson, "Seventy Mile Kid," 13.

78. Albright memorandum to Washington Office of 8/18/31, National Archives, Record Group 79, Entry 6, Box 201.

Alaska Railroad Tour Limousine at Igloo Cabin, 1948. From the Alaska Railroad Collection, AMHA.

Consolidation of the Prewar Park and Postwar Visions of Its Future

The 35 years between 1928 and 1963 traced a shift from meeting McKinley Park's functional necessities to defining the ideals that should shape its future.

Harry Liek, Karstens' hand-picked successor as superintendent, devoted most of his energy to rounding out the early park's geography and completing its basic physical plant. During his tenure the park was enlarged to include Wonder Lake and buffer lands to the northwest, and the lands between the 149th Meridian and the Nenana River to the east. He oversaw completion of the park road, immediately followed by the ARC's construction of the short spur to Kantishna. The park hotel near McKinley Station was built and opened. Crews of the Civilian Conservation Corps (CCCs) built the Wonder Lake Ranger Station—the park's operational anchor at the far end of the road—along with headquarters and other improvements.

Then came World War II. The park closed down its conventional operation and became an Army recreation center. The Park Service presence, severely cut in funds and manpower, was limited to critical maintenance and oversight of the Army occupation.

After the war—which gave Alaska a new transportation infrastructure—interest in Alaska development and tourism surged. National and territorial commissions and boards, expanding on Depression-era programs and studies, conceived Alaska as a giant reservoir of resources to expand the Nation's war-induced industrial might. The territory—visited during the war by a million soldiers, sailors, marines, and airmen, plus unnumbered civilian workers on bases and roads—was now known throughout the land for its unparalleled recreational opportunities: hunting, fishing, and the wild beauty of the Last Frontier.

And this was a different nation from the depression-ridden one before the war: more populous, richer, more powerful, and victorious. Workers, not just the elite, had money and—after peacetime retooling of factories—the mobility of cars and paid vacations. After the deprivations of the past 15 years, they were ready to roll. So Alaska beckoned for industrial development, tourists, and pioneers.

The Park Service responded to these historical forces with development plans of its own, focused on Mount McKinley National Park. The Korean Conflict slowed these plans, but only for awhile.

The prospect of the park's direct connection with Alaska's expanding road system—now connected to the rest of the North American road network—both scared and inspired the park's stewards. That connection would break the pattern of limited and controlled access by rail. Here was a park whose facilities could host only a few thousand visitors a year (the highest prewar number had been 2,200 in 1939). What would happen when the lock of isolation was broken? On the one hand, unless the park's physical plant were expanded (the hotel had less than 100 rooms; campsites were extremely limited) the park would frustrate the expected deluge of visitors. On the other hand, that connection would make the park a democratic institution, a place accessible to working people from both Alaska and the States. Thus historical change brought both threat and opportunity to the Park Service in Alaska.

Park headquarters complex, ca. 1932. From the Denali National Park and Preserve Archive.

Responding to the drumbeat of development and tourism boomers—who were backed by high-level studies and proclamations urging Alaska's integration into the Nation's industrial and recreational systems—Park Service policy-makers and planners envisioned a conventional Stateside park with a lodge at Wonder Lake, more campgrounds, and an upgraded road to accommodate independent auto-borne visitors. The elite would continue to be served tour-and-hotel style; the average family could drive in and camp as at Yellowstone.

The park road—narrow and winding—had been adequate for the low levels of commercially conducted bus and touring-car traffic when visitors were fed into the park by the trains. But it would have to be widened and straightened to handle large numbers of private-car visitors whose eyes would wander in search of wildlife and scenery.

Thus, an improved park road would become the transitional link between old times and new times, between old park and new park.

This planning concept—given funding impetus by the Park Service's MISSION 66 program (a nationwide catch-up in visitor facilities to be completed by the Service's 50th anniversary)—kicked off a lively debate about the park's future both in and out of the Service. Thoughtful people in or closely associated with the Service saw the park's purpose as a wildlife refuge endangered by such plans. Should these plans go forward, they feared the loss of the park's chief charm for visitors: its wild, uncrowded naturalness, its regal animals near and viewable from the low-speed, light-trafficked road because it *was* that kind of a road.

These arguments within were echoed and amplified by a growing conservation constituency without. By 1960 Alaska conservation organizations had become sophisticated and single-minded about not repeating the land-ravaging mistakes that marked the end of frontier Down Below. Mount McKinley National Park became the line in the sand in this struggle. If Alaska's wilderness could not be protected at McKinley Park where would it be safe? National organizations joined this fight, abetting the pressures on the Park Service to rethink its planning concept.

In the end, the road-improvement project and its major accessory developments were scuttled. The park ideal—the combination of wildlife and scenery envisioned by Charles Sheldon—was reaffirmed. The interior of this park would remain a wildlife sanctuary where people came truly as visitors—joining for awhile their mammalian cousins in wilderness adventure.

In this way the early '60s marked a turning point in the park's fate. The organizations and the ideals perfected and affirmed at that time would continue to influence the Nation's sentiments about Alaska's enduring values. This force of ideas would revive and largely prevail during the struggle over the National Interest Lands a decade later.

A CHANGE OF LEADERSHIP

Still superintendent of Yellowstone and assistant field director of the National Park Service in late 1928, Horace Albright recommended his trusted ranger associate Harry Liek as the man to replace Karstens at McKinley. In letters to Director Mather, Albright sketched Liek's dependability and his skill as leader and administrator. Here was a man who could work both sides of the boundary and get the park on a firm footing.[1]

Mather endorsed Liek and got Secretarial approval rapidly. Both Mather and Albright wanted quick action because Alaska's delegate to Congress was pushing local men, including parties to the disputes of the Karstens era.[2]

The park staff greeted Harry Liek's arrival with a sigh of relief. Internal and external strife had frayed the bonds of the park community and relations with neighbors. Toward the end of Karstens' administration, he and Chief Ranger Fritz Nyberg had become enemies. Salvage of Nyberg's usefulness was high on Liek's list of priorities.

In April 1929 Liek sent his first personal report to now Director Albright. He recounted his and Nyberg's trip into the park and their plans to improve existing patrol cabins and build three more along the northwest boundary, as Nyberg had long recommended. Liek relayed concerns about an earlier proposed park-hotel site at Copper Mountain, recommending instead, with Nyberg, a site on Clearwater Creek nearer the mountain. He welcomed the proposed visit of Chief Landscape Architect Tom Vint. Resolution of such planning problems should get the jump on the park road (which would reach Copper Mountain in 1934) or the road's progress would determine park development. Liek ended with an invitation to Albright to visit the park at the same time as Vint. Albright replied that he couldn't make it, but he agreed with the need for Vint's visit and said that he would assure it.[3]

During the winter of 1929-30, Nyberg—a tough Norwegian with his own Sourdough credentials—became critical of the new superintendent. He charged nepotism rampant (Liek's brother and nephew were working at the park), continued miserable conditions for patrol rangers, and misallocation of rangers' time: too much construction work on headquarters and patrol cabins instead of patrols to stop poachers. Continued minuscule appropriations had caught Liek in the bind reflected by Nyberg's

Ranger Bruce Wadlington with Mt. McKinley in the background, 1975. From the Denali National Park and Preserve Archive. NPS photo by William Garry.

inconsistency over the need for, and opposition to ranger construction of, patrol cabins and quarters.

In due course, after Albright had investigated these charges, Nyberg was considered disloyal and suspended, eventually leaving his position. Albright reaffirmed his support for Liek, urging him to get past this episode and carry on.[4]

By January 1931, Albright was frank in his disillusionment with Liek. Why was he spending so much time at headquarters, so little in the park? Could he not drop office detail and get on with the important work? Nyberg had resigned, but Albright regretted that a man so suited to the park had not been salvaged and retained. Albright struck to the heart of the matter with these words to Liek:

I had hoped that you would not only do your work in Mt. McKinley Park in a satisfactory way, in which way I am sure you are doing it, but I had hoped that as an old associate of mine in Yellowstone you would do really conspicuous work that would be enthusiastically talked about by people who come in contact with you. As it is, I hear nothing particularly adverse to you just as I find no particular interest in you or enthusiasm for you. Consequently, I have the impression that while you are minding your own business, doing a fair job of administration and protection, you are doing nothing outstanding and that you are really spending a good deal of time at headquarters instead of moving about the park studying its problems, particularly those of wild life, making plans for the future, gathering data regarding the natural features of the park, etc.

Finally, the Director called for a personal response from Liek explaining "how you think you are getting along," both in the park and in the territory, written in the same spirit "as you would if you were still Assistant Chief Ranger at Yellowstone and I was Superintendent there." He reiterated his continuing interest and affection, and his hope that Liek could do the really big things expected of him.[5]

In another letter two weeks later, Albright referred to Nyberg's charge that rangers spent too much time on construction, particularly around headquarters. The Director recognized Liek's funding bind as the reason for such use of manpower. Nevertheless, discounting emergencies, it was not NPS policy to put rangers on construction work:

You should arrange your work this coming season so that your rangers are used in patrols all the time and you yourself should make all the patrols you can. Mount McKinley National Park is not far enough along to need much in the way of headquarters and aside from the clerk I see no reason why anyone should spend much time at headquarters. I am expecting your men to be on the go right along. If they don't make patrols we will have to assume that their living conditions in the park, in the way of cabins, equipment, etc., were not adequate to support and protect rangers while on patrol and that this was due to the fact that the rangers had no opportunity to get their buildings and equipment in shape for the winter.[6]

Under the gun of Albright's two letters, Harry Liek hastened to reply in early February 1931. His letter covered Albrights criticisms point for point:
❋ Construction of the headquarters complex was the main project when Liek arrived at the park and he could not leave the buildings unfinished.
❋ Funding shortages forced him to draft rangers for construction during a good part of the summer so that the park would be prepared for winter, which would be an emergency without new quarters.
❋ The superintendent, lacking a construction foreman, as was standard in other parks, could not leave project supervision to his clerk; and as disbursing agent for the park, Liek had to be at headquarters periodically to sign checks and vouchers.
❋ Despite these anchors he had tried to make at least one patrol every month to monitor the park's condition, and in fact had been on patrol when Albright's letters arrived, thus the delay in answering them.
❋ The rangers had been in the field since August 15 and had carried out cabin and equipment repairs to facilitate winter patrols.
❋ Both Nyberg and the park clerk had asserted themselves as the old timers who should run the park and tell the new superintendent what to do. When the honeymoon was over, Liek saw that this was not just advice but rather an attempt to usurp his authority as superintendent. Upon refusing further dictates from his subordinates, they got sullen and conspired with others to cause him grief. In this pattern Liek saw a replay of Karstens' troubles.
❋ Liek challenged uncritical evaluations of Nyberg's value to park and Service, asserting that his brusque manner made many enemies.
❋ Liek agreed that he had done nothing conspicuous to put the park on the Alaskan map. He could make little headway with Alaska public opinion because "Alaska people do not visit the park like the people in the states do." He concluded this subject with the remark: "Right now it would be hard for a person to do anything conspicuous here unless it was to climb Mt. McKinley."
❋ Finally, Liek welcomed the Director's trip to the park, planned for summer 1931. Then he could see first hand what the country and the park were like and would not have to take somebody else's word for it. Meanwhile, Harry Liek would keep trying his best "to make a really big job" out of his superintendency.[7]

These exchanges of correspondence between Albright and Liek graphically portrayed McKinley Park's "rob Peter to pay Paul" problems. They also confirmed or set in train a series of important events in the park's history: 1) Tom Vint's 1929 visit and planning concept for the park; 2) Director Albright's 1931 visit; and 3) Liek's answer to Alaskan anonymity, the 1932 double ascent of Mount McKinley.

Upon his accession to the directorship, Horace Albright opened communications with Territorial Governor George Parks. His purpose was to reassure the Governor that the NPS took seriously its charge at McKinley Park, including its contribution to the territory's economic progress. Issues important to the Governor had been outlined in an earlier letter to Director Mather, before illness forced him to resign.

In that letter the governor summarized his discussions in Juneau with Service landscape architect Tom Vint and McKinley Superintendent Harry Liek, who had just conducted a planning reconnaissance in the park. They had agreed that the park could contribute little to the territory's economy until provision of adequate hotels at Seward, McKinley Station, within the park, and Fairbanks. The governor assumed that the park concessioner could finance a hotel or lodge within the park. But the other three hotels would require Outside money. Investors would have to believe in Alaska's future as a tourist Mecca, which depended largely on the park's role as magnet for the pilgrims.

This chicken-and-egg conundrum repeated the usual pattern at McKinley: one could not do the first thing until the second thing was already in place.

The Governor also mentioned park-boundary proposals broached by Vint and Liek. He rejected their idea of an easterly extension to the Nenana River. He stated that the strip between the current boundary (at the 149th Meridian) and the river was too busy with the railroad, landholdings, hunting and trapping, and mineral potential. Any attempt to take over this strip, even as a buffering game refuge, would enflame Alaskans against the government and cause endless administrative annoyance. He insisted that the existing park was big enough, and that development within existing boundaries should be the focus of NPS efforts.[8]

Responding to the Governor, Albright touched on the need for adequate ship service to Alaska and the potentialities of a proposed international road through Canada. He was pessimistic about assurances to hotel investors that the park could be rapidly developed. The Service got only marginal appropriations for stateside parks already crowded with visitors. Remote McKinley Park's uncertain future, especially given the extremely short summer season, would make both Congress and business leery of investment. Albright added that he planned a visit to the park and direct discussions with the Governor before pursuing the boundary issue further.[9] A month later, Albright wrote to the Governor about McKinley Park boundary discussions in the Secretary's Office, where agreement was reached that the boundary should be extended eastward only as far as the railroad right-of way. But no action would be taken pending the promised discussions with the Governor.[10]

The park's economic contributions to the territory would continue to be adduced as a justification for its existence and further development. In an economic-benefits report in 1931, Harry Liek listed these benefits: tourist expenditures on the three main routes through Alaska and the Yukon; replenishment of wild game and furbearers from the protected park to surrounding areas; the park-road project as construction-materials purchaser and employer of about 200 men each year; and upon the road's completion, its expected stimulation of mining activity in the Kantishna district.[11] In 1935 the park attracted 665 railroad tourists who bought tickets and overnighted at the railroad hotel at Curry, 20 miles north of Talkeetna; they also bought lunch at the railroad's Healy lunch stop and made hotel and miscellaneous expenditures at

Fairbanks, Nenana, Anchorage, and Seward—totalling an estimated $60,000 for the year.[12]

Throughout the '30s, because Katmai and Glacier Bay National Monuments (established in 1918 and 1925) were unmanned and rarely visited, there were no statistics from these areas. Sitka National Monument (1910), with only an intermittent custodian, attracted both local people and thousands of tourists from ships, but no expenditure figures were available.[13]

Landscape architect Tom Vint's 1929 reconnaissance at McKinley Park responded primarily to a substantive need: a professional overview to guide park planning and development. The trip also functioned as an earnest to the Governor and other Alaskans that the Service wanted to develop the park for visitor use, which, as a side benefit, would bring dollars to Alaska. With a planning concept at hand the Service stood a better chance of getting funds from Congress. Moreover, lacking such a plan—designed around park principles—the park would fall prey to exploitative development schemes hatched elsewhere.

As previously demonstrated, even in the early days such schemes abounded. And they would continue to surface as the years rolled on. Funds incident to New Deal programs provided the means to do some work in the park, but by then the park's master plan—a direct result of Vint's and subsequent planning—helped screen and channel the projects. As World War II wound down—with victory certain—a whole new generation of Alaska development studies began to proliferate. In the main, through the immediate postwar period, such studies, plans, and petitions treated McKinley Park principally as an economic asset whose yet latent value to Territory and Nation would be measured by the degree of park development and the number of tourists thus attracted.[14]

A postwar letter from Alaska Governor Ernest Gruening to the Interior Department's Office of Territories expressed the frustration shared by many Alaskans over the lack of development in the territory's parks and monuments. The trigger for this letter was a notification from the department that "The National Park Service is taking an increasing interest in tourist development of the Territory of Alaska; they have several people in the field this year studying the area." Gruening exploded:

My own view is that we have been studied ad infinitum, and that we know nearly everything there is to know about recreational facilities in Alaska, including and especially the fact that they continue year after year to be virtually non-existent. We also know that Park Service officials come year after year, survey, inspect, study, look us over, etc., etc. They are fine people, know their business, and we enjoy their company. But they are captains without a ship, officers in the Swiss navy. Their trips, while enjoyed by both us and them, result in nothing but pleasant memories for government officials—at public expense. What we need is some appropriations for facilities. If the money spent on these trips were accumulated we might in time have enough to build a small lodge in Glacier Bay National Monument, or we might be able to build one-half mile of road in Mt. McKinley Park from the long proposed, but non-existent, lodge at Wonder Lake to the Mountain. The trouble with these inspection trips, however, is that they emphasize and call attention to the continued lack of action in bringing about any park development. It is not surprising that a critical attitude had developed in Alaska at the great number of Federal officials who come to Alaska in the summer to "look the situation over."

Hence, while we shall continue to welcome these various Park Service officials at any time, I desire to emphasize with the urgency based on eleven years frustration in getting any favorable results—a frustration which however is much longer than my terms in office, that what we need is action at budgetary and Congressional levels before anything else.

Let us have something besides the wonders of nature for these Park Service inspectors to inspect.

Let us provide some man-made achievements in Alaska's parks and monuments for their study. Let us finally have something in Alaska for the public that pays the bills and is entitled to some return in the way of service.[15]

In reality, beginning with Vint's planning concept and on through the postwar period, the Service was more ally than opponent of the economic rationale for park development—but within certain bounds defined by "the park ideal." The thwarting of additional visitor facilities at McKinley came not from the Service, but from lack of appropriations that only Congress could provide. Mounting frustration bred of no apparent developmental progress in the parks, compounded by Alaska's largely government-inspired boomer psychology in the postwar period, led even enlightened commentators like Governor Gruening to vent outrage against the very principle of preserved lands. Other public land agencies—the Forest Service and the General Land Office (later the Bureau of Land Management)—provided not only recreational uplift but solid economic benefits through timber leases, mining, and land disposals for homesteads, fox farms, and manufacturing sites. In contrast, the Park Service studied but did nothing; meanwhile the huge chunks of Alaska land that it managed produced nothing.

This attitude and perception had deeper roots. Frontier notions—still very much alive in Alaska—that wilderness is the enemy, that the shaping of landscapes to human purpose and profit is the greatest good, offered little support to an institution whose park ideal spoke the opposite. The Service's middle-ground response to development clamor—some development but not too much—suffered public rebuff in the frustration produced by funding deficiencies that aborted even these modest proposals. And by the time the Service did get some appropriations, beginning about 1960, such modest developments were viewed as "too much" by wilderness preservationists, by then coalesced as a national constituency.

So much for context. What of the plans themselves? When Tom Vint came to the park in 1929, he already had a recommendation for a permanent hotel site deep within the park. Following a summer 1927 trip partly to scout such a site, Harry Karstens championed the Clearwater Creek area south of Wonder Lake at the very foot of the mountain. He proclaimed it " . . . the most suitable scenic spot and there are many, many wonderful side trips to be made both for hikers, mountain-climbers or on horseback . . . also the fishing is very good."[16]

Determining the site and type for a permanent hotel or lodge under the loom of the great mountain would continue to occupy park planners and commentators-at-large until 1970 when the idea was finally rejected. Tom Vint's immediate purpose was to provide definitive data for resolution of this issue, but first he must establish the park's place in Alaska:

The Territory of Alaska is a big, new and practically undeveloped country. Some of it is still unexplored. Over 95% of the land area belongs to the Government. The larger portion of this is administered under some bureau of the Department of the Interior. The Government's activities, taken as a whole, form the greatest single influence on the life and the development of the Territory.

The commercial interests are Fishing, Mining, Furs, Pulp and Lumbering. Alaska's possibilities as a recreation area are coming to be a very important element in its development. At present it is generally conceded that commercially, recreation facilities take third place in relative importance in the list named above. It may within a few years creep ahead to second and possibly first place. The outfitting and conducting of big game hunting parties has developed into quite a business. The general tourist trip business is, of course, the largest recreational factor. McKinley Park, it is generally conceded, is the big note of any trip which includes the interior of the territory.

The Park then holds a dominating place in the life of the territory. It contains the most important

Bus at Polychrome Pass, 1967. From the Denali National Park and Preserve Archive. NPS *photo by* P. G. Sanchez.

scenic area. It happens to be located where the park trip becomes the climax of any Alaska trip on which the park is included. This is a strategic position in a country where recreation plays such an important part.

On the other hand, few people will make the park the purpose of their trip. It will be the big note of a trip to Alaska. Its development will influence and equally be influenced by the development of all travel facilities that are used in making the trip from Seattle or Vancouver to the interior of Alaska. In planning and scheduling the development of McKinley Park we are obliged more than [at] any other place to work in accord with the development of the surrounding territory. If we progress too rapidly in providing accommodations, they will remain idle. If we are too slow, tourists will be denied the park trip. This dependence of the various developments is far reaching, for instance, if the steamship companies put on additional boats, hotels at the park and other points must be built and if the hotels are not provided, the additional boats cannot be put on. We find ourselves in one park where we are pioneering in a pioneer country. Our other parks came after the surrounding state was developed.[17]

This exceedingly intelligent statement illuminated much of the park's history and many of its troubles. The park, as a determining factor in the contextual development of Alaska, has never to this day achieved synchrony with its surroundings. In the early years, funding deficiencies held it back; later, and up to the present, preservation and wildlife concerns joined with continuing funding deficiencies to inhibit park developments that would match surrounding paces and pressures.

As "the big note" for Interior Alaska travelers, Mount McKinley/Denali National Park has been placed throughout its history in the incongruous position of commercial pace-setter for much of Alaska and its tour and transportation links with the outer world. But should park development respond willy-nilly to match this external pressure—now at explosive levels—the park's intrinsic values would be lost, particularly in the old park-refuge interior traversed by the park road. As we shall see, modern planning concepts, based on the park's enlargement on the south side, sought an alternative to flooding the park interior with traffic and development. But yet again, funding and decision deficiencies have foiled initiation of conventional park develop-

McKinley Park Station, 1963. From the Alaska Railroad Collection, AMHA.

ments on the less vulnerable south side. So the single road through the park, anchored on ever more powerful commercial winches at either end, stretches ever tauter between them.

Pending southside-development relief, designed to channel commercial pressures *away* from the park interior, Denali National Park will continue to be out of step with its encroaching commercial environment, and vulnerable to destruction of its historic purpose.

After a careful tour of hotel-site potentials with the superintendent and concessioner Jim Galen, including a look at the Clearwater site—which was too distant and difficult of access—Vint chose the well drained plateau below the modern Eielson Visitor Center. Here was firm ground, expansive enough for a major development and easily reached from the route marked out for the park road. It offered excellent views of the mountain and its lesser companions, though Mount Mather was blocked by the near bulk of Copper Mountain.

Vint's general plan included a hotel at McKinley Station, the concessioner facility at Savage River (serving as base camp for east-end wilderness trips), and the Copper Mountain (Mount Eielson as of 1930) hotel deep within the park (with hiking and pack trips toward the mountain). This assemblage, based on the railroad and concessioner-provided access via the park road, offered the choice of short-term or long-term visits, and both sophisticated and rustic facilities to meet differing visitor demands.

Vint saw the inevitability of direct road access to the park, but correctly predicted that private-auto access lay far enough in the future that it need not complicate this first-stage development concept.

The ARC's pioneer construction techniques on the park road worried Vint. He wanted better engineering plans to avoid later rerouting, which would leave unsightly road scars. Neither eventuality came to pass. The road, essentially as built by the ARC (beyond Teklanika), is the road still used today. As noted above, Vint's recommendation to move headquarters back to McKinley Station was rejected by Director Albright.

Pulling a touring car out of Savage River. The tourist camp is in the background. From the Herbert Heller Collection, UAF.

By the 1930s, the concessioner was relying on large tour buses. From the Skinner Collection, ASL.

With the completion of the proposed McKinley Station hotel, the railroad could abandon the Curry hotel as its passenger overnighting facility and rearrange train schedules to allow overnight visits to the park.

Air touring of the park, with its easily attained overviews of McKinley's vast landscapes and mountain architecture, appealed to Vint. He urged approval of a pending aviation permit and an adequate airfield.[18]

Wonder Lake still lay north of the park boundary when Vint was there, so he could not consider it as a hotel or lodge site. In 1929 the Copper Mountain area, with its views of McKinley and easy access to Muldrow Glacier and the range, formed the logical terminus of the park road. The boundary expansion of 1932 took in Wonder Lake, making the lake the logical terminus of the park road, and the preferred site for the interior-park hotel. The Copper Mountain/Mount Eielson site would become an intermediate viewpoint and concessioner camp, and, in later years, the site of an interpretive center.

Excepting that major variation, Vint's concept provided the park's planning frame for nearly 40 years. Lack of funds kept putting off construction of the Wonder Lake hotel/lodge, but it remained in the plans and was periodically revived as a hot project until about 1970.

With the postwar advent of private-auto access (quite modest until 1972), auto campgrounds would replace the concessioner camps of the railroad era. The outer-most of these auto-era campgrounds was established at Wonder Lake, at the south-end site originally reserved for the hotel/lodge.

In terms of actual visitor access and use, Vint's scheme—hinged on the park road, and adjusted for the 1932 boundary change, the failure to build an in-park hotel, and the onset of direct highway access—determined the park's essential infrastructure that is still in place today. In fact, terrain and the railroad determined the park entrance; terrain and in-park objectives determined the route of the park road. Vint's and subsequent planning simply embellished these determinants. Significant private-car access to the park since 1972 has determined all further adjustments, physical and operational. Terrain, transportation, and funding or lack thereof for alternate visitor-use sites will continue to dictate the substance of plans no matter how nicely phrased their rationale. The politics of preservation versus development will determine the real results of such plans. The park ideal will continue hostage so long as an inadequate single-option infrastructure constricts the mounting pressures of commercialization.

Director Albright and his associates in Washington endorsed the substance of Vint's report, the Director calling it "the most useful report that has yet been submitted on this park."[19] After a year's delay Albright visited the park in summer 1931. His appendicitis attack aborted his horse trip to hotel sites, but he flew over all of them, going on to Wonder Lake, which captured his imagination. Seeing it confirmed his intention to expand the park not only on the east end but also to include Wonder Lake and the buffering lands on the northwest boundary. He wanted the park road to extend to the lake and considered it a prime site for a fishing camp for visitors, perhaps even for the hotel. He liked Vint's hotel-site choice but counseled moving slowly for two reasons: First, the concessioner had been hard hit by the Depression-caused dearth of visitors. Thus, Jim Galen, president of the Mt. McKinley Tourist and Transportation Company, lacked finances to build an in-park hotel. Giving him use of the proposed hotel site for a temporary camp would help revive his fortunes, at the same time providing an immediate visitor facility in the heart of the park. Second, because the park was still in the pioneer stage of development such a sequence (camp then hotel) was appropriate. The temporary camp could be easily dismantled and the experience gained from its operation could prove useful for hotel planning.[20]

In another letter, Albright praised Vint's scenic "high line" routing of the park road between the Toklat forks, and the design by Vint's office of the East Fork bridge. Albright praised the park road:

Let me say also that I am very well pleased with the road that is being built in this park. It is frankly a pioneer highway for occasional use mainly by transportation buses. We will not live probably to see the time when many private automobiles

Arthur Gardner and a Fordson grader, along the park road, during the 1930s. From the Herbert Heller Collection, UAF.

*The Savage River cabin of Alaska Road Commission, in the
early 1930s. From the Herbert Heller Collection, UAF.*

*will use this road. No other kind of a highway could have been justified in this park. I am not worried
about curing the scar some decades hence. This country goes back to Nature about as fast as the Great
Smokies. I flew over the park twice, and from the air the highway, except in the passes, is hardly
traceable. So, as long as I am the Director of the Service, I shall hold to the present standards of
highway building, except, of course, in the case of opportunities such as that you seized between the
East Fork and main Toklat. One more thing I am disposed to let the road be built on to Wonder Lake,
provided, of course, we can get an addition to the Park to include the Lake. I want you to cover the
country between your hotel site and Wonder Lake before the road gets too far over that way. . . .*[21]

Both the 1922 and 1932 extensions of the park cited wildlife protection as their
principal rationale. Secondarily, these extensions were proposed to protect key natural features (e.g., Wonder Lake in 1932) and to encompass lands critical to park
administration, particularly on the east end.

In April 1921 Charles Sheldon had talked with Director Stephen T. Mather, Alaska
Delegate to Congress Dan Sutherland, and representatives of the General Land
Office, getting agreement from all of them that the original park boundary (running
north-south near Sanctuary River) should be moved 10 miles east toward McKinley
Station.[22] The 149th Meridian met this criterion and was chosen as the new north-
south line at the park's east end. The headquarters relocation of 1925 would still be
some two miles east and outside of the new boundary, but within the 1922 Executive
Order withdrawal that protected the park entrance.

The Senate Committee report on the 1922 extension noted that the mountainous
area east of the original park boundary, especially the headwaters of Riley and Windy
creeks, were prime breeding grounds for Dall sheep and much frequented by caribou
herds.[23] In an after-the-fact critique of the extension, Col. Frederick Mears, chairman
of the AEC, wanted additional extensions to north, east, and southeast for still more

protection of the game animals, which would be the primary attraction to tourists using the railroad. He warned that delay in moving the east boundary to Nenana River would cause the NPS untold grief by way of annoying and unsightly development in the park's forelands.[24]

As enacted, the January 30, 1922, extension took in the 10-mile strip east of Sanctuary River (but still west of Nenana River and the railroad), plus a narrow slice of land along the southeast boundary that captured the divide of the Alaska Range, giving that side of the park topographic definition. Even this extension was not without its opponents, who argued that further reservations around McKinley Park would deprive hunters and miners of choice land.[25] But the idea of capturing additional gamelands and the park's administrative forelands to the Nenana River, though delayed, would surface again.

The 1932 extension began with a report from Tom Vint to the Director in early 1930, following up on his just-completed planning report. Vint deplored the unnatural boundary formed by the straight line 149th Meridian, pushing instead for extension of protected lands to the natural boundary of the Nenana River. (This proposal revived the idea earlier expressed by Colonel Mears as he was completing construction of the Alaska Railroad.)

Because Governor Parks opposed extension of the park as such, but would accept a game-refuge designation on the park's east end—in effect a protective withdrawal against hunting and random development—the game refuge formed the heart of Vint's proposal. The Park Service would administer the buffer zone to the Nenana, but would not call it a park.[26]

A year later, Director Albright put fresh steam behind the east-extension idea, calling for outright extension of the park to the river. With this support, Vint joined the

*Alaska Road Commission fill work along the main
park road. From the Herbert Heller Collection, UAF.*

The Alaska Road Commission road crew. From the Herbert Heller Collection, UAF.

chorus for direct action. The park extension to the river—excluding the railroad right-of-way—would provide an unambiguous natural boundary and facilitate patrol and game protection. He noted that Governor Parks and General Manager Otto Ohlson of the Alaska Railroad still opposed park extension. Ohlson *wanted* development along this section of railroad as a source of freight revenues for his trains;[27] thus he differed from his predecessor, Colonel Mears, who had seen protected parklands all the way to the Nenana as a lure for tourist traffic. This institutional shift may have reflected differences in temperament between the two men; it surely reflected the deficit-ridden railroad's growing disillusionment with tourist traffic as a significant source of revenue.

Then ensued a series of letters and negotiations between Director Albright and Governor Parks. By late 1931 the Governor had shifted his position. Instead of urging the railroad as the park's eastern boundary, he now counseled Albright to go to the river to avoid "administrative problems that may be exceedingly difficult to control." He was talking about "undesirable citizens [who] have squatted on the lower reaches of Riley Creek and conducted bootlegging establishments to the detriment of the railroad employees and others."[28]

Albright, having become aware of these problems, had meanwhile reversed *his* position and was now loath to go beyond the railroad. There were enough problems even with the line of the railroad, including the Morino homestead, which would have to be bought out. Why acquire more?

At the other end of the park, the Governor had long favored the acquisition of Wonder Lake as a hotel site. He had further urged that lands in the lake's vicinity and along the northwest boundary be taken to capture game-rich but mineral-free hills and drainages. The Anderson homestead and fox farm at Wonder Lake's north end would also have to be acquired in time. Albright eventually acceded to the Governor's views.

With the Governor's support, Judge Wickersham introduced the bill extending the park eastward to the Nenana, northward to include Wonder Lake, and with adjustments northwest and westerly to acquire game ranges in the Kantishna Hills-McKinley River quadrant.[29]

In a memorandum to the Secretary, published in the Senate Committee report on the park-expansion legislation, Director Albright neatly summarized the advantages of these additions, which, when enacted and approved on March 19, 1932, would define the nearly 2-million acre park until 1980:

The east side extension from Windy Creek north brings the park boundary to the right of way of the Alaska Railroad. There are a few isolated tracts lying east of the Alaska Railroad right of way and the west bank of the Nenana River which should also be included in the park, as proposed by amendment No. 4, hereinafter recommended. This would make the west banks of the Nenana River for all practicable purposes a natural boundary line for the park. This extension will bring into the park the administrative headquarters development now constructed on lands withdrawn for this purpose. The National Park Service already maintains roads and trails within this area, and the main park road begins at the railroad station. A new hotel will sooner or later be erected near the railroad and this park road. This hotel should be on park land and built under park policies regarding architecture. Furthermore, better protection can be given the mountain sheep in this section, because the present line is now high up on the side of mountains and can not be observed by hunters to avoid trespass and for the same reason can not be physically patrolled by rangers.

The proposed extension to the northwest will bring Wonder Lake into the park. The shores of this lake would provide an advantageous site for another hotel-lodge development and would afford a finer view of Mount McKinley than any now had in the park. The extension would permit us to continue to this scenic region the road now being constructed. In the most part this area consists of lowlands well adapted for game uses, especially during winter, and will form a better boundary line from a game-protection standpoint. It will also aid in better conserving the moose in the park by giving them winter range protection. An additional benefit from Alaska's standpoint would come from the opening of the Wonder Lake region under the park program. It would then be a comparatively simple matter for the territory to connect up with the Kantishna district making that region accessible.[30]

The administrative problems that came with the new lands made prior warnings about them seem woefully understated. Critical inholdings included: those surrounding McKinley Station (Maurice Morino, 120 acres; Dan Kennedy, 5 acres; and D. E. Stubbs, 35 acres); the 130-acre John Stevens claim at Windy, on the railroad at the park's southeast corner; and the 160-acre Paula Anderson homestead at the north end of Wonder Lake. In addition to these valid homesteads and trading-manufacturing sites were a score or more squatters' cabins tucked into the new park landscapes by wintering miners, hunters and trappers, and bootleggers. Exclusion of the squatters, though a painful and thankless task, occurred fairly rapidly. Most of these cabins—after salvage of the occupants' personal effects, if the men could be found—were burned or dismantled.

But owners with valid holdings made claims for damages incident to the boundary

Morino's Roadhouse and McKinley Park post office, 1938. From the Alaska Railroad Collection.

change: Dan Kennedy complained that his guiding business had been ruined; D. E. Stubbs asserted that park rangers loosed dogs near his fox pens, to the ruination of his fox-farm business. Some of these claims resulted in payment of damages by the government.

Because the private establishments bordering the railroad were derelict and unsightly—as well as being haunts of "undesirable citizens," as Governor Parks had phrased it—negotiations to purchase these properties were recommended by General Land Office investigators. Lack of funds delayed timely purchase by the government, even from the few willing sellers. As these deals dragged out, resentments fanned by Stubbs and others—plus episodes incident to NPS law enforcement, e.g., breaking up stills—embittered the entire process. Resultant condemnations to rid the park of noxious and hazardous establishments clinched the adversarial attitudes. Not until late 1947, with transfer of the deed to the long-contested Morino estate, were all privately owned lands within the park acquired—not counting unpatented mining claims, which did not involve land ownership[31]

It had been 15 years of stress and strain for all involved. As the years went on, new judges and juries rendered condemnation judgments. Apparent inconsistencies of legal interpretation and land prices, plus overt political interventions, produced widely varying judgments: thousands of dollars awarded in one case, paltry hundreds in another. Indeed, there was pain and attrition on both sides of these land dealings as the voluminous records of the cases indicate. For the park people, these unpleasant and seemingly endless tasks were the price paid to cohere the park and assure its legally mandated protection.[32]

After the war—with Morino long dead and buried at the park (March 1937),[33] and the bitter days fading into the past—the pioneer roles of Maurice Morino and his roadhouse spurred then-Supt. Frank Been to consider the building's preservation as a historic site. Investigation of the collapsing remains by an NPS landscape architect in 1948 put a damper on this idea: they were dilapidated beyond repair and an eyesore at the very entrance to the park. The issue was resolved when Jessie L. Shelton, bumming through the park on May 30, 1950, took shelter in the roadhouse and, while reposed on a cot, dropped a cigarette on the littered floor. Perhaps in gratitude for his beneficent arson—and in practical recognition of his destitution—Jessie was not prosecuted.[34] Remains of the charred ruin were razed in 1951.[35]

CLIMBING THE MOUNTAIN TO MAKE A POINT

It will be recalled that Harry Liek's debut as superintendent struck Horace Albright as a bit plodding. He wanted Liek to do something outstanding and conspicuous to get the park back in the good graces of Alaskans. Liek replied that in Alaska's climate

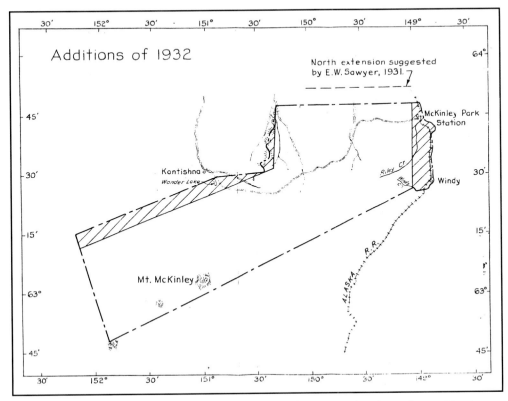

A *map showing 1932 park addition. From* Mount McKinley National Park, *Kauffmann, Map 4.*

A few rugged tourists took pack trips to McGonagall Pass, or to the ice formations at Muldrow Glacier. This photo of a Muldrow Glacier ice bridge was taken in 1931. From the J. C. Reed Collection, USGS.

of opinion he would have to climb Mount McKinley to make a mark.

So that is what he did, in 1932, with Minneapolis attorney Alfred Lindley, Norwegian skier Erling Strom, and park ranger Grant Pearson. This last of the old-time mountaineering expeditions used dog teams to freight supplies to the 11,000-foot camp on Muldrow Glacier. These were the first men to ascend both peaks, climbing South Peak via Karstens Ridge and Harper Glacier, then traversing Denali Pass to North Peak.

On their return to Muldrow Glacier they found the abandoned camp of the 1932 Cosmic Ray Party, led by Allen Carpé. A research engineer and mountaineer, Carpé had been commissioned by the University of Chicago to measure cosmic rays on Mount McKinley's high flanks. The Lindley-Liek group searched the camp vicinity and found the body of Theodore Koven, Carpé's assistant. Apparently he had died from exposure after being injured in a nearby crevasse, where signs pointed also to Carpé's fate: ski tracks, a broken snow bridge, and silent, blue depths. Study of this scene indicated that Koven, in trying to help Carpé, had injured himself. Koven's body was eventually retrieved from the mountain, but Carpé had to remain in his tomb of ice.

These were the first fatalities on Mount McKinley. The Cosmic Ray Party also inaugurated the technique of air transport and glacier landings by ski plane. Bush pilot Joe Crosson had set them down at the 5,700-foot level on Muldrow. This mode of access broke the logistical lock on Mount McKinley and became standard practice for later expeditions.

In 1934 the Charles Houston party made the first ascent of Mount Foraker, using pack horses for the overland approach. Bradford Washburn of Boston's Museum of Science began his long association with the mountain in 1936. Sponsored by the National Geographic Society and Pan American Airways, he made an aerial photographic exploration of the massif, taking 200 photographs that revealed the mountain's most remote and intricate secrets. On this trip he discovered the Kahiltna Glacier-West Buttress route to South Peak, which he would pioneer 15 years later.

Washburn joined the U.S. Army Alaskan Test Expedition of 1942, led by Lt. Col. Frank Marchman. This 17-member party camped in the high basin of Harper Glacier for lengthy testing of cold-weather food, tents, and clothing. Seven members, including Washburn and Terris Moore, chronicler of the pioneer climbs, made the third ascent of South Peak.

In succeeding years, the pace of climbing and route pioneering accelerated. Glacier landings gave access to high base camps that would have been inaccessible by ground approach. The massif's secondary peaks and isolate features were climbed by parties seeking "firsts" in mountaineering annals.

Highlights include:

❊ 1947, first ascent of Mount McKinley (both peaks) by a woman, Barbara Washburn. On this expedition Brad Washburn performed survey observations from the peaks, and cosmic ray studies at Denali Pass.

❊ 1951, Brad Washburn and Moore land on Kahiltna Glacier during mapping expedition, setting stage for Washburn's South Peak ascent via West Buttress a month later.

❊ 1954, Glacier Pilot Don Sheldon makes first commercial flight from Talkeetna to Kahiltna Glacier, thenceforth the standard approach for McKinley climbers.

❊ 1960, Brad Washburn's map of Mount McKinley published by Boston Museum of Science,

Secretary of the Interior Harold L. Ickes, during his 1938 visit, near Camp Eielson. From the "Alaska Railroad Album, 1938," AMHA.

177

American Academy of Arts and Sciences, and Swiss Foundation for Alpine Research. The result of 15 years of exploration, survey, and laboratory work, this masterful cartographic and artistic production remains the standard map for climbers.

✻ 1961, Italian Alpine Club party ascends South Peak via its sheer 6,000-foot ice-and-granite south face, called by Brad Washburn at the time "the greatest achievement in American mountaineering history."

✻ 1963, a seven-man party led by Henry Abrons climbs North Peak via the 14,000-foot Wickersham Wall.

✻ 1967, Art Davidson, Raymond E. Genet, and David Johnston make first winter ascent of South Peak, via West Buttress.

✻ 1967, seven members of Muldrow Glacier-South Peak expedition die in storm during descent, the worst McKinley climbing disaster.

✻ 1970, first solo ascent of South Peak by Naomi Uemura of Japan (who would die in 1984, on descent, after first winter solo ascent of South Peak).

From the mid-'60s on, climbing at McKinley began to proliferate and fall into broad categories: 1) standard guided climbs by parties following established, non-technical routes; 2) expedition parties seeking to pioneer ever more difficult routes, including climbs of highly technical features and lesser peaks; and 3) party and solo climbs and traverses that sought "firsts" in new combinations of mode (skis, dogs, hang-gliders, etc.), route, difficulty, and season.

All categories suffered increasing fatalities. More and more people climbed the standard routes, which were less demanding technically, but killed by storm, exposure, altitude sickness, and simple fatigue that led to accidents. As more experts stretched human capabilities to break point with technical feats and innovative combinations, more of them died, too.

All of these hazards came together in 1976—the Nation's Bicentennial—when 95 expeditions assaulted the massif. That year 33 climbers, out of 671 registered, suffered accidents—10 of them fatal. They required 21 separate rescue operations at great cost to the taxpayers.[36]

The NPS has been criticized both for *imposing* climbing regulations and experience-equipment screening, and for *lack* of screening and control over climbers. Improved procedures and facilities, spurred by the 1976 crisis, have saved many. These improvements include the ranger station-reception center at Talkeetna, with its specialized mountaineering rangers; medical camps on the mountain; and a network of public and private rescue groups who regularly accomplish prodigies of skill and courage—and sometimes die in their attempts to rescue others.

Modern mountaineering at McKinley has become a philosophical thicket: attitudes toward the mountain (conquest? caper? or spiritual quest?); freedom vs. restraint; life and death, for one's self and perhaps others; and the issue of park and wilderness ideals. Does freedom include freedom from rescue and from the Service's obligation to rescue? How far must people go to prove themselves against this enduring mountain? How bizarre their methods? And at what cost to the mountain's dignity, to rescuers, and to the taxpayer? Seeking the balances between mountaineering freedom and social responsibility, between intrinsic park values and transient human exploit will go on, probably indefinitely, but we must leave it here.[37]

Harry Liek's 1932 climb did help him gain public acceptance as "a real Alaskan." His association with Alaskan leaders on Depression-era commissions, boards, and recreation and economic surveys gave him access to public gatherings where he could push the park message and achieve first-name recognition in the territory's higher councils.[38]

Meanwhile, day-by-day work at the park moved along. Liek queried Washington about his jurisdiction over hunting in the railroad right-of-way, now included in the expanded park. The departmental solicitor's opinion held that it was the intent of Congress that the right-of-way ". . . should be subject to the provisions of law and regulations, applicable to lands within the National Park, not inconsistent with the operation and maintenance of the railroad."[39]

A 1935 report by the Interior Department's division of investigations indicated that Superintendent Liek had worked constructively with concessioner Jim Galen to provide adequate and comfortable visitor facilities at the Savage River camp, which now contained 100 "thoroughly clean and sanitary" tent houses, "10 x 12 feet, with board floors and sides and canvas roof. They contain two single iron beds, a small wood-burning stove, and table and chairs." Meals cost $5.50 a day, tents $3 per person, $4 for two. Round-trip transportation between station and camp cost $7.50.

Train service had been adjusted so that visitors could stay at least 24 hours in the park. Two package auto-touring trips, including lodging and meals, (24 hours at $25; 48 hours at $42.50) gave visitors access to Polychrome Pass or farther on to Eielson for close-up views of Mount McKinley. Guided horseback trips cost $15 per day. The flight-seeing trip from Savage River camp to the mountain cost $35.

Special Agent S. E. Guthrey gave high marks to park administration and to the propriety of the superintendent's dealings with the concessioner and with cinematographers employed for a promotional film by the Alaska Steamship Company. Questions on these matters had caused the investigation.[40]

In 1935 Liek proposed a number of physical improvements to be funded by the Public Works Administration, a New Deal agency that provided work for the jobless. In addition to employee quarters and housekeeping items, he wanted a radio telephone system for connections with outlying patrol cabins, a new administration building to replace the old one-room office, an interpretive museum at Eielson, and a ranger station at the Wonder Lake end of the road. He also wanted straight poles for the telephone line between headquarters and Eielson camp because the tripods supporting the line kept blowing down. These improvements were disapproved but would be revived under the CCC's program a few years later.[41]

By 1937, Washington officials, concerned that McKinley Park's purpose as a game preserve continued to be eroded by remote-area poaching, advocated aerial patrols. Living quarters for park personnel were still inadequate for the park's climate. And there were rumblings about a road connection to the park from Richardson Highway that would require significant changes at the park.[42]

That same year the American Consulate General in Calcutta, India, wrote to now Director, Arno B. Cammerer:

I was interested especially in one statement in . . . [your] press release in which it was pointed out that Mt. McKinley rises higher than any other mountain in the world above its own base. That this was so insofar as North American mountains are concerned, I already knew, but from the world standpoint this statement does not stand. I thought you would be interested to know that the famous Himalayan peak, Nanga Parbat, rises to an even greater height on its northern side than the total height of Mt. McKinley. Where the Indus washes the northern base of Nanga Parbat, the river has an elevation of just under 3,500 ft., and less than ten miles back from the river Nanga Parbat pushes its head into the blue to an elevation of 26,620 ft., thus at this point there is a sheer elevation of 23,120 ft., which so far as I am aware is the greatest sheer elevation attained by any mountain above its base. I have not yet had the good fortune to see this mighty spectacle, but I am still hoping that it will be possible before I leave India.

A cryptic and perhaps glum marginal note on this letter states: "verified by U.S.G.S."[43]

Matters of deeper substance also simmered during these years. The National Park Service had inherited a congeries of new areas under the Government Reorganization Act of 1933: many historical areas and a number of lesser reserves that, in the opinion of critics, did not match up to the pure parks created under the original National Parks impulse. The watchdog National Parks Association in 1936 tackled this problem with a paper on "The Place of Primeval Parks in the Reorganized National Park System." Robert Marshall and Robert Sterling Yard stated the gist of the association's thinking: The great primeval parks constitute a separate, superior class, which by title, mode of administration, and permitted uses must always stand distinct from parklands that bear the human signature. The association denied any deprecation of other park types in this segregation. They had their useful purposes, but they were different purposes.

Of the great parks the writers said: "The brilliance of these primeval areas results from their unaltered condition of descent from the beginning. There is no mistaking primeval quality." As modern civilization and exploitation cut across America's wild landscapes only remnants of the primitive remained—the few primeval parks (including Mount McKinley) and certain unexploited segments of National Forests.[44]

Of course this was an old idea, the notion that Nature untrammeled, unaltered by human purpose was yet of value to humans for the uplifting of the spirit inspired by untamed majesty and beauty. This concept treated not only of esthetics, but also of ethics and science. The Deists of the late eighteenth century—a number of them founders of the nation—conceived Nature as a great watch assembled and set in motion by the Deity. It was only proper that some zones should run on Nature's time, that human beings should respect and care for the Creator's creation. In such zones scientists could study Nature's unmodified processes and the relationships between its parts. In this view ecology became a sort of intellectualized mysticism.

Thus was revived in the '30s—a time of desperation, Dust Bowl, and reflections on the Nation's plundered patrimony—the distinction between Nature and natural resources, between superior value and economic benefit, between awe and board feet. This split in conservation philosophy played out a fascinating subset at McKinley Park—a struggle that helped to save it as a National Primeval Park.

THE WOLF-SHEEP CONTROVERSY

As the result of a series of unusually hard winters at McKinley Park in the late '20s and early '30s, the Dall sheep population dropped precipitately.[45] Extremely deep snows and severe cold prevented the usual wind-clearing of snow cover from the high ridges where sheep found their winter forage. Many sheep died of starvation and those that survived faced the next hard winter in weakened condition. This condition, only partly recouped each summer, made the sheep easier prey for disease and wolves. Here was a classic combination for a population "crash," which came with a vengeance. Where there had been thousands of sheep, suddenly there were scattered hundreds.

The organizations that had helped found the park had focused their interest on the big game animals, particularly Dall sheep and caribou. The sheep, given Charles Sheldon's interest in them, symbolized the park for the game-protection groups that

Dall Rams. From the Denali National Park and Preserve Archive.

had worked so hard for its establishment. Responding to Alaskan reports that as many as 1,000 sheep and an equal number of caribou had been killed by wolves over the 1930-31 winter, William B. Greeley of the Camp Fire Club of America enquired of Director Albright in July 1931 how he planned to control predators and preserve the game animals. Greeley's letter ended with a pointed comment that the club's conservation committee ". . . does not in the least share the views of those sentimentalists who would rather let the mountain sheep be wiped out by depredators than to destroy any of the depredators."[46]

This letter and line of argument kicked off a jurisdictional and philosophical struggle that lasted 20 years. The main questions were: Did the Founding Father game-protection groups run this park, or did the NPS? Was specific game-species management—with its corollary of predator control—the proper management scheme for a National Park? Or were all native species protected under an ecosystem-management concept in which predators, by culling the weaker ungulates, kept those species vital and healthy over the long term?

Early on the Service defined its position as one of "preserving all forms of wildlife in their natural relationship."[47] Opponents of this position marshalled alarming figures on McKinley game-species deaths by predation, which could not be proved and were considered suspect by the NPS. The Service attributed declining wildlife populations to weather, migration patterns, and other natural dynamics, including predation as a contributing cause. Next the NPS was accused of bureaucratic foot-dragging in predator control; its theoretical and romantic approach toward predators produced carnage on the ground, leading to destruction of the park's choice game animals.[48] This position fitted well with prevailing game-management and bounty-hunter attitudes in Alaska. Thus, ironically, the Eastern game-protection elite, which had chastised Alaska's "wanton killers of game" during the earlier Alaska Game Law debates, now found itself aligned with the locals against the NPS.[49]

It must be understood that both sides to this controversy, bitter though it became, were moved by the highest motives. Moreover, the successive NPS directors drawn into this maelstrom had no interest whatsoever in alienating the game-protection groups whose efforts had led to McKinley Park's establishment. The differences between them were philosophical at base. These differences were fanned by other parties, for example by those Alaskans who wanted predator control both to increase huntable game and to keep bounty income flowing. But it was the difference in philosophy that counted. The depth and political volatility of the controversy forced the Service to refine its all-species-in-natural-relationship position through scientific studies. In aid of this work, the Service solicited help from some of the Nation's leading mammologists and ecologists. To avoid threatened imposition of statutory requirements for control of wolves, the Service compromised with a limited wolf-control program, a course legitimized by Adolph Murie in 1945. It is to the Service's evolving philosophical position, and the use of science to support it, that we now turn.

Responding to alarming figures for game animals, especially sheep, published by the game protection alliance, Supt. Harry Liek in 1935 made an aerial survey with Alaska game warden-pilot Sam White. They estimated 3,000 sheep in the park. Liek thought that this represented neither a decrease nor a significant increase from the past few years, but rather a restabilization of the sheep population at a lower level after the crash.[50]

In 1938 the Service announced publication of Joseph Dixon's *Birds and Mammals of Mount McKinley National Park*, using that opportunity to further explain a natural regime in which variations of animal populations follow cycles dictated by habitat conditions and other dynamics. "Preservation of the native values of wilderness life," said author Dixon, is the ideal that differentiates NPS policy from those of sister agencies. The National Parks, as Director Cammerer had frequently stated, allow wild animals to behave like wild animals in their natural settings.[51] This let-Nature-take-its-course philosophy might register some disturbing perturbations, such as animal-population crashes. But this non-manipulative approach took the long view of natural rhythms and balances, and was the price of preserving the naturalness that gave ultimate meaning to wilderness parks.

In 1939 the Service sent Dr. Adolph Murie to the park to study predator-prey relationships. Exaggerated accounts of wolf numbers and their slaughter of wildlife would not die. The Service realized that it must develop a sound, science-based rationale for its hands-off (in reality, its light hands-on) wolf/sheep policy, or political pressure would force wolf extermination at the park. NPS biologist L.J. Palmer emphasized the importance of Murie's work both for McKinley Park and for other parks facing similar problems. Only accurate and complete data would validate Service policy and provide precedent across the country.[52]

The voluminous files of the wolf-sheep controversy furnish a fascinating case study of this ecologically motivated agency moving across fields of fire directed by the entrenched attitudes of an earlier age. The notion of favored animals derived from an older philosophy, manifested in game preserves and game-management practices of Europe's hunting nobility. Predators and particularly wolves symbolized the antithesis of Man's rationality imposed on chaotic Nature; to allow them free rein was to regress to pre-civilized times. For the advocates of wilderness and naturalness—called forth by the destructive impacts of industrialized civilization—opponents of the inclusive tenets of ecology were themselves regressive. Into this ideological maelstrom marched Doctor Murie who, respected on all sides, would do his best to reconcile these differences in thought.

Murie's conclusions, after field research in 1939-41, acknowledged that the sheep population was down and had not recovered from the hard winters of the 1927-32 period. But the current relationship between sheep and wolves seemed to have reached equilibrium. In fact, the limited predation by wolves probably had a salutary effect on the sheep, as a population, by eliminating weak and sick animals from the stock.[53]

As a result of Murie's analysis the Service decided to terminate a limited wolf-control program that had been in effect since 1929.[54] This change of policy created a virulent backlash. A petition to the President and the Congress from the Alaska Legislature, backed by nearly all public and private organizations in the territory, called for extermination of wolves in McKinley Park and other NPS areas which, said the petition, served as sanctuaries for breeding wolves that migrated and spread havoc across the land.[55] NPS Director Newton B. Drury, though a strong supporter of his biologists' ecosystem approach, read the signs of the petition and coincident drumming for a wolf-control law by stateside game protectionists as omens too strong to ignore. In an ironic note to his chief biologist, Victor H. Cahalane, he asked, "Hadn't something better be thrown to the wolves?"[56]

This message coincided and comported with the results of Murie's second survey, which rang alarm bells. In 1945 Murie counted only 500 sheep in the park. This was getting close to a critical population that might not be able to sustain any further shocks—including wolf depredations—without danger of extinction from the park.[57]

Interior Secretary Harold L. Ickes joined Drury in advocating resumption of limited wolf control with his endorsement of a program that called for destruction of 15 wolves in the park. This control program would be conducted under direction of Adolph Murie, who would become the park's resident biologist.[58]

The rules of the wolf-sheep controversy changed qualitatively with introduction of H.R. 5004 in December 1945. This bill would require the Service to rigidly control wolves and other predators in McKinley Park in favor of game animals.[59] As a precedent with System-wide implications, this proposed legislation posed great danger. It would sabotage the Service's painfully established policy of preserving all native flora and fauna as necessary elements of the ecosystem. This challenge forced the Service beyond compromise and delaying tactics, for the very foundation of its wildlife philosophy now came under fire.

Director Drury and his associates worked with key friends of the Service to mobilize opposition. In May 1946 esteemed scientist Aldo Leopold of the University of Wisconsin joined the fight against the bill, volunteering his willingness "to do anything I can within reason to help kill it."[60] Ira N. Gabrielson of the Wildlife Restoration Institute responded positively to Drury's plea for assistance. Kenneth A. Reid of the Izaak Walton League of America urged Congress to reject the legislation on the basis that executive agencies could not respond to changing wildlife conditions if their discretionary powers were abrogated by gross statutory control over Nature's "minute mechanics." The Boone & Crockett Club, though ambivalent on the issue, refused to endorse the bill. William Sheldon, the principal Founder's son, argued not only the biological case but also the ethical and aesthetic ones for keeping wolves in Nature's sanctuaries. For him the park's 500 sheep with wolves was better than more sheep without wolves, for "the wolf is the essence of what we refer to when we speak of 'wild' animals." He concluded with the formula: Necessary control, yes, in the present critical situation; but extirpation, no. With this support at hand, in April 1947, Interior Secretary Julius A. Krug recommended against the bill, pledging such administrative control of wolves as necessary to preserve McKinley's sheep and other ungulates.[61]

Though the wolf-sheep controversy and limited wolf control continued for a few more years, the legislative threat was dead. The Service had threaded its way through both biological and political thickets. By 1952, with noticeable recovery of the sheep and a reduced wolf population, the control program was ended, having destroyed some 70 wolves since 1929.

Among a series of reports from distinguished biologists, solicited by the Service at the height of the controversy, was one by Dr. Harold E. Anthony, Chairman and Curator of the American Museum of Natural History. He advocated the Murie concept of wolf control—for both biological and political reasons—for the term necessary to assure sheep recovery. He made the distinction between beneficial, manipulative control to rectify an extreme natural situation, and the atavistic drive to *exterminate* wolves as a malignant species—the view that had clouded the wolf-control debates. In the letter forwarding his report to Director Drury, Doctor Anthony neatly summed up the Service's stresses and compromises, and the formula finally adopted for surviving this crisis:

I know [Victor] Cahalane has been holding out valiantly for the principle involved in this problem. He believes the wolf has just as much right in the Park as the sheep. I agree with him on that if this can be kept as a matter of theory. Unfortunately, the situation in the Park, for more reasons than one, has passed to the stage where the average man will not accept it on a theoretical basis. Furthermore, I consider that when one really believes in a principle he should maintain it and not make concessions to expediency. But if a conservationist is trying to get the best possible break on any particular issue, he may reach the point where it is necessary to decide whether he will take a stand that calls for all or nothing. Personally, I fear for the future of the wolf in the Park unless some concession in the way of active control is made now. And I really believe that the welfare of the sheep at this time requires it.[62]

A byproduct of Adolph Murie's assignment to the park during the wolf-sheep controversy was publication of his reports and observations in The Wolves of Mount McKinley (1944). Its portraits of the wolf and associated predator and prey species comprise a brilliant tapestry whose interwoven threads lead painlessly to ecological

The McKinley Park Hotel under construction, 1938. The hotel
opened in June 1, 1939. From the Ray B. Dame Collection, AMHA.

understanding. In his footsteps the distinguished wolf authority, Dr. L. David Mech, today continues studies of Denali's wolves and the ecosystem that sustains them. It seems that all students of this singular animal—so highly social, so symbolic, so powerful and cunning—fall under the spell of its primeval cry, the very essence of that which is wild.

THE HOTEL PROJECT

Wrapping up the first-stage development of the park occupied the last few years before World War II. Critical to McKinley Park's function as a partner in Alaska's economic development—via attraction of tourists to the territory—was construction of a first-class hotel at the McKinley Station entrance. Alaska Governor Ernest Gruening and Interior Secretary Harold Ickes worked together to get funding for the hotel through the Works Progress Administration, with $350,000 appropriated in 1937.[63]

Interior of the McKinley Park Hotel, 1946. From the Hickock Collection, USGS.

Two principles framed Secretary Ickes' approach to this project: As a staunch New Dealer he believed that visitor facilities in the National Parks should be government-owned and -operated to avoid any deviation from the public purposes of such accommodations. On a broader scale, he felt that Alaska had flirted long enough with the gambling psychology of mining. If the territory were to advance to statehood, thus avoiding the fate of a vast, abandoned mining camp, it must ". . . build up a civilization based upon a more stable and widely prevailing economy." Because of its many charms and splendors Alaska should look to tourism as the long-term base for permanent development.[64]

As affirmed by an NPS-conducted Alaska recreation survey of 1937, the plans for McKinley Park visitor accommodations called for a hotel at McKinley Station and a lodge at Wonder Lake. Planning Chief Tom Vint's office drew up preliminary plans for the rustic-design buildings. Money problems cut out the lodge and forced a revised, spartan design for the hotel.[65]

Following Secretary Ickes' principle of public ownership and operation, the Alaska Railroad was directed to use the WPA funds for construction of the hotel, and was charged with its operation once built. The NPS acted as the railroad's agent for design and construction.[66]

When Secretary Ickes visited Alaska in August 1938 he met with NPS and Alaska Railroad officials at McKinley Park to inspect the hotel project. He expressed great disappointment in the hotel's design, saying it looked like a factory and he expected to hear a shift-change whistle blow. With Tom Vint and the railroad's Otto Ohlson in tow, Ickes strode through the site demanding modifications of the building—more rooms, enlargement of lobby and dining areas—and told them they were to see to it personally and directly. This story and that of the devolution of the hotel's design—caused by too little money and too many bosses—are told in Tom Vint's chagrined report to the Director on the Secretary's visit.[67]

Colonel Ohlson had been loath to have the railroad take over the hotel's operation because the park's short season assured losses for the operator. But under the Secretary's orders, he complied.

The new hotel opened on June 1, 1939, with accommodations for a maximum of 200 guests. For the first time visitors to the park could enjoy the amenities typical of stateside railroad parks, including ranger-conducted interpretive programs at the hotel and on the tour buses into the park.

To avoid competition with the railroad hotel, the Mt. McKinley Tourist and Transportation Company was ordered to shift its main operation from Savage Camp to Camp Eielson, 66 miles from McKinley Station.[68] (In 1953 the Alaska Railroad dumped the red-ink hotel; the NPS took over and contracted with a concessioner for its operation.)

THE CIVILIAN CONSERVATION CORPS DIGS IN

With further assistance from Governor Gruening, always alert for Alaska's development, McKinley Park benefitted from another New Deal program, the Civilian Conservation Corps. Perhaps the most popular of President Franklin D. Roosevelt's relief programs, the CCC provided work, training, discipline, and moral environments for 2.5 million young men who otherwise would have passed the jobless years on Depression street corners. After recruitment of enrollees by the Labor Department, the U.S. Army operated and supervised the CCC camps, including transportation and basic training. The Forest Service and the Park Service provided the conservation projects, including forest-fire suppression, reforestation, road and trail building, landscaping, and construction of recreational structures.[69]

For two seasons in 1938 and 1939 the 200-man CCC crew at McKinley Park did all

The Civilian Conservation Corps camp (location of present-day seasonal employee complex), 1938. Courtesy of AMHA.

Dog and food barn, in park headquarters complex, 1950.
From the Denali National Park and Preserve Archive.

of these things. A summary of CCC accomplishments by Supt. Frank Been—who replaced Harry Liek in June 1939—listed scores of projects that helped complete the park's prewar development. With the impetus of relief-program funding, work was done in those two short seasons that would have taken many years under the regular appropriation route. At Park Headquarters the CCC's built employee housing, garages, the machine shop, a new 40-dog kennel and equipment house for sled dogs, and completed sewer, waterline, telephone, and powerline installations. The hotel grounds were landscaped and a deep waterline was laid to avert freezing problems. Fire hazards were removed along the park road by clean-up and burning of slash and other construction debris. And the much-needed Wonder Lake ranger station-residence was built by a special crew in 1939, providing a district headquarters for the park's deep interior.

Superintendent Been extolled the CCC program not only for its material accomplishments but also for the great opportunity it provided the young men of the Pacific Northwest to experience Alaska and carry their enthusiasms for the territory back home. Several of the camp supervisors, and later some of the CCC enrollees, became productive citizens of Alaska.[70]

The human story of the camps—from 6 a.m. reveille and calisthenics to after-hours sports and educational sessions—has been told by many of the enrollees, who in later years returned to the park to view the products of their labors, still very much in use. Adventures and companionship with campmates is a recurring theme of these reminiscences. Most of the CCC's lauded the Army-camp routines and the physical conditioning from outdoor work and solid food as valuable preparation for their service in the war.

With virtual completion of its first-stage physical development and with inauguration of formal interpretive programs—dog-team demonstrations at the kennels, lectures at the hotel and along the park road—McKinley Park at last was ready to entertain visitors in a manner approximating that already standardized in the stateside parks. Ground-patrol bases at the new Wonder Lake district headquarters and scattered boundary cabins, along with the 1940 start of air patrols over the park's remote sections, finally gave the superintendent and his rangers a handle on protection. But then threats of war and war itself came along to interrupt this new dawning with a rising sun of another sort.

THE U.S. ARMY ARRIVES

The December 7, 1941, attack on Pearl Harbor propelled Alaska from preparations for war into war itself. The feared Japanese assault on Alaska came in June 1942 with air attacks on Dutch Harbor at the east end of the Aleutian Islands and occupation of the far western islands. Immediately travel to Alaska came under military control and McKinley Park operations closed down to a basic maintenance schedule. Local people could visit the park, but all facilities were either mothballed or, as at Savage and Eielson camps, held open on a do-it-yourself basis.[71]

Military reinforcements and civilian construction crews flowed into Alaska by the scores of thousands, transported in ships whose passage up the coast was threatened by Japanese submarines. Completion of defensive bases that had been started before Pearl Harbor made possible an island-hopping offensive campaign across the stormy 1200-mile-long Aleutian chain. A triumph of logistics as much as of battle, this northern warfare finally evicted the invaders from the westernmost islands of Kiska and Attu. All across Alaska major and emergency airfields sprang up overnight, one of them at McKinley Station. Army and Navy bases, coastal defense installations, fuel lines, and supply depots proliferated. The Army engineers began building the Alaska-Canada Highway, the Alcan, to secure lines of supply from the risky sea passage.

Suddenly Alaska had several hundred thousand more people than ever before. Soldiers on leave or recuperating from the miseries of Aleutian campaigning needed some place to go. McKinley Park with its hotel, rustic camps, and healthy outdoor recreation opportunities offered such a place—happily removed from the boom-town temptations of Fairbanks and Anchorage.

After a flurry of correspondence and negotiations between Governor Gruening, Maj. Gen. Simon B. Buckner, Commanding General of the Alaska Defense Command, and Interior Department and NPS officials, McKinley Park's conversion as an Army recreation camp was consummated.[72]

A phase of the negotiations warrants further notice: General Buckner, a driving, take-over commander, had been authorized by the President to declare Alaska a military area, subject to military control as a war zone. His plans for McKinley Park—once he became convinced of its advantages as an Army recreation camp—had the ring of battle orders. He wanted major construction of camp facilities, extension of roads, and other improvements that would have turned the park into a military reservation. NPS Director Drury, working through the Secretaries of War and Interior, quickly scotched these plans. He maintained that the National Parks would pitch in for the war effort in all ways compatible with their status as National Parks, but not in ways that would jeopardize that status. The parks were symbols of our national greatness, civilized institutions that must be defended from ourselves as well as from our attackers during wartime. The National Parks would survive the war and exist unimpaired after the war. They would not be sacrificed to it.[73]

With this sparring over, the Service entered into McKinley's war effort with enthusiasm. The hotel and the camps were, in effect, loaned to the Army, which staffed and ran them for the soldiers' benefit. Hundreds of men piled off every train—6,000 to 8,000 per month during the peak year of 1943. Fishing, hiking, and horseback expeditions were favorite summer activities. A small ski-slope near headquarters, plus unexcelled cross-country expanses, skating rinks, and dog teams provided winter sport. The Army's special services branch, aided by volunteer hostesses and Red Cross women, presented dances, parties, and special events—including the usual World War II hilarity of brawny soldiers cavorting as hula dancers in slit-paper "grass" skirts. This was a place where fighting men could forget the Army and G.I. drill. Men and officers here fraternized as friends. All in all, McKinley was "heaven" after the sodden, fog bound Aleutians.[74]

The Army also held small-scale winter maneuvers at the park and conducted the previously noted cold-weather tests of food, clothes, and equipment high on the mountain.[75] But these exercises involved only small numbers of men. It was the thousands who came as recreationists that filled the park in numbers never before recorded.[76] With hardly an exception the visiting soldiers became missionaries of Alaska's splendors. Many of them converted themselves and settled in Alaska after the war. The Army's funding and administration of "visitor services," with a guaranteed clientele, made McKinley a park for all seasons, including winter, as never before or since.[77]

During the war park personnel, depleted by the war effort—several of the staff having volunteered for military service—maintained a sort of shadow presence in the park. They showed off the sights and clarified the park's regulations for the Army special services staff, including the ban on hunting. They and the ARC did what they could with pittance money and manpower to keep the road passable for the Army trucks and buses that took soldiers into the park. Patrol schedules suffered; but this was less a problem than it might have been given the wartime dearth of population surrounding the park. Custodial management—just holding the park together until after the war—occupied nearly all the energies of the skeletal staff.[78]

The Army's pumping in large numbers of visitors solved one problem that had bothered Supt. Frank Been since his transfer north from Sequoia, where he had been park naturalist. A critical congressman had added up total expenditures for the park road ($1.5 million), then divided that figure by the number of park visitors in 1940 (1,202), yielding a cost per visitor of more than $1,000. Been wrote to Washington that construction of a park approach road would solve this problem by encouraging low-income, local people to come to the park.[79] In 1943 Acting Director Hillory Tolson urged the park's acting superintendent, Grant Pearson (Been had left for military service), to get a release from the Army to use military-visitor numbers in NPS travel tabulations. These hefty transfusions would help justify the park's budget requests. Though these numbers were common knowledge in Alaska, the Army refused their publication because of war-zone security.[80]

Before Been left for Army duty in January 1943, his park-naturalist urge to do something more for visitors resulted in approved plans for three east-end trails still used today: Horseshoe Lake (built in 1943), and the Headquarters-to-Hotel, and Yanert (Triple) Lakes, trails completed in the late '40s.[81]

As acting superintendent in Been's place, Grant Pearson made a big hit. He was the old timer, the last of the pioneer rangers. His credentials as a bona fide Alaskan ranked as high as anyone's in or out of the Service. A field man par excellence, he had

Grant Pearson (fourth from right) with a group of government officials and Kantishna prospectors, 1931. Pearson began as a ranger in 1926, and was active in park affairs for the next 30 years. From the J. C. Reed Collection, USGS.

seen most of the park's far corners and he was a proven leader in tough places. In 1944 he had another chance to prove his mettle.

An Army transport plane crashed on September 18 some 16 miles east of Mount McKinley in the tangle of peaks at the head of Eldridge Glacier. Aerial reconnaissance indicated no survivors among the 19 on board. The Army asked Pearson to lead an expedition to the crash site to try to determine the cause and to recover the bodies. Pearson wanted a small team to reach the site quickly, before snow covered bodies and crash remains. But the insistence on body removal meant a large expedition, ponderous in organization and logistics. With the aid of Sgt. James Gale of Elmendorf Field's Search and Rescue Squadron (a still functioning outfit operating out of Anchorage) and Brad Washburn—called in from the Army's cold-weather test camp— Pearson took the 40-man party to and from the crash vicinity without loss or injury during a 43-day trek, 25 days of it above timber in arctic ice and snow in the teeth of winter. Twelve men of the party, led by Pearson, arrived at the crash site on October 10, roping down a precipitous ice slope after crossing the range from the park side. As best they could determine, the plane hit high on Mount Deception, then plunged 1,600 feet down the ice to its final resting place. An engine near the point of impact protruded from the ice nearly 12,000 feet above sea level. Deep snow, 10 feet fallen since the crash, frustrated all efforts to find bodies. Only a bloodstain on a piece of fuselage and the co-pilot's B-4 bag, dug out of a drift, connected the scattered plane to its vanished occupants.

A few months later, after a memorial service at Ladd Field in Fairbanks, a sister transport craft dropped three floral wreaths over the snow-covered mountain where the bodies lay buried beyond recovery. The Army awarded Pearson the Medal of Freedom for this extraordinary mountaineering exploit. Following Been's return after the war, and subsequent transfer in 1949, Pearson assumed the full superintendency of the park. He retired after 31 years of service in 1956 and became a leader in the Alaska Legislature.[82]

WORLD WAR II SPURS MINING

When the 90-mile-long park road and the ARC spur to Kantishna were completed in 1938, miners began hauling equipment and ore between that district and the railroad, as contemplated in the 1922 agreement between ARC President James Steese and NPS Director Stephen T. Mather. Opening of this direct transportation link coincided with and significantly promoted the expansion of lode mining that led to the Kantishna's most productive era.

At first this commercial use of the scenic park road caused perturbations in the Service's Washington Office. The quid-pro-quo terms of the ARC-NPS agreement had been lost in the shuffle of years. But eventually the dual-use concept of the road—as park road and commercial road—was rediscovered in park and Washington files. The park's jurisdiction over that part of the road within its boundaries, and the miners' use of it as an industrial link between mines and railroad, was accommodated by the park's issuance of nominal-fee permits. These documents stipulated load limits, size of equipment, and seasonal-and-hours-of-use regulations that safeguarded the primary scenic-road purpose and the integrity of the roadbed.[83]

The government virtually banned gold mining as nonessential during World War II, but prospecting and production of strategic minerals was pushed hard. The U.S. Geological Survey and its sister Interior Department agency, the Bureau of Mines, conducted strategic-mineral surveys across the country and provided technical assistance and other subsidies to mines that could produce these critical war materials. One of these was the Stampede Mine, which ranked as Alaska's prime producer of antimony—an alloy of great importance in aircraft and other war production.

The Stampede Mine, 45 miles west of park headquarters, was just a few miles outside the park until the expansion of 1978-80. Discovered during the early Kantishna Hills prospecting, Stampede's isolated lode of stibnite—the ore of antimony—lay essentially fallow until Earl Pilgrim took over operations in 1936. He had acquired the claims and transferred them to a subsidiary of the National Lead Company, which provided financial muscle for mine development. By 1939 a used 40-ton mill and ancillary facilities were in operation. But technical difficulties and commodity-price fluctuations limited operations to "high grading" or hand-picking only the richest ore for shipment. By Spring 1941 transportation costs forced closure of the isolated mine, located many miles from the park road. The long ore haul by caterpillar tractor and double-enders over the Stampede winter trail to the railroad at Lignite—then on to stateside smelters—simply would not pay.

In 1942 Pilgrim rehabilitated the old mill with new equipment and machinery, operating until the fall of that year when the water supply froze. Meanwhile the USGS performed geological mapping and the Bureau of Mines did extensive testing and drifting to locate the most promising ores. With this boost Pilgrim continued mining and shipping high-grade ore, along with development of new ore bodies.[84]

Transportation costs continued to plague Pilgrim throughout the years of his Stampede Mine operations, which lasted into the early '70s.[85] As an alternative to the winter-trail haul, he pioneered air transport of ore concentrates from the airstrip he built at the junction of Stampede Creek and the Clearwater Fork of Toklat River, 2 1/2 miles below the mine.

During the war Pilgrim proposed a constructed road paralleling Toklat River that would give him trucking access to the railroad via the park road.[86] After clarifying correspondence with Superintendent Been, Director Drury authorized this road as a war-emergency measure, for use only during that emergency, and to be routed on the river bars rather than cross-country.[87] Pilgrim abandoned this idea in 1944 for lack of funds, but renewed it in 1948, when it was again approved. Pilgrim let the project lapse when the ARC failed to subsidize it.

Park rangers at Stony Creek ranger cabin, 1931. Built in 1926, the cabin is now in ruins. From the J. C. Reed Collection, USGS.

Pilgrim next revived the project in 1954 when he was operating the mine under contract with the Defense Minerals Exploration Agency. The Stampede end of the proposed route would be bulldozed across country, thus saving 6 or 8 miles over the riverbed route.[88] Supt. Grant Pearson saw advantages to the park in such a road: It would not mar scenery near the park road (where Pilgrim's route did follow the riverbed) and it would give the park vehicular access to its Toklat boundary cabin, which could be used as a supply point for patrols on the remote north boundary. Pearson recommended approval,[89] as did the Alaska Railroad, always alert for more freight-traffic revenue.[90] Approval from Washington followed, based on Pearson's foreseen advantages and permit stipulations that required landscape-architect approvals of route, culverts, and bridges. Again the ARC could not come up with subsidizing funds and the project lapsed.[91]

Three years later Pilgrim renewed the struggle. But by then NPS personnel had changed, including appointment of a new superintendent. The new men considered the road project inimical to park purposes and values. The NPS offered some solace to Pilgrim, citing new road plans of the Bureau of Public Roads (which had assumed ARC functions) that would intersect the Stampede winter trail.[92]

Meanwhile, Olaus Murie and other conservationists had publicly deplored the proposed mining road through the park. On the other hand, the interminable Pilgrim road case had made the old miner a martyr to bureaucratic caprice in the arena of public opinion. After all, the NPS had thrice approved the project in past years. The Service took this heat alone, for territorial highway people—who had opposed in the past and continued to oppose using their scant funds for a costly road to one faltering mine operation—did not have to expose that sentiment so long as the Service refused to grant Pilgrim a permit.[93]

Park Superintendent Duane Jacobs summed up all this crossfire in a memorandum of April 1958. He, too, strongly opposed the road, if that position would not expose the Service to undue criticism and opposition. His philosophical views were buttressed by a potent practical consideration: He feared that the 18 miles of road routed in the riverbed, which would be washed out with every flood, would inevitably be relocated to bordering terraces if the road were ever established; i.e., a dozed and constructed road throughout.[94] Regional Director Lawrence Merriam relayed Jacobs' analysis to the Director—emphasizing the superintendent's last point, and questioning the utility of such a road given the fluctuating market price of antimony. This letter implied the need for a once-and-for-all executive decision to

Savage River cabin and cache, 1946. Both were built in 1931; the cache is no longer standing. From the C. A. Hickock Collection, USGS.

refuse further consideration of the Toklat road permit.[95]

Evidently Washington did so decide, for by 1960 Pilgrim had given up on a road through the park. Now he fastened onto the new State of Alaska pioneer-road program, specifically designed to bring remote mines into production.[96] This program lived a brief and futile life. Its first and only accomplishment was the pioneer road to Stampede, built in 1965. According to former Alaska Highway Commissioner Bruce Campbell, this road traversed the same wet ground—fit only for winter trails—rejected by road engineer Hawley Sterling during his 1920 survey of routes to the Kantishna. Earl Pilgrim, who had advised the 1965 road builders to take a better route on the terraces, could not contain his rage. As Campbell relates the story, the project inspector traversed the new track by four-wheel-drive vehicle with great difficulty. When he got to Pilgrim's mine road at the Stampede airstrip, he found the aged and armed miner astride a blocking bulldozer, waving him away and cursing road engineers in general. The inspector's disappointing trip out to Stampede was, by all accounts, the only full traverse ever made by a wheeled vehicle. The "road" reverted to bog almost instantly over the greater part of its length.[97]

Bowed by age and frustration, but not beaten, Earl Pilgrim ran his mine and cat-trained his ore intermittently for another 7 years, depending on the price of antimony. With a forge, piles of salvaged parts, and a couple of cranky generators the venerable miner kept things going. He was a certified mining engineer and had been the first professor of mining at Alaska's A&M college in Fairbanks. Beyond that he had practiced mining of all kinds in Alaska's hinterlands. He was a genius at improvisation. One who knew him figured that he could fashion a moving part from a chunk of rock, if necessary. Machines, circuits, piping, and tools were interlocked with the personality of the man at the Stampede Mine site, as demonstrated by a local anecdote: When Pilgrim finally divested himself of the mine in 1978, the new company sent in its by-the-book engineers; they simply could not make the place run. Without

Earl Pilgrim's personal coaxing, all of these ingenious hookups and fabrications refused to mesh into the system that he had made.[98]

In December 1979, Stampede Mine, Ltd.—which had acquired the property from Earl Pilgrim—donated its real estate rights and interests to the National Park Service and its mineral rights and interests to the University of Alaska. Under the conditions of the quitclaim deeds the new owners were charged to cooperatively use the site as a mining study area for development of efficient and environmentally sound mining methods consonant with the Mining in the Parks Act of 1976.

In the process of surveying the mine and developing work proposals under the subsequent NPS-UAF agreement, hazardous materials were discovered. The Service agreed to rid the site of these materials, including explosives. In pursuit of this task, a major dump of explosives stored at the mill was targeted for demolition by an Army ordnance detachment. Miscalculation of the course and effects of this demolition on April 30, 1987, resulted in a major explosion that severely damaged the mill and nearby structures. Subsequent investigation showed procedural faults and miscommunication among the NPS and Army personnel involved. Revised demolition procedures and management controls put in force by the NPS since this explosion will prevent future episodes of this kind at the many abandoned mine sites on NPS lands in Alaska. But the integrity of Earl Pilgrim's legacy was sorely diminished. (Mercifully, Earl Pilgrim was living out his final days at the time and was beyond cognition of this event.) Pending development of historic preservation plans for Stampede, the park has stabilized and weather-sealed key structures and maintains custodial protection of the site.[99]

POLITICAL POLICY

As World War II wound down, plans and promotions for Alaska's postwar development wound up. Completion of the Alcan Highway during the war—with roadside recreation plans already drafted by U.S. and Canadian park services—called for beefing up Alaska's inadequate internal road system to meet the expected flood of auto tourists from the States. Tourism—seen as Alaska's long-term steady industry, the counter to extractive-industry boom and bust cycles—called for new recreation and camping sites, and full development of existing national parks and monuments in Alaska.

Mixed in with the large doses of profit motive in these schemes were altruistic and common-welfare concerns. The nation had gotten used to public-works projects during the Depression. Now, with 16 million servicemen and women about to be demobilized into the job market, which would be further flooded by war workers displaced during the transition to peacetime production, public works would again come to the fore. Both public and private interests scrambled to get plans and drawings prepared so they could be first in line when projects were passed out.[100]

The NPS submitted initial-development plans for Glacier Bay and Katmai National Monuments and looked to McKinley as the flagship of its Alaska parklands. The park hotel would be expanded and the long-sought Wonder Lake Lodge would be built by the Alaska Railroad, based on plans and specifications provided by the NPS.[101]

As it turned out neither the Alaska Railroad nor the NPS could come up with funds for these developments, though budget requests were sent to Congress each year. Without specific appropriations from Congress, the Service was helpless to proceed. When Governor Gruening said sacrifice something else and give Alaska a break, Director Drury was forced to respond that the patched and tattered prewar facilities in stateside parks—by now flooded with real, rather than Alaska's potential, visitors—demanded every dime of the minuscule NPS construction funds. Despite these stresses, Gruening and Drury maintained close contact and collaborated in efforts to get NPS funds for Alaska.

These efforts proved futile. The NPS reality in Alaska, to 1950, was no progress: Glacier Bay and Katmai remained unmanned and undeveloped; McKinley limped along at a custodial-maintenance pace. The park's biggest problem in the immediate postwar years was the deteriorated park road. Lacking basic maintenance during the war years it had suffered from both the elements—especially spring thaws and eroding runoffs—and the heavy traffic of the Army recreation camp. To this fundamental necessity the park devoted nearly all of the minimal funds left over from operations, salaries, and headquarters upkeep[102]

Then came the Korean Conflict. Interior Secretary Oscar Chapman clamped the lid on Alaska park developments—in an August 1950 response to another Governor Gruening plea—with these words: "In calling for a review of our programs, the President has directed that all civil public work projects be screened with the objective of deferring projects which do not directly contribute to national defense . . . ."[103] At the same time, internal budget documents froze NPS expenditures to a level that allowed only minimal operations and maintenance—no new construction.[104]

As earlier noted, Governor Gruening, ceaselessly laboring for Alaska's development and settlement, and—by virtue of the financial and political power these would

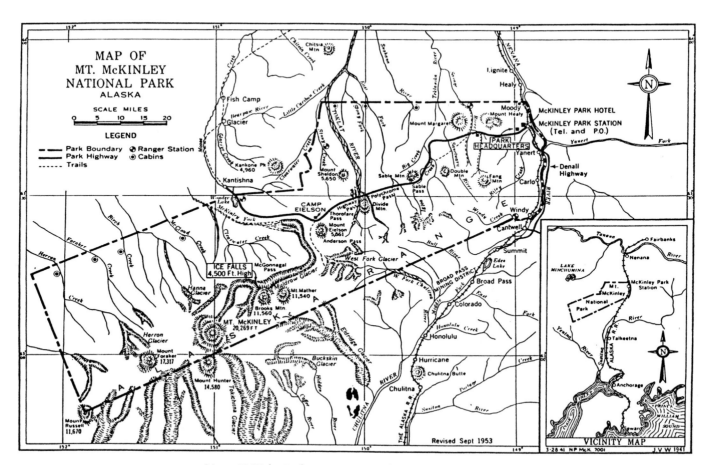

Mount McKinley Park, 1953. Courtesy of NPS, in DENA Archives.

bring—its statehood, became ever more cynical of Washington's statements of good intentions. Granted that the Korean Conflict had snarled progress in the parks, why was the chief safety engineer of the National Park Service coming to Alaska? Gruening directed his latest salvo at Joseph T. Flakne of Interior's Office of Territories. What were the functions of a chief safety engineer, the Governor asked, and was he bringing money for park improvements?[105] The sympathetic Flakne responded that his office lacked the research capabilities to determine the duties of such an officer, but wryly assured the Governor that doubtless his mission would "help save the Alaskans." Moreover, had the Governor changed his stripes; was he not in favor of tourism, even at the taxpayers' expense? Getting serious, Flakne joined the Governor in wanting more action and fewer survey-and-report junkets.[106]

These letters got circulated in the department and prompted a memorandum from the NPS director to the secretary's office. The director cited the Service's good-faith intentions in Alaska and its repeated frustration at the hands of Congress. The Service had coordinated the U.S. phase of the Alcan Highway recreation studies. Since the war it had annually proposed multimillion dollar development programs for Alaska parklands, only to have them killed in Congress, then deferred by the Korean affair. At present (1951) the Service was conducting the Alaska Recreation Survey under the direction of NPS planner George Collins—a direct response to the governor's plugging of tourism as Alaska's long-term salvation. The criticized "junkets" by NPS scientists and planners gave on-site substance to NPS requests for programs and money aimed at developing Alaska's tourism business. The funds spent for such necessary field work did not come from construction accounts (so shrunken as to be useless anyway) and could not have been used for construction in any event. Such studies and reports gave the Service its only means to focus Congressional attention on Alaska's needs.[107]

With the accession of Conrad L. Wirth to the NPS directorship, Governor Gruening turned a new leaf in his campaign to get McKinley Park caught up with the expectations and demands long placed upon it by Alaskans and the tourism industry. His correspondence with Wirth is quoted and paraphrased below, for it sets the scene for the policy disputes that have racked the park's recent history. First, Gruening's opening letter:

As you know for many years there has been almost no new construction in Alaska's National Parks and Monuments. Within a year or two the highway connecting the continental highway system with Mt. McKinley Park will be completed and we can certainly expect a tremendous influx of automobiles bearing tourists. It seems to me essential that we make some plans to meet this situation.

At present there is only one stretch of road extending from the entrance of the Park to Wonder Lake, approximately ninety miles. The most important project, it seems to me, in the Park would be to start building a road from somewhere near the western terminus of this highway toward Mt. McKinley. It is a project that has been long urged by so enthusiastic an Alaskan rooter and mountaineer as Bradford Washburn. Certainly a beginning should be made of this road in the coming budget. It would involve a trestle bridge across the McKinley River, and beyond that point the road could be extended for the time being at a reasonably low standard and at a reasonable cost. It would open up, for the tourists and others, a region of incomparable interest and beauty, dotted by many small ponds and a great abundance of game. It would heighten the recreational value of the Park.

Please recall that no new mileage has been built in the Park for at least fifteen years. I strongly urge that the Park Service make every effort to get some sort of appropriation for this project for fiscal year 1954. I am confident that the Alaska Road Commission will get the greatest value for the money appropriated for that purpose. If this is not begun now we shall lose much of the benefit of the road which will connect the entire continental highway system to the Park. Could you not find it *possible to squeeze out $150,000, or at least $100,000, for this very desirable undertaking?*[108]

In his response Wirth acknowledged the coming influence of the Denali Highway. This 170-mile-long graveled road—coming west from Paxson on the Richardson Highway to Cantwell and McKinley—would open in 1957. It gave private motorists their first direct access to McKinley Park. Because of the length and primitive condition of this road it produced more a flow than a flood of auto traffic at the park. Thus it was a relatively gentle prelude—both in numbers and modified park operations—to the exponential onslaught that came in 1972 with the paved Parks Highway between Anchorage and Fairbanks. But the Denali Highway served as an omen of what was to come. So this Gruening-Wirth correspondence of 1951 previews the modern condition.

After agreeing with Gruening that the park must prepare for motoring tourists, Wirth stated that improvement of the existing park road must take precedence over any new mileage. The temporary bridges inherited from ARC-construction days had to be replaced with permanent structures or the park road itself would have to be closed. Instead of a new road to the base of the mountain—with an expensive 600-to-800-foot-long bridge across McKinley River—Wirth advocated a trail from Wonder Lake to McGonagall Pass, a project already on the park's list. This trail would complement the proposed Wonder Lake Lodge development.[109]

Gruening replied in haste, citing Henry David Thoreau's injunction to "aim high":

I insist that the Park Service should be out fighting for something more all the time. It should not be content merely to maintain or "improve" the negligible facilities it has long had. . . . I regret to see from your letter that the situation under your leadership, which I for one and many others hoped would presage a change in attitude, appears not to be altered. . . . I think it is not too late for you to raise your sights.[110]

Wirth, too, responded with alacrity. He forwarded his 1954 budget estimates, which contained nearly $1.5 million for roads and trails in Glacier Bay and Mount McKinley, and more than $700,000 for other physical improvements.[111] These amounts were chopped by the Bureau of the Budget, and further pared by Congress.[112] So grim reality set in again. Incremental replacement of park-road bridges—a matter of life and safety—continued to define new construction work at the park.

Despite these delays and deferrals, here was beginning to play out the scenario foreseen by Tom Vint in 1929. McKinley Park, "the big note in Alaska," could not escape the spotlight. From here on out, to the present day, the themes defined in the Gruening-Wirth correspondence would frame the political and policy debates over the park's future.

In the frustrated atmosphere of 1951—with the insulations of distance, deficient transportation, and chronic lack of funds still in force—neither man saw any threat to the park's basic integrity. Both men did see the park's inevitable linkage to the continental highway system as a turning point in the park's history and as a rationale for its further development. But only the passage of years could reveal the full implications of that linkage—which would break the park's protective isolation and, with gathering momentum, indeed threaten its integrity.

Within a decade a countering force would begin to gather. Both locally and nationally the conservation community began defining a question of a different order: Did the intrinsic values of the park command its fate, as mandated by Congress, or was the park to be sacrificed to the demands of private motorists and the tourism industry which viewed the park as its central economic asset in Alaska?

The Service's MISSION 66 program to upgrade park facilities across the land brought the first phase of McKinley Park's preservation-versus-development debate to a head. This program—laudable and undeniably necessary in its broad objectives—produced many conflicts over specific projects in the National Parks. During the 25 years of Depression and wars since 1930, park construction had been limited to bare, rustic necessities. During this period the concept of wilderness preservation had gained force and public recognition through the efforts of such national organizations as the Wilderness Society, the Sierra Club, the National Parks Association and, locally, the Alaska Conservation Society. Their select and politically potent members had become used to the parks in their rustic and relatively undeveloped condition. The paucity of development funds had coincided with the evolution of a wilderness preservation movement.

In 1948, NPS Director Newton B. Drury—himself a California preservation leader before coming to the Park Service—applied the wilderness idea to the great parklands of America and the world:

Phrases like "nature protection," "recreation," "wilderness values," "the unity of nature," "sanctuaries for native animals and plants," imply the recognition, by those concerned with the good earth and the fullness thereof, of the fact that land is used to minister not only to man's physical well-being, but also to his mind and spirit—that man "does not live by bread alone"; that some lands, in the Americas and throughout the world, should be preserved for what they are, as well as for what they will produce; preserved with all their wealth of flora and fauna and geological formations, with all their beauty and wonder and significance, in the perfection that nature gave them, unchanged by man.[113]

Drury introduced the new wave within the Service. He was the first director not of the Mather generation of parkmen—and the first one to face the qualitatively different world of the postwar era with its infinite demands upon the National Park System driven by popular possession of the automobile. Drury's second successor, Conrad L. Wirth—creator of the MISSION 66 program—came from the old school, whose Mather-Albright philosophy emphasized more the "pleasuring ground" concept embedded in the original Yellowstone legislation than the fragile-wilderness one now emerging. As translated into criteria for park development, these different emphases were perceptible enough to cause tensions both within the Service and in the larger world.

As applied to McKinley Park, beginning in the late '50s, the MISSION 66 program resulted in three major categories of construction: the interpretive center at the site of the phased-out Camp Eielson; campground and headquarters-area improvements—including some employee quarters to replace the deteriorated health hazards that park people had been living in; and, most important, upgrading of the park road to meet the increase in auto traffic and assure visitor safety. It was the road project that ignited controversy.

In the midst of this controversy, in 1963, the NPS chief of design and construction, Clark Stratton, issued a "party line" memorandum to guide park people in their responses to the mounting criticism of road reconstruction. In summary the road improvements would produce "telescoping standards" as follows:

1. The first 30 miles would have a 20-foot paved driving surface with 3-foot shoulders.
2. The middle section, about 40 miles in length, would have a 20-foot driving surface with minimal shoulders, oiled and possibly paved later.
3. The last 18-mile-long section from Eielson to Wonder Lake would remain a primitive gravel road with sufficient base to support the thinned out traffic at that end.
Whenever possible, the reconstructed road would follow the original alignment.[114]

Stratton's memorandum responded generally to the mounting criticism over the road and other MISSION 66 projects, and specifically to publication of an article by Olaus Murie, now president of the Wilderness Society. Murie had long believed that the machine was ruling our civilization, that science and society had become victims of the technologists.[115] He remembered the pristine days when he had studied Denali's caribou, when—by dog-team and on foot—he had wandered through a land entirely natural. For him, the road as built in the early years had already crossed the threshold of the acceptable. It allowed the sanctuary to be invaded by noisy machines. To compound this desecration by "improving" the road would give free rein to speed and numbers, with attendant scarification of the landscape and destruction of the silence that once had been punctuated only by distant calls of wild creatures and rustling winds.[116]

The *National Parks Magazine* became the forum for a running symposium on MISSION 66 projects at McKinley Park. In a May 1963 article, the authors traced the planning history of the park and the mounting pressures for its development. They implied that the NPS response to the opening of the Denali Highway in 1957, and its MISSION 66 preparations for the opening of the Parks Highway—already in 1963 in the initial construction phase—smacked of a simple numbers game: expand park facilities to meet whatever visitor numbers the statisticians estimate. Campgrounds and cabins at Wonder Lake; expansion of the hotel at McKinley Station; the trail to McGonagall Pass with its McKinley River bridge and shelter cabins in the hills—and above all the straightened park-road speedway now abuilding—seemed to be exercises in quantification without philosophy or thought of the park's deeper purposes. The road reconstruction would take $14 million of a total $20 million park-construction budget over the period 1957-73. Thus the road became the focus of the preservationists' attention. It was the umbilical that would feed all other growth. If the road-improvement program could be stopped, much of the other in-park development would remain on the drawing boards, and needed facilities—responding to real visitors, not anticipating them—could be developed outside the park.[117]

In the introduction to a September 1963 symposium of preservationists' views, the editors of *National Parks Magazine* called for reassurance from the Park Service that it " . . . is not selling its soul to the public demand for easy comfort and amusement." They called for high aesthetic standards at McKinley, where uplifting education and the continuing right of people to participate in the park's natural wonders should define management objectives—which must match in taste and judgment the park's scenic beauty and natural harmony.[118]

One biologist in this symposium, after urging the park's expansion based on scientific determination of wildlife ranges, advocated screening by naturalists of all development projects to control their ecological impacts. The engineering mentality should not prevail. He concluded:

The really important thing to keep foremost in consideration of developmental activities in Mount McKinley National Park is that the plant and animal communities are exceedingly delicate and that traditional temperate-zone construction and management techniques are frequently not applicable. If those who administer this park can acquire an appreciation of the delicacy of these plant and animal communities then most of the problems will not occur.[119]

These thoughts echoed an earlier critique of McKinley's MISSION 66 program by Adolph Murie. His 14-page analysis covered every facet of the development schedule, judging them all against the values that Murie believed should guide planning at the park:

It is difficult to properly express the human values in McKinley Park. But we can say that in McKinley we have the highest, most majestic, and impressive mountain in North America. There are other snowclad mountains in the Park, and many extensive but lesser spur ranges, any one of which can vie with the Tetons or similar spectacular ranges elsewhere. The charming sheep ridges, the myriads of tundra ponds, the glacial streams and river bars, the immense glaciers, make this northern area a

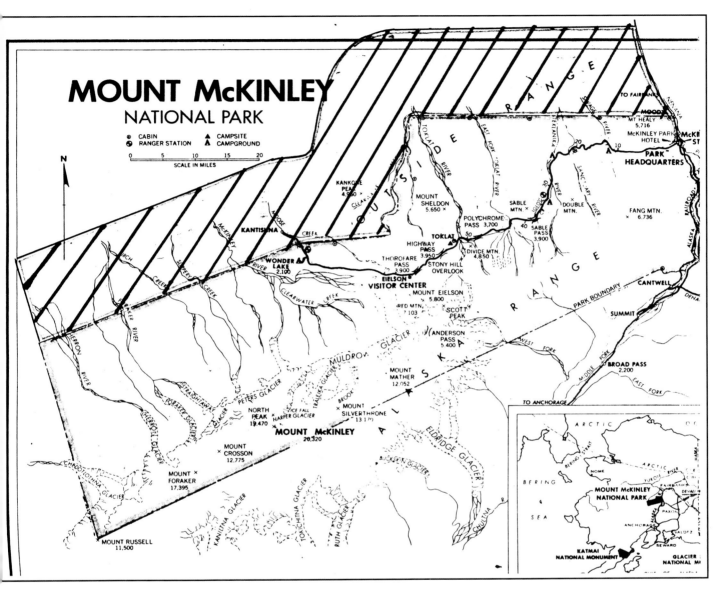

Adolph Murie's park expansion proposal, 1965. Boundary Adjustments, MOMC, 1965–1966. File L1417, ARO.

veritable fairy land. And in this varied scenery is a flora and fauna characteristic of the north.

It would perhaps not tax our ingenuity to save the above physical features. However, in all of them there is a wilderness spirit that concerns us. I am sure that many of those who are planning recognize that our big task is to preserve this wilderness spirit. But there will be wide difference in planning nevertheless. Some will seek ends that are destructive to the wilderness feeling, believing that their ends justify the additional intrusion. Some will think that the highway should be intensively labeled like a museum, even though each label will detract from the wilderness. Some will want to bring accommodations into the midst of the scenery, instead of a simple and delicate approach from the edge of things. Some will want to have structures on a prominence, rather than tucked away unobtrusively.

These differences will have to be worked out in discussions. I recognize that my point of view will stress intruding and injuring the spirit of wilderness as little as possible, with sometimes a little inconvenience resulting. I would rather err in that direction. But I hasten to add that I am not alone in this point of view.

I am stating my opinions with, I hope, proper humility, but forthright, and in an effort to get the best possible planning. For fear of being considered too captious in this report, I wish to point out that the wilderness standards in McKinley must be maintained on a higher level than anything we have attempted in the States. Because McKinley is a wilderness within a vast northern wilderness, the ill effect of any intrusion will here be proportionately greater; and any "dressing up" will be more incongruous, will clash more with the wilderness spirit, than would be true in any of our areas in the States. And since wilderness is recognized as one of the foremost values in the Park, it must be given special consideration in order to maintain its purity. Fortunately the visitation is far below what outside parks are subjected to, hence we are able to strive for and maintain a high standard of quality in Denali. I would urge all planners to strive for quality in this Alaska wilderness. The people expect it.[120]

Following this lead, Adolph Murie called for minimalist intrusion on all counts. The road should remain primitive, a wilderness adventure in its own right for those visitors bound to their cars; only tucked-away campgrounds in the park—no lodges or cabins; Charles Sheldon's Tolkat cabin should not be preserved (to do so would violate Charles Sheldon's own love of the pristine); airplane touring, with its uniquely intrusive and noisy probing into the wild corners reached only with difficulty by trekkers, should be banned; and the park should be expanded north of Wonder Lake, both to provide protected range for wildlife and to prevent helter-skelter private development in the critical Kantishna sector.

Another noted conservationist, Sigurd F. Olson, later wrote to Murie saying that he agreed on almost everything in Murie's MISSION 66 critique. He was disappointed in the architectural esthetics of the new Eielson Visitor Center and commented generally on in-park developments:

The reason McKinley is such a wonderful game sanctuary is because there are no interior developments beyond those at Denali and Headquarters. Start developing elsewhere and the charm and wildness will be gone.

Here then is a great opportunity to do the very thing that should have been done in other parks, keeping all developments outside. That is the ultimate goal of the park service, something that will take a long time to realize in the parks that have been built up, but in McKinley this is paramount and if there must be new developments they should stay outside the park boundaries.[121]

For a few more years the Service's official position continued to stress the park-road improvements as a necessity, based on increasing private-car access and visitor safety. But by 1966 road reconstruction had been effectively halted. Widening and paving had been completed to Savage River, and widening with gravel surface had reached Teklanika, 30 miles into the park. Beyond that point, bridge replacement and maintenance-level upgrading would prevail.[122]

In a February 1972 letter to Alaska Congressman Nick Begich, NPS Assistant Director Lawrence Hadley stated the Service's evolved policy on the park road:

As you are aware, the new State Highway 3 [Parks Highway] will provide much greater access to Mount McKinley than has been the case in the past. In order to properly plan for this increase in travel and to fulfill our responsibilities for the management of the national park, it has been necessary for us to concern ourselves with the proper management technique involving the 87-mile-long park road. As you know, the road is narrow and winding for the last 57 miles. The first 30 miles to the Teklanika River were realigned and constructed to two-lane-road standards during the decade of the 1960's. Fourteen miles of the road from the McKinley Park Hotel to the Savage River were paved a few years ago.

Further improvement of the road has been somewhat controversial, because of the nature of the resources of the park, the appeal of the old road, the abundance of wildlife, the generally high-quality experience received by visitors, and the potential intrusion on the aesthetic and primitive scene likely to result from further road reconstruction.

Planning for visitor use in a national park always constitutes consideration of balance between the manner and means of use and enjoyment and conserving the resources unimpaired for future generations. Mount McKinley National Park was established to preserve an outstanding display of wildlife in a setting of scenic and geologic splendor, including the highest mountain in North America.

The maintaining of opportunities for the viewing of wildlife in its natural setting appears to be paramount if a visit to the park is to retain its high quality. There are doubts that this can be done if the remainder of the road is improved and unlimited automobile use permitted in the future.

Unlimited automobile use cannot be permitted without road improvement, because of safety involving the narrowness of the road, sharp curves, rough or slippery surface, and frequent clouds of dust.

The suggestion has been made that a flexible, free public transportation system be implemented to provide for the various types of park users. Such a system would mean that persons arriving in their automobiles or recreation vehicles would camp or stay in public accommodations at or near the east side of the park. Private vehicles would be parked at this end of the park while their owners were conveyed by public vehicles to various destinations in the park for day trips, or to get to the small existing campgrounds with tent camping equipment, if desired. Variations on this theme are being studied.

Development of such a system would have several advantages:

1. Road improvement would be minimal and less expensive with no additional scarring of the natural scene.

2. Disturbance of wildlife will be lessened, and good opportunities for viewing wildlife maintained.

3. Opportunities for development of campgrounds and other accommodations by private individuals outside but near the park would be stimulated.

4. Traffic congestion on the road would generally be reduced.

5. A visit to the park would be something out of the ordinary, and a quality experience more likely maintained.

Our planning, however, does not envision the restricting of reasonable access to privately owned facilities.

Hadley went on to say that the Service had "finally learned" from experience in Lower 48 parks that "the solution is not to provide more and more roads for more and more automobiles." The first step to ease pressure on the park's sensitive interior would be the bus transportation system on the park road. The second step would be the proposed southerly expansion that would join McKinley Park with the new Denali State Park. In this area, where the two parks flanked the route of the new State Highway, both public and private developments could accommodate the exploding recreation demands in the Denali region. Thus, McKinley Park would be able to zone and manage for both recreation development and wilderness. Heretofore, the single-option park—that option defined by the park road—had been unable to balance its two obligations to the public: preservation and use. With controlled access and no further development in the wilderness interior, and cooperative development and management for expanded recreation uses along the Parks Highway, appropriate balances in both zones could be achieved.[123]

THE VISION FOR THE FUTURE

This statement of policy, the upshot of years of controversy and in-Service soul searching, effectively set the planning and management framework for the park through the 1978-80 expansion and into the present. It established the principle of a bus transportation system to limit road traffic, with the objective of maintaining the viewability of wildlife for park visitors. The inauguration of this bus system in 1972 was a critical turning point that established the operational precedent of finite limits, most recently reaffirmed in the park's 1986 General Management Plan (which significantly strengthened restrictions on buses and cars). On a broader front, the Hadley policy statement recognized the "two-park" concept of the undeveloped interior wildlife-wilderness preserve and the southside scenic borderland where more conventional park development and recreation activity could occur. Until that dual-park concept achieves reality—at this writing the southside project is still blocked by funding and planning delays—the preservation-development politics of the park will continue to focus on its single option, the park road, and threaten its integrity.

✳

Notes: Chapter 8

1. Albright letters to Mather of 10/11 and 10/13/28, NationalArchives, Record Group 79, Entry 6, Box 369.
2. Ibid.; Mather letter to Albright of 10/19/28, National Archives, Record Group 79, Entry 6, Box 369.
3. Liek letter to Albright of 4/11/29; Albright letter to Liek of 5/2/29, National Archives, Record Group 79, Entry 6, Box 374.
4. Albright letter to Liek of 10/23/30, Denali NP&P Archives.
5. Albright letter to Liek of 1/2/31, National Archives, Record Group 79, Entry 6, Box 370.
6. Albright letter to Liek of 2/17/31, National Archives, Record Group 79, Entry 6, Box 370.
7. Liek letter to Albright of 2/3/31, National Archives, Record Group 79, Entry 6, Box 370.
8. Parks letter to Mather of 6/6/29, State Archives, Record Group 101, Box 306.
9. Albright letter to Parks of 10/23/29, State Archives, Record Group 101, Box 306.
10. Albright letter to Parks of 11/29/29, State Archives, Record Group 101, Box 306.
11. Liek report to Director of 10/16/31, National Archives, Record Group 79, Entry 6, Box 370.
12. Liek report to Director of 12/10/35, National Archives, Record Group 79, Entry 7, Box 1403.
13. Cammerer memo to Scott of 5/28/31, National Archives, Record Group 79, Entry 6, Box 374.
14. See George A. Parks, "Alaska—A Record of Progress and Enterprise," Pan Pacific Progress (March 1930), for early context; Franklin D. Roosevelt, "Alaska—Its Resources and Development," Message from the President of the United States, House of Representatives, 75th Cong., 3d Sess., Doc. No. 485 (Jan. 20, 1938), 133-135, for New Deal context; Gov. Ernest Gruening corres. with NPS and Interior Department, State Archives, Record Group 101, Ser. 79-35, Box 468, for postwar context; with additional postwar attitudes and premises in Joint Economic Committees, Canada-United States, "The North Pacific Planning Project, Report of Progress—May 1943," Denali NP&P Archives; Harry S Truman, "Message to Congress on Development and Settlement of Alaska," White House press release of 5/21/48, and Statement of Interior Asst. Sec. W. E. Warne before Interior Appropriations Subcommittee of 2/19/48, Denali NP&P Archives.
15. Gruening letter to J. T. Flakne of 6/1/51, State Archives, Record Group 101, Ser.79-35, Box 468.
16. Karstens letter to Mather of 9/19/27, National Archives, Record Group 79, Entry 6, Box 370.
17. Thomas C. Vint, "Report on Mt. McKinley National Park," December 26, 1929, National Archives (San Bruno, Calif.), Record Group 79, Box 9, 1.
18. Ibid., passim.
19. Albright letter to Vint of 3/17/30, National Archives, Record Group 79, Entry 6, Box 370.
20. Albright letter to Vint of 8/18/31 (a), Denali NP&P Archives.
21. Albright letter to Vint of 8/18/31 (b), Denali NP&P Archives.
22. Sheldon letter to Grinnell of 4/25/21, Sheldon Collection, Box 1, University of Alaska, Fairbanks, Archives.
23. Quoted in John M. Kauffmann, "Mount McKinley National Park, Alaska, A History of its Establishment and Revision of its Boundaries," 1954, MS on file at Alaska Regional Office.
24. Mears letter to Interior Secretary Fall of 5/29/22, National Archives, Record Group 79, Entry 6, Box 381.
25. Kauffmann, "History of Boundaries," 14-20.
26. Vint letter to Director of 3/24/30, National Archives, Record Group 79, Entry 6, Box 370.
27. Gov. Parks letter to Albright of 7/9/31, State Archives, Record Group 101, Box 336.
28. Gov. Parks letter to Albright of 10/24/31, State Archives, Record Group 101, Box 336.
29. Kauffmann, "History of Boundaries," 20-31.
30. Albright memo to Interior Secretary of 1/20/32, in Senate Report 379 (Calendar No. 398), 72d Cong., 1st Sess., 3/2/32, 2.
31. Fairbanks Daily News-Miner, 6/1/42; Wirth memo to Regional Director, Region Four of 11/3/47, National Archives San Bruno, Record Group 79, Box 79.
32. The records of these land cases comprise several thousand pages of reports, correspondence, and legal documents and exhibits; they provide an invaluable history of early settlement on the fringes of the park. See Lands Files, Alaska Regional Office general files (to be archived at National Archives Anchorage). A convenient summary of the land holdings and their histories is provided in the 17-page April 26, 1933,

report (with attached maps and exhibits) by H. K. Carlisle, Examiner, General Land Office, National Archives, Record Group 79, Entry 7, Box 1403 (copy in Denali NP&P Archives).

33. Fairbanks *Daily News-Miner*, 3/12/37.

34. Conrad L. Wirth memo to Assoc. Director of 3/4/48; Diedrick memo to Wirth of 3/8/48, National Archives, Record Group 79, Entry 7, Box 1419. File on Morino Roadhouse fire, May-June 1950, National Archives San Bruno, Record Group 79, Box 85.

35. Maier telegram to Supt. Pearson of 10/3/51, National Archives San Bruno, Record Group 79, Box 79.

36. Ralph Baldwin, "The Crisis on Denali," *Off Belay* (Dec. 1976), 2-10.

37. The temptation to dwell on the human adventure on this mountain, and on the ethical problems it presents, is made nearly irresistible by the rich climbing literature of success, tragedy, and heroic rescue. Convenient summaries used in this chronology are Grant Pearson, *The Taming of Denali* (Los Altos, Calif.: self published, 1957) and Bradford Washburn, "Chronology of Events Related to the Exploration of the McKinley Massif, Alaska" (through 1984), draft copy in Denali NP&P Archives. See Frances Saunders Randall, *Denali Diary, Letters from McKinley* (Seattle: Cloudcap Press, 1987), for an intimate look at modern mountaineering on McKinley. Randall spent the summers of 1976 through 1983 at Kahiltna base camp, where, as a volunteer, she performed all the duties that merited her unofficial title, "Guardian Angel of McKinley."

38. See Governor's corres. files in State Archives, Record Group 101, Ser. 30, Boxes 315 and 321, and National Archives, Record Group 79, Entry 7, Boxes 1403 and 1404 for examples of such duties.

39. Solicitor's memo of 12/19/32, National Archives, Record Group 79, Entry 6, Box 370.

40. Guthrey report to Director of Investigations of 10/24/35, National Archives, Record Group 79, Entry 7, Box 1404.

41. Liek letter to Director of 1/7/35 and Tolson replies of 10/14 and 12/11/35, National Archives, Record Group 79, Entry 7, Box 1412.

42. Endersbee memo to Cameron of 11/20/37, National Archives, Record Group 79, Entry 7, Box 1403.

43. E. M. Gorton letter to Cammerer of 7/27/37, National Archives, Record Group 79, Entry 7, Box 1409.

44. National Parks Association News Service release Number 41 of 6/8/36, State Archives, Record Group 101, Box 468.

45. See Chief Ranger Reports 1927, et seq., Denali NP&P Archives.

46. Greeley letter to Albright of 7/13/31, National Archives, Record Group 79, Entry 6, Box 374.

47. Act. Dir. Demaray letter to W. N. Beach of 10/15/37, National Archives, Record Group 79, Entry 7, Box 1414.

48. For the history of this controversy from the game-protectionists viewpoint, see Charles Banks Belt, comp., *History of the Committee on Conservation of Forests and Wildlife of the Camp Fire Club of America* 1909-1956, 36-38, Denali NP&P Archives.

49. Corres. on Wolf Controversy, 1935-1945, National Archives, Record Group 79, Entry 7, Box 1414 and 1415.

50. Liek letter to Director of 11/11/37; Liek letter to W. N. Beach of 2/17/38, National Archives, Record Group 79, Entry 7, Box 1414.

51. NPS memo for the press of 1/6/38, National Archives, Record Group 79, Entry 7, Box 1414.

52. Palmer report of 12/6/39, National Archives, Record Group 79, Entry 7, Box 1415.

53. V. H. Cahalane report to Director of 1/25/43; National Archives, Record Group 79, Entry 7, Box 1415.

54. Tolson memo to Reg. Dir., Region 4 of 5/10/43; Director Drury memo to Reg. Dir., Region 4 of 12/10/43, National Archives, Record Group 79, Entry 7, Box 1415.

55. Reg. Dir., Region 4 memo to Director of 3/9/45 w/petition enclosure, National Archives, Record Group 7, Box 1415.

56. Drury note to Cahalane of 3/13/45, National Archives, Record Group 79, Entry 7, Box 1415.

57. Director Drury statement on "The Wolf Problem in Mount McKinley National Park," enclosure with Drury letter to Gov. Gruening of 1/11/46, State Archives, Record Group 101, Ser. 79-35, Box 468.

58. Drury memo to Ickes of 11/20/45; Cahalane control-program memo of 11/16/45; Ickes memo to Drury of 11/12/45, National Archives, Record Group 79, Entry 7, Box 1414.

59. J. E. Price memo to Director of 12/29/45, National Archives, Record Group 79, Entry 7, Box 1414.

60. Leopold letter to Drury of 5/15/46, National Archives, Record Group 79, Entry 7, Box 1414.

61. See wolf controversy documents in National Archives, Record Group 79, Entry 7, Box 1414 for corres. and reports cited.

62. Anthony letter to Drury of 12/9/48, National Archives, Record Group 79, Entry 7, Box 1415.

63. Stroud, "History of the Concession," 8.

64. Harold L. Ickes, *The Secret Diary of Harold Ickes*, Vol. II, (New York: Simon and Schuster, 1954), 453.

65. Dir. Drury letter to Rev. Bentley of 3/4/47, National Archives, Record Group 79, Entry 7, Box 1410.

66. Ibid.

67. Vint letter to Director of 8/18/38, National Archives, Record Group 79, Entry 7, Box 371.

68. Stroud, "History of the Concession," 8-10.

69. John A. Salmond, *The Civilian Conservation Corps*, 1933-1942 (Durham, N.C.: Duke University Press, 1967); Southwest Regional Office Div. of History, "A History of the Civilian Conservation Corps" (1989).

70. Mount McKinley NP press bulletin of 4/18/41, Denali NP&P Archives.

71. Interior Dept. telegram to Gov. Gruening of 12/30/41, State Archives, Record Group 101, Ser. 79-35, Box 368; Drury-Swope memo to Int. Sec. of 3/19/42, National Archives, Record Group 79, Entry 7, Box 1417.

72. Governor Gruening's wartime corres. files provide a summary picture of this conversion, in State Archives, Record Group 101, Ser. 79-35, Box 468; see Jean Potter, *Alaska Under Arms* (New York: Macmillan Co., 1942) for contemporary wartime atmosphere.

73. Gen. Buckner letter to Supt. Been of 9/28/41; Drury letter to H. B. Miller of 12/1/42, Denali NP&P Archives; Gen. Buckner Public Proclamation No. 1 of 4/7/42, State Archives, Record Group 101, Ser. 79-35, Box 468.

74. Cpl. Paul B. Lowney, "Soldier's Dreamland," *Alaska Life* (March 1944), 25-26; Sgt. C. E. Davidson, "McKinley Park Recreation Camp," *Alaska Life* (March 1945), 52-53. See the Army handbook, "Mount McKinley Army Recreation Camp" (produced at the park, 1943,) National Archives, Record Group 79, Entry 7, Box 1404, and George L. Hall, *Sometime Again* (Seattle: Superior Pub. Co., 1945), for detail on the camp and the park during wartime.

75. See Robert H. Bates, "Mt. McKinley, 1942," *The American Alpine Journal*, Vol. 5, No. 1 (Jan. 1943), 1-13, for an account of the 1942 cold-weather test expedition.

76. NPS press release of 7/4/43, National Archives, Record Group 79, Entry 7, Box 1408.

77. Supt. Been memo to Reg. Dir., Region 4, of 9/24/47, National Archives, Record Group 79, Entry 7, Box 1420.

78. Superintendent's monthly reports for war years, Denali NP&P Archives.

79. Been memo to Director of 6/25/41, National Archives, Record Group 79, Entry 7, Box 1408.

80. Tolson memo to Act. Superintendent of 8/7/43, National Archives, Record Group 79, Entry 7, Box 1408.

81. Been telegram to Reg. Dir., Region 4, of 6/4/40; Vint memo to National Resources Planning Board of 9/4/40, National Archives San Bruno, Record Group 79, Box 80; postwar development schedules, National Archives, Record Group 79, Entry 7, Box 1420.

82. Pearson, "History of Mount McKinley NP," 50-52; Dir. Drury letter to Gov. Gruening of 4/8/46 and enclosed undated news clipping re: Medal of Freedom Award, National Archives/San Bruno, Record Group 79, Box 77.

83. See park road and road jurisdiction files, Denali NP&P Archives; Act. Dir. Demaray letter to Alaska Delegate A. J. Dimond of 6/13/41, National Archives, Record Group 79, Central Files, 1907-1949, Mount McKinley; mining permit files, National Archives San Bruno, Record Group 79, Box 79; Dir. Cammerer-Supt. Liek letters of 11/8/38 and 12/5/38, National Archives, Record Group 79, Entry 7, File 630 (Roads).

84. William E. Brown, "Cultural Resources Survey of Stampede Mine, May 14, 1987," 16-page typed report for Alaska Regional Office, NPS, Anchorage, Alaska; Donald E. White, "Antimony Deposits of the Stampede Creek Area, Kantishna District, Alaska,"USGS Bulletin 936-N (Washington: GPO, 1942), 331-348; Norman Ebbley, Jr., and Wilford S. Wright, "Antimony Deposits in Alaska," Bureau of Mines Report of Investigations 4173 (1948), 3-20.

85. Earl R. Pilgrim testimony, "Antimony Brief," submitted to Senate Interior and Insular Affairs Committee, 3/26/58, NPS Alaska Regional Office file L3027 (Pilgrim Road), to be retained in National Archives Sand Point, hereinafter: Pilgrim Road File.

86. Pilgrim letter to Ike Taylor, ARC, of 11/27/42, Pilgrim Road File.

87. Drury letter to Reg. Dir., Region 4, of 1/6/43, Pilgrim Road File.

88. Pilgrim letter to Supt. Pearson of 7/27/54, Pilgrim Road File.

89. Pearson letter to Reg. Dir., Region 4, 8/10/54, Pilgrim Road File.

90. Kabaugh (ARR) letter to Pearson of 8/19/54, Pilgrim Road File.

91. Reg. Dir. Maier telegram to Pearson of 8/23/54, Pilgrim Road File.

92. King letter to Pilgrim of 10/4/57, Pilgrim Road File.

93. Various 1957 corres. in Pilgrim Road File.

94. Jacobs memo to Reg. Dir., Region 4, of 4/25/58, Pilgrim Road File.

95. Reg. Dir. letter to Director of 5/1/58, Pilgrim Road File.

96. Supt. King memo to Reg. Director, Region 4, of 9/19/60, Pilgrim Road File.

97. Bruce Campbell interview with author of 9/23/87.

98. Gordon Harrison interview with author of 5/14/87.

99. "Investigation Report: Stampede Mine, Denali NP&P," NPS Alaska Regional Office (May 1987).

100. See remarks of P. B. Fleming, Administrator, Federal Works Agency, in "The Role of Construction in the Post War Period," *The Constructor* (July 1943), cited in Gov. Gruening's broadcast letter to municipal, territorial, and federal agencies of 9/15/45, State Archives, Ser. 130, Box 573, Postwar Plans.

101. Drury memo to Under Secretary of the Interior of 12/28/45; Drury memo to Director, Division of Territories (DOI) of 10/3/45; Otto Ohlson (ARR) memo to Director, Division of Territories of 10/22/45; Gov. Gruening memo to Interior Secretary of 11/26/45, National Archives, Record Group 79, Entry 7, Box 1420.

102. Budget and program documents of late '40s; Superintendent's monthly reports, Denali NP&P Archives.

103. Chapman letter to Gruening of 8/24/50, National Archives San Bruno, Record Group 79, Box 78.

104. Reg. Dir. Merriam wire to Superintendent, McKinley Park of 12/13/50, National Archives San Bruno, Record Group 79, Box 78.

105. Gruening letter to Flakne of 6/15/51, State Archives, Record Group 101, Ser. 79-35, Box 468.

106. Flakne letter to Gruening of 6/22/51, State Archives, Record Group 101, Ser. 79-35, Box 468.

107. NPS Director letter to Asst. Secretary of 6/29/50, State Archives, Record Group 101, Ser. 79-35, Box 468.

108. Gruening letter to Wirth of 4/2/52, State Archives, Record Group 101, Ser. 79-35, Box 468.

109. Wirth letter to Gruening of 6/2/52, State Archives, Record Group 101, Ser. 79-35, Box 468.

110. Gruening letter to Wirth of 6/5/52, State Archives, Record Group 101, Ser. 79-35, Box 468.

111. Wirth letter to Gruening of 6/11/52, State Archives, Record Group 101, Ser. 79-35, Box 468.

112. Wirth letter to Gruening of 12/21/52, State Archives, Record Group 101, Ser. 79-35, Box 468.

113. N. B. Drury, "National Park Policies," *National Parks Magazine*, Vol. 23, No. 97 (Apr.-June 1948), 28–34, quote on 28.

114. Stratton memo to Director, et al., of 6/17/63, Denali NP&P archive.

115. O. Murie letter to F. Masland of 11/20/60, Univ. of Alaska, Fairbanks, Archives, A. Murie Collection, Box 14.

116. O. Murie, "Mount McKinley, Wilderness Park of the North Country," *National Parks Magazine*, Vol. 37, No. 187 (Apr. 1963), 4-7.

118. "Some Views Concerning the Development of Mount McKinley National Park," *National Parks Magazine*, Vol. 37, No. 192 (Sept. 1963), 18–19, 21.

119. Ibid., 19.

120. Adolph Murie, "Comments on Mission 66 Plans, and on Policies Pertaining to Mount McKinley National Park, " 14-page critique attached to Murie letter to Supt. of 11/8/56, Denali NP&P archive.

121. S. Olsen letter to A. Murie of 9/6/60, Univ. of Alaska, Fairbanks, Archives, Adolph Murie Collection, Box 12.

122. Federal Highway Administration, "McKinley Park Highway 1978 Study Report," Appendix A, 12–13, Denali NP&P archive; abstract of road-project correspondence, 1950–69, Denali NP&P archive.

123. Hadley letter to Begich of 2/1/72, Denali NP&P archive.

An aerial view of caribou on the snow. From the Denali National Park and Preserve Archive.

McKinley Becomes Denali with Dubious Future

The park-road controversy had been the sharpest spur forcing reaffirmation of the McKinley Park ideal. But it had not operated alone. Threats of mining and related industrial incursions—e.g., building-stone prospects on Riley Creek near the railroad bridge, and limestone claims on upper Windy Creek near Cantwell, which augured a cement plant within the park—had aroused the Service's protective instincts.[1] The possibility of commercial development in the Kantishna area, where several business-site applications had been filed with the Bureau of Land Management,[2] increased the sense of a closing industrial-commercial environment crowding upon this park so recently secluded in wilderness. The mining developments would impair the park itself; all commercialization would bring more people to park boundaries with attendant environmental and hunting pressures, which, among other things, would interdict the migration routes of park wildlife moving to and from their trans-park ranges.

The first line of defense was to tighten the park's mining regulations to control surface uses.[3] Next came administrative withdrawals near McKinley Station and along the park road to protect against new mining entries in those areas most important for visitor use.[4] One protective withdrawal covered the limestone-cement plant area. But the Service suffered severe political damage on this score, both in Alaska and in the Department, where sister agencies—the Bureau of Mines and the Alaska Railroad—fought the withdrawal. The Service considered deleting this area from the park should the cement venture prove economically feasible, which, fortunately for park integrity, it did not.[5] In 1965 the Service worked with the Bureau of Land Management to get a protective withdrawal of 9,000 acres in the Kantishna vicinity. Though this withdrawal was not formalized because of another political storm, it still stopped new mining entries in this area, to which BLM assigned high recreation potential and the likelihood of inclusion in the park in the future.[6]

The NPS recognized that these remedies were partial and ameliorative. They were spot solutions in a changing world that demanded systematic and comprehensive solutions. Shortly, these concerns over borderland developments united with long-desired park-expansion proposals to chart a new course for park protection.

As early as 1931 the prescient Tom Vint had seen the need for a southern expansion of the park to encompass the spectacular glaciers and gorges that fronted the high mountains, only the peaks of which lay within the park. People on the trains had the impression of passing by the park, then losing sight of it—an ephemeral vision that could not be grasped. Yet, on the southside, excellent views and diverse forelands-recreation opportunities abounded. He concluded, nearly 60 years ago, with words that form the thrust of the park's modern planning: "If such an extension is found advisable McKinley Park would ultimately have two systems of tourist facilities, one north of the range the other south."[7]

Similarly, informed observers early noted the inadequacies of the boundary in the Wonder Lake area. Caribou and other animals drifted northerly from the park as the seasons dictated. The lowlands stretching toward Lake Minchumina and Kantishna

River, and the hills and mountains curving north and east from Wonder Lake formed the other half of the wildlife ecosystem. The expansion of 1932 had caught only the fringe of this extended range.[8]

Because of concerted opposition to any further expansion of the park, these ideas lay dormant until after the war. But the wildlife studies of Adolph Murie and other biologists in the '40s kept the complete-ecosystem concept alive as an aspiration.

In 1963, consulting naturalist Sigurd Olson and NPS planner Ted Swem visited the park during an Alaska parklands survey requested by the Interior Secretary and the NPS Director. This was one of a series of agency studies stemming from George Collins' recommendations in the 1950-54 Alaska Recreation Survey. By the late '60s these studies, in aggregate, would mark out a comprehensive park and conservation system for Alaska, the blueprint for the landmark National Interest Lands legislation of 1980.[9]

Sig Olson's report on McKinley Park stated that it was an elongated rectangle ". . . whose boundaries cut across normal game habitats irrespective of migration routes or breeding requirements." Both in winter and during spring birthing the animals strayed beyond the boundaries and had no protection. Ecologically, the park was simply too small. The Kantishna area brought the problem into focus. There, mining activities scarred the landscape; alienation of 5-acre tracts by BLM boded developments inimical to the park and its wildlife. These problems brought into the open ". . . the constant threat to the land near the borders of the park and the need of zoning, extensions, or cooperative programs with other agencies."[10] Olson's report was instrumental in the NPS-BLM negotiations that led to the Kantishna protective withdrawal in 1965.

PIONEERS OF ALASKA, 1965

Not only biologists and bureaucrats concerned themselves with McKinley Park. In September 1965 the Fairbanks Igloo No. 4 of the Pioneers of Alaska wrote to Secretary of the Interior Stewart Udall urging protective expansion of the park before the new wave of commercial development engulfed it. This branch of the Pioneers, an association of old-time Alaskans, unanimously recommended a near doubling of the park's area by means of a "U"-shaped addition from the Kantishna Hills along the northwest boundary, around the west end, and back up the south boundary nearly to Cantwell. On the north, this extension would protect wildlife wintering range (in a wide band similar to the coincidental proposal by Adolph Murie); on the west end, prime sheep habitat; on the south, the glaciers and gorges.[11]

At the same time the founders of Camp Denali, Celia Hunter and Ginny Hill Wood, proposed a modest buffer to protect Wonder Lake's biological and viewshed values.

The two adventurous women had migrated to Alaska after the war (during which they were aircraft ferry pilots for the Army Air Force). With Ginny's husband, Woody, they staked land in 1951 on the ridge overlooking Moose Creek Canyon and Wonder Lake, just north of the park boundary. Here they established a wilderness camp that yet today offers quality experiences to that limited clientele that forms "the adventurous fringe" of the traveling public. Their determination to forego tinsel comforts and immerse their visitors in the Alaskan wild is captured in a paragraph from their promotional literature:

With wilderness fast disappearing in the "first 48" states, Alaska . . . offers the last large, unspoiled outdoor laboratory for the study and appreciation of undisturbed nature. Here you may still have the experience of the frontiersmen and explorers who first gazed on unbroken prairies,

East Fork of the Toklat River, 1966. From the Denali National Park and Preserve Archive. NPS photo by P. G. Sanchez.

unharnessed rivers and undiminished wildlife."

Wilderness advocate Roderick Nash, in his history of Alaska tourism, credits them with establishing and popularizing "wilderness touring" as a new category of recreational adventuring, made possible by "the remarkable expansion of interest in wilderness" in the decades following the war.[12]

In their critique of the Kantishna withdrawal and the ambitious expansion proposals of 1965, Celia Hunter and Ginny Wood warned of political backlash from mining interests. Moreover, they wanted Camp Denali to remain outside the park, for they feared regulatory interference with their operation. A small buffer zone defined by the line of Moose and Willow creeks would protect the physiographic setting of Wonder Lake. It would also leave out the disturbed mining landscape of the Kantishna district, which they deemed unqualified for parkland.[13]

Over the next few years—with benefit of formal boundary studies and endorsements by the Secretary's Advisory Board on National Parks—the more generous boundary proposals gained official status. In terms of rationale they boiled down to inclusion of the outstanding southside physiography and forelands-recreation potential, and the extended northside wildlife range that would complete the park's ecosystem.[14]

By this time George B. Hartzog had become Director of the National Park Service. Sensing the quickening pace of development in Alaska—given impetus by signs of major oil discoveries soon to come—Hartzog wanted action. Alaska was the last place where giant accessions to the Nation's parklands could occur. With strong backing from Secretary of Interior Stewart Udall, himself spurred by President Lyndon B. Johnson's espousal of the "new conservation," the energetic Director looked to a systems solution in Alaska. Individual park and site studies began to coalesce into an Alaska-wide plan of action. Coordination of this effort became the task of now Assistant Director Ted Swem. Hartzog then appointed a special Alaska task force, directed by George Collins, to define an "entire park complex" that would meet the long-term park and recreation needs of the American people on their last frontier.[15]

The expansion of McKinley Park now became part of what was shaping into a larger movement—pushed by the Service, other conservation agencies, and the forming Alaska Coalition, which over the next decade would focus private conservation groups on the Alaska issue. In what proved to be a premature expression of that movement, Hartzog and Udall in January 1969 presented to President Johnson seven National Monument proclamations, which, upon his signature, would constitute the outgoing president's "parting gift to future generations." Among them was a 2.2-million-acre addition to McKinley Park. Johnson rejected this and a 4-million-acre Gates of the Arctic (in Alaska's Brooks Range) proclamation because, in his view, Secretary Udall had failed to properly prepare Congress for such large-acreage executive actions.[16]

Meanwhile, historic changes were coming to a head in Alaska. The Statehood Act of 1958 had granted Alaska the right to select 104 million acres of the state's 375-million-acre total to be used as its economic and natural-resource base. The state's initial selections aroused the ire of Alaska Natives, whose traditional lands were threatened by wholesale alienation. Political mobilization by the Natives—Indians, Eskimos, Aleuts—resulted in a land freeze first imposed in 1966 by Interior Secretary Udall, pending resolution of the Native land-claims issue by Congress. The freeze stopped dead the parcelling out of Alaska's land. Thus was halted the great shift from an unbounded and almost totally public domain owned by the Federal Government to a diversified land tenure system—from open range to "fenced" range.

Coincidentally, the hints of giant oil discoveries became reality in extreme northern Alaska, at Prudhoe Bay. Transfer of the oil from the ice-bound Arctic to an ice-free port in southern Alaska required a pipeline, and the pipeline required an 800-mile-long right-of-way. The land freeze frustrated acquisition of this right, and temporarily put on hold Alaska's greatest bonanza.

The resultant remorseless and building pressures gave birth to a second system and a third system for divvying up Alaska's land base. Under the terms of the Alaska Native Claims Settlement Act of 1971, Alaska Natives would select 44 million acres of traditional and resource lands for their cultural and economic stake in Alaska. Under pressure from conservation agencies and organizations, Congress included a provision in the act, Section 17(d)(2)—"d-2" in popular parlance—that mandated recommendations from the conservation agencies to Congress for the setting aside of National Interest Lands Conservation Units: parks, wildlife refuges, wild and scenic rivers, and forests.

The Settlement Act lifted the land freeze. State, Native, and National Interest selections soon blanketed the map of Alaska with a kaleidoscopic array of multicolored, 36-square-mile townships. Each of these 16,000-plus townships got its color code at the price of political, economic, and ideological struggle. In particular, the d-2 townships, including 11 park proposals—one of them being the additions to McKinley Park—caused storms of development-vs.-preservation conflict. It took nine years of intense scrutiny, strife, horse-trading, and political maneuvering for the Nation to sift out its vision for Alaska. This was only proper, the price of constitutional government, the way we as a people compromise our conflicts.

ALASKA NATIONAL INTEREST LANDS CONSERVATION ACT OF 1980

In the end, after the episode of the blanket National Monument proclamations of 1978—a holding-action to spur Congress to fulfill its own mandate—the legislators passed the Alaska National Interest Lands Conservation Act of 1980.[17] ANILCA, as the law is acronymed, set aside 106 million acres of conservation units, nearly 44 million of them in new and expanded national parklands. Close to 4 million acres were added to McKinley Park, tripling its size. The new complex of park and preserve lands was designated Denali National Park and Preserve. Old McKinley Park forms the wilderness-wildlife core of the complex. The 2.4-million-acre National Park additions extend north, northwest, and south; two National Preserves—lands on which sport hunting is allowed—rim the National Park to the northwest, west, and southwest.

These additions—the joint product of NPS and Alaska Coalition efforts, and confirmed by Congress—incorporated and expanded upon the Murie-Pioneers of Alaska recommendations of 1965. They capture the northern wildlife range so important to Ade Murie and the other biologists who have studied the park; the south flank and recreation forelands of the range; and the spectacular Cathedral Spires and neighboring mountainous areas to the southwest.

Included in the lands immediately north of Wonder Lake is the Kantishna district, where nearly 1,000 acres of patented private lands give prospect of major resort development. This old but new-in-scale prospect is part of an evolution stemming from the effects of the Mining in the Parks Act of 1976 and a recent conservationist lawsuit that forces tighter environmental controls over mining. For marginal operators, these stricter regulations make mining unattractive. But resort investors will bid high on privately owned acreage that is retired from mining.

How ironic it would be if major in-park facilities—long proposed and only recently firmly rejected by the NPS—were developed at Kantishna. Then the stresses on the "narrow and winding" park road, plus constant air access, would break the lock on the wilderness, *despite* the vast, buffering additions of 1980.

Solution of the Kantishna problem—which builds toward irresistible pressures for unrestricted access upon and inevitable "improvement" of the park road—paired with provision of a politically palatable southside alternative to the current single-option, interior-park visitor use, are the prerequisites of the park's salvation. Lacking these critical and costly moves the park road will become a stake in the park's heart.

Then the vision of Charles Sheldon, even now faded from his original ideal, will vanish entirely. And the park's potentially great role as an International Biosphere Reserve will be aborted. And the visitors who come to see the bears and caribou and wolves and moose and sheep will see them no more.

Bull Moose. From the Denali National Park and Preserve Archive. NPS photo by Rick McIntyre.

THE UNANSWERED QUESTION

In the midst of all these complications, threats, and imperatives, the question posed 30 years ago by Adolph Murie still remains unanswered: Will this park survive as symbol and standard of our civilization's higher aspirations, or will it be sacrificed to the lowest common denominator? The absolute relevance of this question today testifies to the enduring themes of the park's history, and its meaning to a society still trying to find its way.'

✳

1. Building-stone and limestone claim files, National Archives San Bruno, Record Group 79, Box 78.
2. Reg. Director, Region 4, letter to L. Puckett (BLM) of 7/27/51, National Archives San Bruno, Record Group 79, Box 79.
3. Drury memo to Secretary of Interior of 2/7/49, National Archives San Bruno, Record Group 79, Box 79.
4. Reg. Director, Region 4 memo to Director of 2/19/53, National Archives San Bruno, Record Group 79, Box 79; *Federal Register*, 6/28/58, 4811.
5. Director memo to Asst. Secretary of Interior of 11/26/48, National Archives San Bruno, Record Group 79, Box 79; Kauffmann, "History of Boundaries," 37-38.
6. Kantishna Withdrawal File, Denali NP&P Archives.
7. Kauffmann, "History of the Boundaries," 33.
8. Ibid., 27, et seq.
9. Theodore Swem, "National Park Service Interest in Alaska" (1972), 7-page typescript narrative and bibliography in Denali NP&P Archives.
10. Sigurd F. Olson, "Report on Alaska," (1954), excerpt in Denali NP&P Archives.
11. Pioneers of Alaska, Igloo No. 4 letter to Sec. Stewart Udall of 9/20/65, Alaska Regional Office Gen. Files (L1417), to be permanently stored in historical files, National Archives Anchorage.
12. Roderick Nash, "Tourism, Parks and the Wildness Idea in the History of Alaska," *Alaska in Perspective*, Vol. 4, No. 1 (1981), 18.
13. Celia M. Hunter and Ginny Hill Wood letter to Ross Youngblood (BLM) of 9/27/65, Alaska Regional Office General Files (L1417).
14. See, e.g., "Mount McKinley National Park Study" of August 1966, and special report to Secretary by Asst. Secretary Stanley A. Cain on Advisory Board trip to Alaska, 1965, in Denali NP&P Archives.
15. G. Frank Williss, "Do Things Right the First Time": The National Park Service and the Alaska National Interest Lands Conservation Act of 1980 (Denver: National Park Service, 1985), 34-41; George B. Hartzog, *Battling for the National Parks* (Mt. Kisco, N.Y.: Moyer Bell, Ltd., 1988), 205-206.
16. Williss, "Do Things Right" 56-58.
17. From a vast array of "d-2" literature, the author chooses the following core references for further reading: G. Frank Williss' administrative history of the Park Service part in the struggle, previously cited; Celia Hunter, et al. "Alaska National Interest Lands," *Alaska Geographic*, Vol. 8, No. 4 (1981); Federal-State Land Use Planning Commission for Alaska, "The D-2 Book," Lands of National Interest in Alaska (Anchorage: 1977); Robert Arnold, et al., *Alaska Native Land Claims* (Anchorage: Alaska Native Foundation, 1976); Robert B. Weeden, *Alaska, Promises to Keep* (Boston: Houghton Mifflin Co., 1978); Robert Cahn, *The Fight to Save Wild Alaska* (Audubon special issue, 1982).

Mount McKinley from Camp Eielson (location of present-day Eielson Visitor Center). Courtesy of the Eide Collection, AMHA.

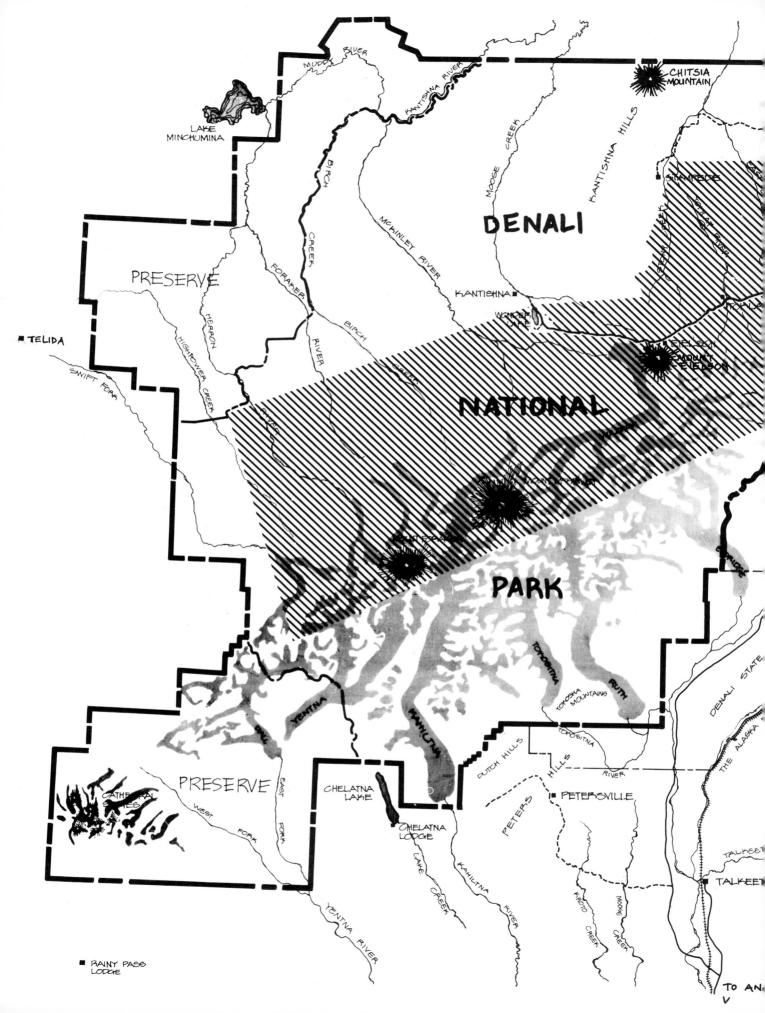

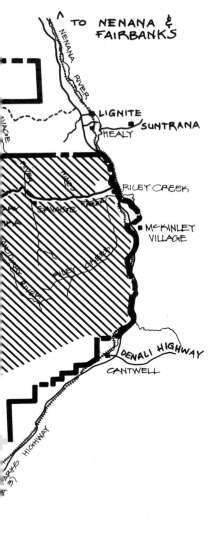

TO NENANA &
FAIRBANKS

NENANA RIVER

LIGNITE
SUNTRANA
HEALY

RILEY CREEK

McKINLEY
VILLAGE

SAVAGE CREEK

RILEY CREEK

DENALI HIGHWAY
CANTWELL

(PARKS) HIGHWAY

RIVER

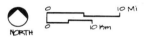

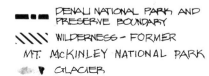

NORTH

0 ——————— 10 Mi
0 ——————— 10 Km

REGION
Denali National Park and Preserve

— — — DENALI NATIONAL PARK AND
PRESERVE BOUNDARY

\\\\\ WILDERNESS - FORMER
MT. McKINLEY NATIONAL PARK

GLACIER

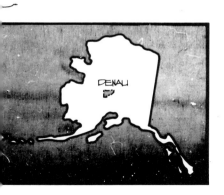

DENALI

Bibliography

I. Archival Collections

Alaska Regional Office, National Park Service
General Records: MOMC Lands Files, L1417 and L3027 (Pilgrim Road File).

Alaska State Archives, Juneau:
RG 101 (Governor's Correspondence with the NPS), Box 172, 195, 219, 246, 306, 315, 321, 336, 368, 468, and 573.

Bruce Campbell Collection, Anchorage.

Denali National Park and Preserve Archives (DENA).

*National Archives, San Bruno, Calif.:*RG 79 (Records of the National Park Service), Box 9, 77, 78, 79, and 85.

National Archives, Washington, D.C.:
RG 79 (Records of the National Park Service), Entry 6 (General Files, NPS, Mount McKinley NP, up to 1933), Box 201, 369, 370, 374, 379, and 381 through 385; Entry 7 (same subject, after 1933), Boxes 371, 630, 1403, 1404, 1408, 1410, 1412, 1414, 1415, 1417, 1419, and 1420.

University of Alaska, Fairbanks:
Lee R. Dice Collection.
Col. Frederick Mears Collection.
Adolph Murie Collection, Box 12 and 14.
Olaus J. Murie Collection, Box 2, 4 and 7.
Oral History Archive: Slim Carlson interviews, 1965, and Robert Rose, 1985.
Reprint File: Falcon Joslin address.
Charles Sheldon Collection: Box 1 and 4.

USGS Technical Data File, Menlo Park, Calif.:
Prindle, L.M., Field Notebook 133-A.

II. Theses, Dissertations, Government Agency Reports and Unpublished Reports

Alaska Department of Transportation and Public Facilities, "Historical Profile of the Alaska Railroad," contract report of September 1980, available at Alaska State Library.

Bishop, Richard H., *Subsistence Resource Use in the Proposed North Addition to Mt. McKinley National Park*, Occasional Paper Number 17, Anthropology and Historic Preservation, Cooperative Park Studies Unit (Fairbanks: University of Alaska), 1978.

Brooker, Edgar, Jr., [Brooker family biographies], n.d., in DENA archives.

Brown, C. M., "The Alaska Railroad: Probing the Interior," report for the History and Archeology Branch of the Alaska Division of Parks (Anchorage), October 1975.

Buzzell, Rolfe, "Overview of Mining in the Kantishna District, 1903-1968," 1989; MS on file at Alaska Regional Office, NPS.

Dice, Lee R., "Interior Alaska in 1911 and 1912: Observations by a Naturalist," MS in Dice Collection, UAF Archives.

Evans, Gail E. H., "From Myth to Reality: Travel Experiences and Landscape Perceptions in the Shadow of Mount McKinley, Alaska, 1876-1938," master of arts thesis (Santa Barbara: University of California), 1987.

Grinnell, George Bird, "Charles Sheldon," MS in William Sheldon Collection, copied from research files of Gail Evans, DENA.

Gudgel-Holmes, Dianne, comp. and ed., "Kantishna Oral History Project," report prepared for National Park Service (Anchorage: Gudgel & Holmes Associates), 1983.

Gudgel-Holmes, Dianne, "Kantishna Oral History Project - Interviews with native Elders," typescript report for the NPS, 1988.

Gudgel-Holmes, Dianne, "Predictive Model of Aboriginal Site Types and Locations for a Catchment Basin along the Denali Park Road within Denali National Park and Preserve," typescript report for National Park Service, Alaska Region, 1989.

Guthrie, R. Dale, "Paleoecology of the Site and it Implications for Early Hunters," in W. Roger Powers, et al., *Dry Creek, Archeology and Paleoecology of a Late Pleistocene Alaskan Hunting Camp*, report prepared for the National Park Service (Fairbanks: University of Alaska), 1983.

Holthaus, Gary H. and Raymond Collins, "Education in the North: Its Effect on Athapascan Culture" (typescript), 1971, in DENA archive.

LaFleur, Harold [historical architect], "Building Inventory" for Mount McKinley National Park, September 16, 1975, in DENA archive.

Mitchell, Beverly, "An Early History of the Healy Valley," unpublished college term paper, May 1989, in author's collection.

Morton, Susan, "Geese House Report," prepared for the Doyon Cemetery and Historic Sites Committee (Fairbanks: Anthropology and Historic Preservation, Cooperative Park Studies Unit, University of Alaska), 1983.

Neilson, J. M., "Focus on Interior History," typescript report prepared for Alaska Historical Commission (Anchorage), 1980.

Oswalt, Wendell H., "Historical Settlements Along the Kuskokwim River, Alaska," Alaska State Library Historical Monograph No. 7 (Juneau: Alaska Department of Education), 1980.

Pearson, Grant H., "A History of Mount McKinley National Park, Alaska,"typescript administrative history prepared by the superintendent, 1953.

Plaskett, David Charles, "The Nenana River Gorge Site: a Late Prehistoric Athapaskan Campsite in Central Alaska," master's thesis, UAF, December 1977.

Sheldon, William G., "Biographical Notes on Charles Sheldon," MS in Charles Sheldon Papers, UAF.

Stanek, Ronald T., "Historical and Contemporary Trapping in the Western Susitna Basin," Technical Paper No. 134 (Anchorage: Alaska Department of Fish and Game, Subsistence Division), 1987.

Stroud, George S., "History of the Concession at Denali National Park (formerly Mount McKinley National Park)," typescript report for the National Park Service Anchorage), 1985.

Vint, Thomas C., "Report on Mt. McKinley National Park," December 26, 1929, at FARC San Bruno.

Washburn, Bradford, "Chronology of Events Related to the Exploration of the McKinley Massif, Alaska," draft typescript (Boston: Museum of Science), 1988.

Washburn, Bradford, "Guide to the Muldrow Glacier Route" (typescript), n.d., at DENA.

Washburn, Bradford, ed., "A Map of Mount McKinley: (Boston: The Museum of Science), 1977.

III. Public Documents
United States Documents - Listed by Author

Berg, Henry C. and Edward H. Cobb, *Metalliferous Lode Deposits of Alaska*, USGS Bulletin 1246 (Washington: GPO), 1967.

Brooks, Alfred Hulse, "An Exploration to Mount McKinley, America's Highest Mountain," in the *Smithsonian Report* for 1903 (Washington: GPO, 1904), 407-425. Also published in the Journal of Geography 2 (November 1903), 418-421.

Brooks, Alfred Hulse, *The Mount McKinley Region, Alaska*, USGS Professional Paper 70 (Washington: GPO), 1911.

Brown, William E., "Cultural Resources Survey of Stampede Mine," May 14, 1987, typescript on file at Alaska Regional Office, NPS.

Capps, Stephen R., *Geology of the Alaska Railroad Region*, USGS Bulletin 907 (Washington: GPO), 1940.

Capps, Stephen R., *The Kantishna Region, Alaska*, USGS Bulletin 687 (Washington: GPO), 1919.

Cobb, Edward H., *Placer Deposits of Alaska*, USGS Bulletin 1374 (Washington: GPO) 1973.

Davis, J. A., "Coal Mining in the Nenana Field, Alaska," in *Annual Report of the Mine Inspector to the Governor of Alaska* (Juneau: Territory of Alaska), 1922.

Dessauer, P. F. and D. W. Harvey, "An Historical Resource Study of the Valdez Creek Mining District," typescript report for Bureau of Land Management (Anchorage), 1980.

Dixon, Joseph S., *Birds & Mammals of Mount McKinley National Park, Alaska*, National Park Service Fauna Series, No. 3 (Washington: GPO), 1938.

Ebbley, Norman, Jr. and Wilford S. Wright, "Antimony Deposits in Alaska," Bureau of Mines Report of Investigations 4173 (1948), 3-20.

Fitzgerald, G., "Surveying and Mapping in Alaska," USGS Circular 101 (Washington: USGS), February 1951.

Glenn, E. F. (with subreports by William Yanert, George Vanschoonoven, George B. Thomas and H. G. Learnard), in *Compilation of Narratives of Exploration in Alaska*, Senate Reports, 56th Cong., 1st Sess., No. 1023, 1900.

Herron, Joseph S., *Explorations in Alaska*, 1899 (Washington, War Department), 1901.

Kauffmann, John M., "Mount McKinley National Park, Alaska, A History of its Establishment and Revision of its Boundaries," 1954, MS on file at Alaska Regional Office.

Mackintosh, Barry, *The National Parks: Shaping the System* (Washington, D.C.: National Park Service), 1985.

Olson, Sigurd F., "Report on Alaska," 1954, excerpt in DENA archive.

Orth, Donald J., *Dictionary of Alaska Place Names*, U.S. Geological Survey Professional Paper 567 (Washington: GPO), 1967.

Prindle, L. M., "The Bonnifield and Kantishna Regions," in *Progress of Investigations of Mineral Resources of Alaska in 1906*, USGS Bulletin 314 (Washington: GPO), 1907.

Roosevelt, Franklin D., "Alaska—Its Resources and Development," Message from the President of the United States, House of Representatives, 75th Cong., 3rd Sess., Doc. 485, January 20, 1938.

Schneider, William, Dianne Gudgel-Holmes, and John Dalle-Molle, *Land Use in the North Additions of Denali National Park and Preserve: An Historical Perspective*, Research/Resources Management Report AR-9 (Anchorage: National Park Service), 1984.

Snow, Dave, Gail Evans, Robert Spude and Paul Gleeson, Historic Structure Report, Mt. McKinley Park Headquarters District & Wonder Lake, 3 vols. (Anchorage: NPS, Alaska Regional Office), 1987.

Swem, Theodore, "National Park Service Interest in Alaska," 1972, typescript in DENA archive.

Truman, Harry S, "Message to Congress on Development and Settlement of Alaska," DENA archive.

White, Donald E., "Antimony Deposits of the Stampede Creek Area, Kantishna District, Alaska," USGS Bulletin 936-N (Washington: GPO, 1942), 331-348.

Williss, G. Frank, *"Do Things Right the First Time": The National Park Service and the Alaska National Interest Lands Conservation Act of 1980* (Denver: National Park Service), 1985.

Wright, George M., Joseph S. Dixon and Ben H. Thompson, *Fauna of the United States*, National Park Service Fauna Series, No. 3 (Washington: GPO), 1933.

United States Documents - General

Alaska Road Commission, *Annual Report* for 1917, 1921 and 1922.

Federal Highway Administration, "McKinley Park Highway 1978 Study Report," in DENA archive.

Federal-State Land Use Planning Commission for Alaska, "*The D-2 Book*," *Lands of National Interest in Alaska* (Anchorage), 1977.

Joint Economic Committees, Canada-United States, "The North Pacific Planning Project, Report of Progress," May 1943, DENA archive.

Mount McKinley National Park, *Superintendent's Monthly Report*, May 1923 through October 1943.

National Park Service, Alaska Regional Office, "Investigation Report: Stampede Mine, DENA," May 1987 in ARO files.

National Park Service, *Director's Annual Report, 1919* (Washington: GPO), 1920.

National Park Service, *Director's Annual Report, 1923* (Washington: GPO), 1924.

National Park Service, *Proceedings of the National Park Conference, January 2-6, 1917* (Washington: GPO), 1917.

[NPS,] Southwest Regional Office, Division of History, "A History of the Civilian Conservation Corps," 1989.

Secretary of the Interior, *Annual Report of the Secretary of the Interior, 1923* (Washington: GPO), 1924.

U.S. Code, Title 16 (1982 edition).

U.S. Congress. House. Mount McKinley National Park, Alaska. Report No. 1273, 64th Cong., 2nd Sess., January 10, 1917.

U.S. Congress. House. Subcommittee of the Committee on Public Lands. Hearing on a Bill to Establish Mount McKinley National Park, 64th Cong., 1st Sess., May 4, 1916.

U.S. Congress. Senate. Committee on Territories. Hearing on the Establishment of Mount McKinley National Park, 64th Cong., 1st Sess., May 5, 1916.

U.S. Congress. Senate Report 379 (Calendar No. 398), 72nd Cong., 1st Sess., March 2, 1932.

U.S. Statutes at Large, Mount McKinley National Park Act, February 26, 1917, 39 Stat. 938.

U.S. Statutes at Large, 46 Stat. 1043 and 90 Stat. 1342.

IV. BOOKS

Albright, Horace M., *The Birth of the National Park Service: The Founding Years, 1913-1933* (Salt Lake City: Howe Brothers), 1985.

Albright, Horace M., *"Oh, Ranger!" A Book About the National Parks* (New York: Dodd, Mead & Co.), 1947.

Arnold, Robert, et. al., *Alaska Native Land Claims* (Anchorage: Alaska Native Foundation), 1976.

Belt, Charles Banks, comp., *History of the Committee on Conservation of Forests and Wildlife of the Camp Fire Club of America, 1909-1956*, in DENA archive.

Brooks, Alfred Hulse, *Blazing Alaska's Trails* (Fairbanks: University of Alaska and the Arctic Institute of North America), 1973.

Browne, Belmore, *The Conquest of Mount McKinley* (Boston: Houghton Mifflin Co.), 1956. (First published in 1913.)

Cahn, Robert, *The Fight to Save Wild Alaska* (special issue of *Audubon Magazine*), 1982.

Cole, Terrence, ed., *The Sourdough Expedition, Stories of the Pioneer Alaskans Who Climbed Mount McKinley in 1910* Anchorage: Alaska Northwest), 1985.

Cook, Frederick A., *To the Top of the Continent* (New York: Doubleday, Page & Co.), 1908.

Cruikshank, Moses, *The Life I've Been Living* (Fairbanks: University of Alaska), 1986.

Davis, Mary Lee, *We Are Alaskans* (Boston: W. A. Wilde Co.), 1931.

Dean, David M., *Breaking Trail, Hudson Stuck of Texas and Alaska* (Athens: Ohio University Press), 1988.

Dunn, Robert, *The Shameless Diary of an Explorer* (New York: The Outing Pub. Co.), 1907.

Greeley, Maj.-Gen. A. W., *Handbook of Alaska: Its Resources, Products and Attractions in 1924* (Port Washington, N.Y.: Kennikat Press), 1970.

Gruening, Ernest, *The State of Alaska* (New York: Random House), 1954.

Hall, George, *Sometime Again* (Seattle: Superior Pub. Co.), 1945.

Hartzog, George B., *Battling for the National Parks* (Mt. Kisco, N.Y.: Moyer Bell, Ltd.), 1988.

Helm, June, ed., *Handbook of North American Indians, Volume 6, Subarctic*, Alaska Plateau and South of the Alaska Range sections (Washington: Smithsonian Institution), 1981.

Hinckley, Ted C., *The Americanization of Alaska, 1867-1897* (Palo Alto, Calif.: Pacific Books), 1972.

Holmes, Charles E., *Lake Minchumina Prehistory: An Archeological Analysis*, in

Aurora, Alaska Anthropological Association Monograph Series #2, 1986.

Hunter, Celia, et al., "Alaska National Interest Lands," *Alaska Geographic* 8:4, 1981.

Ickes, Harold L., *The Secret Diary of Harold Ickes*, Vol. II (New York: Simon and Schuster), 1954.

Mackenzie, Clara Childs, *Wolf Smeller (Zhoh Gwatsan), A Biography of John Fredson, Native Alaskan* (Anchorage: Alaska Pacific University Press), 1985.

Moore, Terris, *Mt. McKinley: The Pioneer Climbs* (Fairbanks: University of Alaska), 1967.

Nelson, Richard K., *Make Prayers to the Raven, A Koyukon View of the Northern Forest* (Chicago: University of Chicago Press), 1983.

Pearson, Grant, *My Life of High Adventure* (Englewood Cliffs, N.J.: Prentice Hall, Inc.), 1962.

Pearson, Grant, "The Seventy Mile Kid," (Los Altos, Calif.: the author), 1957.

Pearson, Grant, *The Taming of Denali* (Los Altos, Calif.: the author), 1957.

Potter, Jean, *Alaska Under Arms* (New York: Macmillan Co.), 1942.

Prince, Bernadine L., *The Alaska Railroad in Pictures, 1914-1964* (Anchorage: Ken Wray Print Shop), 1964.

Rand McNally and Co., *Rand McNally Guide to Alaska and Yukon* (New York: the author), 1922.

Randall, Frances Saunders, *Denali Diary, Letters from McKinley* (Seattle: Cloudcap Press), 1987.

Salmond, John A., *The Civilian Conservation Corps, 1933-1942* (Durham, N.C.: Duke University Press), 1967.

Sheldon, Charles, *The Wilderness of Denali* (New York, Charles Scribner's Sons), 1930.

Sherwood, Morgan B., *Big Game in Alaska: A History of Wildlife and People* (New Haven: Yale University Press), 1961.

Sherwood, Morgan B., *Exploration of Alaska, 1865-1900* (New Haven: Yale University Press), 1981.

Stuck, Hudson, *The Ascent of Denali* (New York: Scribner's), 1914.

Trefethen, James B., *An American Crusade for Wildlife* (Alexandria, Va.: Boone and Crockett Club), 1975.

Trefethen, James B., *Crusade for Wildlife* (Harrisburg, Penn.: Stackpole Co.), 1961.

VanStone, James, *Athapaskan Adaptations, Hunters and Fishermen of the Subarctic Forests* (Arlington Heights, Ill.: AHM Publishing Corp.), 1974.

Washburn, Brad, *Mount McKinley and the Alaska Range in Literature, A Descriptive Bibliography* (Boston: The Museum of Science), 1951.

Webb, Melody, *The Last Frontier, A History of the Yukon Basin of Canada and Alaska* (Albuquerque: University of New Mexico Press), 1985.

Weeden, Robert B., *Alaska, Promises to Keep* (Boston: Houghton Mifflin Co.), 1978.

West, Frederick Hadleigh, "Excavations at Two Sites on the Teklanika River, Mount McKinley National Park, Alaska" (Fairbanks: University of Alaska), 1965.

Wickersham, James, *Old Yukon: Tales—Trails—and Trials* (Washington, D.C.: Washington Law Book Co.), 1938.

Wilcox, Joe, *White Winds* (Los Alamitos, Calif.: Hwong Pub. Co.), 1981.

Williams, Howell, ed., *Landscapes of Alaska* (Berkeley, University of California Press), 1958.

V. NEWSPAPER AND PERIODICAL ARTICLES

Aigner, Jean, "Footprints on the Land," in Jean S. Aigner, et al., *Interior Alaska, A Journey Through Time* (Anchorage: The Alaska Geographic Society), 1986.

"Alaska Government Railroad, The," *The Pathfinder*, 3:3 (January 1922, 1-6.

Albright, Horace, interview in *Boone and Crockett News*, 4:2 (Spring 1987), 4.

Amesbury, E. G., "Erection of Hurricane Gulch Arch Bridge in Alaska," *Engineering News-Record*, 88:4 (January 26, 1922), 144-146.

Baldwin, Ralph, "The Crisis on Denali," *Off Belay* (December 1976), 2-10.

Bates, Robert H., "Mt. McKinley 1942," *The American Alpine Journal*, 5:1 (January 1943), 1-13.

Brown, C. M., "American Alaska," in *Writing Alaska's History*, Vol. I (Anchorage: Alaska Historical Commission), 1974.

Browne, Belmore, "Hitting the Home Trail from Mount McKinley," *Outing*, 62:4 (July 1913), 387-404.

Bundtzen, Thomas K., "A History of Mining in the Kantishna Hills," *The Alaska Journal*, 8:2 (Spring 1978), 151-161.

Davidson, Sgt. C. E., "McKinley Park Recreation Camp," *Alaska Life* (March 1945), 52-53.

Dose, H. F., "Report on Trail from Nenana Watershed to End of Steel on Susitna River," *Alaska Railroad Record*, II:14 (February 12, 1918), 110-111.

Drury, N. B., "National Park Policies," *National Parks Magazine*, 23:97 (April-June 1948), 28-34.

Episcopal Church, "St. Mark's Mission, Nenana," *Alaskan Epiphany*, I:1,2, and 3 (1980).

Fairbanks News-Miner, March 12, 1937, June 1, 1942 and November 29, 1955.

Farquhar, Francis P., "The Exploration and First Ascents of Mount McKinley," *Sierra Club Bulletin*, June 1949, 95-109.

Federal Register, June 28, 1958, 4811.

Fleming, P. B. [administrator, Federal Works Agency], "The Role of Construction in the Post War Period," *The Constructor*, July 1943.

Grant, Madison, "The Establishment of Mount McKinley National Park," in G. B. Grinnell and Charles Sheldon, eds., *Hunting and Conservation: The Book of the Boone and Crockett Club* (New Haven: Yale University Press), 1925.

Haley, Dorothy E., "The Steel Trail into the Heart of Alaska," *The Pathfinder of Alaska*, 6:6 (April 1924), 19-20.

Kari, James, "The Tenada-Denali-Mount McKinley Controversy," *Names*, 34:3 (September 1986), 347-350.

Loftus, Jule, "Corralling Caribou—a Wilder West Sport," *Farthest-North Collegian*, 2:1 (1924), 20-21.

Lowney, Cpl. Paul B., "Soldier's Dreamland," *Alaska Life* (March 1944), 25-26.

Marchand, Leslie, "Mount McKinley," *Farthest-North Collegian*, 5:1 (1927), 5-6, in UAF Archives.

Mayse, Charley, "Scion of the Mountain Men," *The Alaska Journal, a 1981 Collection* (Anchorage: Alaska Northwest, 1981), 66-71.

McConnell, Grant, "The Conservation Movement—Past and Present," *Western Political Quarterly*, 7:1 (September 1954), 463-478.

Merriam, C. Hart, "Introduction," in Charles Sheldon, *The Wilderness of Denali* (New York, Charles Scribner's Sons), 1930.

"Mount McKinley National Park, The," *Field and Stream* (April 1917), 171.

Murie, O. J., "Mount McKinley, Wilderness Park of the North Country," *National Parks Magazine*, 37:187 (April 1963), 4-7.

Nash, Roderick, "Tourism, Parks, and the Wilderness Idea in the History of Alaska," *Alaska in Perspective*, 4:1 (1981), 1-27.

Naske, Claus-M. and Don M. Triplehorn, "The Federal Government and Alaska's Coal," *The Northern Engineer*, 12:3 (Fall 1980), 20-21.

Nelson, E. W., "Charles Sheldon," *American Forests* (November 1928), 659-660.

"Nenana, the Hub City of Interior Alaska," *The Pathfinder*, 2:5 (April 1921), 1-9.)

Norris, Frank, "Showing Off Alaska: the Northern Tourist Trade, 1878-1941," *Alaska History*, 2:2 (Fall 1987), 1-18.

Parks, George A., "Alaska—A Record of Progress and Enterprise," *Pan Pacific Progress*, March 1930.

Roosevelt, Theodore, "The American Hunter-Naturalist," *The Outlook*, 99:15 (December 9, 1911), 854-856.

Rusk, Claude E., "On the Trail of Dr. Cook," *Pacific Monthly*, issues of October and November 1910 and January 1911.

Schneider, William, "Chief Sesui and Lieutenant Herron: A Story of Who Controls the Bacon," *Alaska History*, 1:2 (Fall-Winter 1985-86), 1-18.

Schneider, William, "On the Back Slough," in Jean S. Aigner, et al.,

Interior Alaska, A. Journey Through Time (Anchorage: The Alaska Geographic Society, 1986), 147-194.

Secrist, T. W., "Alaska Railroad Surveys Through Broad Pass," *Engineering News-Record*, 86:15 (April 14, 1921), 632-633.

Sheldon, Charles, "List of Birds Observed on the Upper Toklat River near Mount McKinley, Alaska," *Auk*, 26 (January 1909), 66.

Shives, Jim, "The Sled Dogs of McKinley," *Alaska Magazine*, 44 (October 1978), 6-8.

"Some Views Concerning the Development of Mount McKinley National Park," *National Parks Magazine*, 37:192 (September 1963), 18-19, 21.

Steese, Col. J. G., "Across Alaska by Automobile," *American Motorist* (March 1923), 12-13, 24.

Steese, Col. J. G., "Road Construction Under the Alaska Road Commission," *The Highway Magazine*, January 1923, 11-12.

Steese, Col. J. G., "Building Roads to Develop Alaska," *The Highway Magazine*, December 1924, 13-15.

Thompson, Paul E., "Who Was Hudson Stuck?" *Alaska Journal*, 10:1 (Winter 1980), 62-65.

Thorson, Robert M., "The Ceaseless Contest," in Jean S. Aigner, et al., *Interior Alaska, A Journey Through Time* (Anchorage: The Alaska Geographic Society). 1986.

Tilden, Paul M. and Nancy L. Machler, "The Development of Mount McKinley National Park," *National Parks Magazine*, 37:188 (May 1963), 10-15.

Washburn, Bradford, "Doctor Cook and Mount McKinley," *American Alpine Journal* (1958), 1-30.

Washburn, Bradford, "The First Ascent of Mount McKinley, 1913, A Verbatim Copy of the Diary of Harry P. Karstens," *The American Alpine Journal* (1969), 339-348.

Wilson, William H., "The Alaska Railroad and Tourism, 1924-1941," *Alaska Journal*, 7:1 (Winter 1977), 18-24.

VI. INTERVIEWS

Campbell, Bruce, by author, September 23, 1987.
Harrison, Gordon, by author, May 14, 1987.

Index

About the Author

Bill Brown, now retired and residing in Gustavus, Alaska, served as historian in the National Park Service for more than 30 years. His assignments as survey and field historian included long tours in the Southwest and in Alaska, where he wrote major histories for Gates of the Arctic and Denali National Parks. On sabbaticals in the '70s, he worked as an environmental activist (Southwest) and with Arctic Coast Eskimos preparing cultural landscape plans (Alaska). Still active in Park Service and conservation affairs, he writes and volunteers in the parks from his Gustavus home base near the mouth of Glacier Bay. He has five sons, the younger two still at home.